Three Anarchical Fallacies

An Essay on Political Authority

How is a legitimate state possible? Obedience, coercion, and intrusion are three ideas that seem inseparable from all government and seem to render state authority presumptively illegitimate. This book exposes three fallacies inspired by these ideas and in doing so challenges assumptions shared by liberals, libertarians, cultural conservatives, moderates, and Marxists.

The first fallacy links the state's right to rule to its subjects' having a duty to obey. If legitimacy entails a right to rule, doubts about the duty to obey seem to foreclose a legitimate state. The second fallacy assumes that the law is coercive. This assumption appears to entail that the state bears the burden of justifying its own existence and that state inaction is preferable to action. The third fallacy depicts morality as two concentric circles, of which the law may police only the outer one. In a clear and tightly argued essay William Edmundson dispels these fallacies and shows that living in a just state remains a worthy ideal.

This is an important book for all philosophers, political scientists, and legal theorists, as well as other readers interested in the views of Rawls, Dworkin, and Nozick, many of whose central ideas are subjected to rigorous critique.

William A. Edmundson is Professor of Law at the College of Law, Georgia State University.

Cambridge Studies in Philosophy and Law

GENERAL EDITOR: Gerald Postema (University of North Carolina, Chapel Hill)

ADVISORY BOARD

Jules Coleman (Yale Law School)
Antony Duff (University of Stirling)
David Lyons (Boston University)
Neil MacCormick (University of Edinburgh)
Stephen Munzer (U.C.L.A. Law School)
Phillip Pettit (Australian National University)
Joseph Raz (University of Oxford)
Jeremy Waldron (Columbia Law School)

Three Anarchical Fallacies

An Essay on Political Authority

WILLIAM A. EDMUNDSON

PUBLISHED BY THE PRESS SYNDICATE OF THE UNIVERSITY OF CAMBRIDGE
The Pitt Building, Trumpington Street, Cambridge CB2 1RP, United Kingdom

CAMBRIDGE UNIVERSITY PRESS
The Edinburgh Building, Cambridge CB2 2RU, UK   http://www.cup.cam.ac.uk
40 West 20th Street, New York, NY 10011-4211, USA   http://www.cup.org
10 Stamford Road, Oakleigh, Melbourne 3166, Australia

First published 1998

Printed in the United States of America

Typeface Palatino 10/12 pt.   *System* Quark XPress™   [BB]

A catalog record for this book is available from the British Library

Library of Congress Cataloging in Publication Data
Edmundson, William A. (William Atkins). 1948–
Three anarchical fallacies : an essay on political authority /
William A. Edmundson.
   p.   cm. – (Cambridge studies in philosophy and law)
Includes index.
ISBN 0-521-62454-1 (hardcover)
1. Legitimacy of governments.   2. Authority.   3. Political
obligation.   4. Anarchism.   I. Title.   II. Series.
        JC497.E35   1998
   306.2–dc21   98-20690
                                        CIP

ISBN 0 521 62454 1 hardback

For Ann

Contents

Acknowledgments

A Henry M. Phillips Research Grant in Jurisprudence from the American Philosophical Society, along with the generous support of the Georgia State University College of Law, helped make this book possible. Beth Bercaw's able research support is gratefully acknowledged.

The argument in Part One has been improved by my opportunity to respond to challenges by Kit Wellman. For their helpful comments on Part Two, thanks are due to Larry Alexander, Linda Bell, David Blumenfeld, Mike Hoffheimer, Doug Husak, and Hans Oberdiek. I owe a special debt to Alan Wertheimer's work and his patient readings of mine. Part Three is the product of a number of years' thought, conversation, and correspondence. I thank Stephen Shute, Jim Peterman, Nick Fotion, and Mike Hoffheimer, for their suggestions, and Richard Nunan and Bonnie Steinbock for having provoked me to begin the line of thought I lay out here. The influence of the late Ferdie Schoeman may be obvious enough, but I gratefully acknowledge it anyway.

I am especially indebted to George Rainbolt, Steve Rieber, Chuck Marvin, John Simmons, Jack Sanders, Les Green, Jerry Postema, Charlie Silver, and Paul Milich, and to my research assistants, Jeffrey Tucker and Vincent Anderson, each of whom commented on the entire manuscript. Portions of Part Two appeared in *Legal Theory;* portions of Part Three appeared in the *Brigham Young University Journal of Public Law.*

My thanks do not convey any responsibility for my obstinacy; only I am to blame for the errors remaining.

Introduction

"Tired: Blaming your parents; *Wired:* Blaming the government."
—*Wired* magazine

As the century and millennium draw to a close, it is hard not to notice how visions of the "end" of various things have come to dominate popular thinking.[1] As never before, we are impatient to get on with the future and be done with whatever is stale, makeshift, or established. Even the staider print journalists seem unable to conceive a topic except in terms of walls crumbling, bastions falling, myths exploding, highways to the future opening out. And of all the bric-a-brac of the past, nothing seems quite so dated, quite so discredited, quite so stifling, as government.

Manifestations of our antistate Zeitgeist range from the lawful (such as deregulation and privatization in the industrialized democracies), to the ragged (such as the devolution and disintegration of the Soviet bloc), to the apocalyptic (such as the Oklahoma City bombing). Underlying these instances is a fundamental *distrust* of state power. Auschwitz, the Gulag, and even (if you insist) Waco and Ruby Ridge should and will refresh this distrust. Suspicion of state power has a long and venerable intellectual pedigree, encompassing figures ranging from Locke, Jefferson, Madison, and Mill to antibureaucratic Marxists, libertarians, and Rawlsian liberals. But when chronic suspicions combine with millenarian enthusiasm, damage can result. As Garry Wills has put it, "Where the heated deny legitimacy and the cool are doubtful of it, a crisis is in the making."[2]

My intention in writing this book is to reinforce – or, if necessary, reestablish – your conviction that legitimate political authority is

---

[1]   See, e.g., John Lancaster in *The New Yorker,* December 25, 1995, p. 9.
[2]   "The New Revolutionaries," *The New York Review of Books,* August 10, 1995, p. 55.

1

possible and that living in a just state is a worthy ideal. If necessary, I also hope to persuade you that thinking about legitimacy is not a mere "pastime to be resisted,"[3] as Laurence Tribe has claimed, but a responsibility that we are capable of meeting, and one that we would shirk at our own and each other's peril. A democratic state can only be vitiated by popular doubts about its right to exist, and a weakened state is to that extent less able to do what only it can do, for example, protect the weak and meek against the strong and loud. But confidence is no substitute for wisdom; nothing I say here is meant in any way to lead anyone to think that state power is a panacea, or that it has somehow expended its capacity to do great harm.

Specifically, in this book I address three views that I impertinently call *anarchical fallacies* – I add to the impertinence by shamelessly stealing a phrase of Jeremy Bentham's.[4] By "fallacy" I mean an example of bad reasoning; by "anarchical" I mean tending to undermine confidence in the legitimacy of the state.

The first fallacy trades on an abstract linkage between the idea of the state having a *right to rule* and the idea that its subjects have a *duty to obey* its commands. It is natural enough to think of a *legitimate* state as one that has, in some sense, the right to rule. Once we begin to scrutinize the scope and nature of the duty to obey, doubts accrue, and they appear to accrue directly against the state's reserve of legitimacy. If these doubts are taken as seriously as many contemporary thinkers have taken them, the very possibility of a legitimate state is foreclosed.

The second fallacy rests on the commonsense thought that law – the distinctive tool of civilized states – is distinctively *coercive*. From this apparently uncontroversial datum it is tempting to infer that the state bears some special burden of justifying its existence. It is also tempting to infer that state inaction is, in general, preferable to action. "State interference is an evil, where it cannot be shown to be a good," as Oliver Wendell Holmes, Jr., put it.[5] Even the most popular and beneficial measures a state might undertake remain, therefore, somehow tainted because whenever, wherever the state acts, somebody, somewhere, has to have been coerced.

---

[3] Laurence H. Tribe, *Constitutional Choices* 6 n.9 (Cambridge, Mass.: Harvard University Press, 1985).

[4] Jeremy Bentham, "Anarchical Fallacies" in vol. 2 of *The Works of Jeremy Bentham*, John Bowring, ed., 491–534 (Edinburgh, 1843).

[5] Oliver Wendell Holmes, Jr., *The Common Law* 96 (Boston: Little, Brown, 1881).

The third fallacy involves a certain view of the relation between law and morality. Morality is divided into two concentric spheres, an inner and an outer. The outer sphere is one that the law may help police, but the inner sphere the law may not enter. What goes on in the inner sphere is subject to appraisal as right or wrong and may be policed by the informal pressures of opinion and ostracism, but morality itself forbids the law from taking a hand.

The anarchical fallacies I am concerned with are not confined to the thinking of anarchists – they would be of limited interest if they were. As it happens, though, ACLU liberals, cultural conservatives, middle-of-the-roaders, free-marketeers, libertarians, and Marxists seem to be equally susceptible to them. And you? If at this moment you are saying to yourself, "Yes, I think I understand what these three views are, but what in the world is supposed to be 'fallacious' about them?" you are ready to proceed.

I cannot claim that once the three fallacies have been exposed we will find ourselves occupying a single, synoptic point of view from which we might together survey the whole field of political and legal philosophy. I will conclude the book, however, by suggesting some ways in which the state might be valuable to us – ways that, no longer cast as mere compensating benefits, we might be able to appreciate afresh. Thus, although the book is largely devoted to the task of clearing conceptual underbrush, I hope the effort of reading it will expose some of the capabilities of an estate that is usually lovelier when viewed from a distance.

Part One

The Fallacious Argument from the
Failure of Political Obligation

"Government and obedience go hand in hand."
Bentham, *Anarchical Fallacies*, 504

Chapter 1

Legitimacy and the Duty to Obey

In 1970, Robert Paul Wolff pronounced that "the fundamental problem of political philosophy [is] how the moral autonomy of the individual can be made compatible with the legitimate authority of the state." The reconciliation proved impossible for Wolff because "the defining mark of the state is authority, the right to rule[, while] the primary obligation of man is autonomy, the refusal to be ruled." The state, in Wolff's view, is necessarily illegitimate, and "political philosophy, as the study of that legitimate political authority which distinguishes civil society from the state of nature, is dead." Although political philosophy has not died, it has not yet recovered from Wolff's assault.[1]

Wolff and others have been able to persuade most of their attentive colleagues that the idea that citizens owe the state, even a just state, a duty of obedience – even only a provisional, nonabsolute, prima facie duty – has to be given up. Accordingly, one might say that the fundamental problem confronting political philosophy today is that of explaining how the state can be legitimate if there is no general duty to obey its laws. This is the problem that I will attack. What I hope to show is that we can make sense of the idea of a legitimate political authority without positing the existence of a general duty to obey the law.

---

[1] Robert Paul Wolff, *In Defense of Anarchism*, 2d ed., vii, 18, 110 (New York: Harper & Row, 1976) [hereafter, Wolff, *In Defense of Anarchism*]. Throughout the early postwar period it was widely reported in Anglo-American philosophical circles that political philosophy had died of its own linguistic confusion. See, e.g., John Plamenatz, "The Use of Political Theory," and P. H. Partridge, "Politics, Philosophy, Ideology," in Anthony Quinton, ed., *Political Philosophy* 19, 32 (Oxford: Oxford University Press, 1967).

AN INCONSISTENT TRIAD

The problem I want to address can be put another way. Consider the following set of propositions:

1. A state is legitimate only if it claims to impose and, in fact, does impose on its subjects a general, at least prima facie, duty to obey its laws.
2. There is no general, even prima facie, duty to obey the laws of a state, not even those of a just state.
3. Legitimate states are not only possible, but actual.

A logical tension within this set should be plain. This is an example of what has been called an "inconsistent triad" of propositions. It is so called because the truth of any pair of the three entails the falsity of the third. The three cannot be all true together, although any pair taken from among them can. Two or even all three may be given up as false, of course, but if our aim is simply to resolve the logical tension within this set, we should be reluctant to do more than reject its most dubious member.

Of the three, only the second seems to lack initial plausibility. No general duty, not even a prima facie one, to obey the laws of a just state? On what grounds have "mainstream" philosophers embraced so radical a proposition?

DOUBTS ABOUT THE EXISTENCE OF A PRIMA FACIE DUTY TO OBEY THE LAW

Philosophical doubts about the existence of a general, prima facie duty to obey the law have had four chief sources. The first source is the difficulty of stating such a duty precisely without reducing its scope and force so drastically that it ceases to have significant practical "bite." The second is the difficulty of resisting the subsumption of such a duty to deeper, more general moral principles that make such a duty superfluous. The third is the difficulty of reconciling such a duty with other moral values, such as personal autonomy. The fourth is the difficulty of providing a satisfactory foundation for such a duty. Let us consider each of these four sources in turn.

The Duty Eroded by Its Qualifications and Exceptions

The duty to obey the law cannot be a duty incumbent upon everyone, everywhere, to obey every law, every time. In other words,

8

unlike some moral duties, the duty to obey the law cannot be an absolute and universal one. Laws differ from jurisdiction to jurisdiction and one cannot be expected to obey the laws of every jurisdiction, especially if they conflict. One is normally expected to obey only the laws of the state where one resides or is present. If one happens to be in an inhabited place beyond the territorial claims of any state, then there may be no law for one to obey – although the demands of morality are not so limited.

So, the duty to obey the law has to be understood to bind individuals to the laws of the states in which they dwell or visit, or at the very least to those with which they deal. Even so, the duty cannot be an absolute one. If there were an absolute duty to obey the law, then the German people would have had a duty to obey Nazi laws implementing the final solution to the Jewish problem. Of course there was no such duty. One might say that there was no such duty because there was no such law, in the proper sense of the word, but merely a command backed by threats. One might, in other words, take the "natural law" position that an unjust law is no law,[2] and maintain the view that a subject has a duty to obey every law that is law properly so called.

But circumstances can easily be imagined in which even a just law ought not to be obeyed. If, for example, my wife is in difficult labor and must be rushed to the hospital, the *moral* duty to observe the speed limit that I would otherwise have might not apply even if the legal duty were unaffected. Laws are normally drafted in general terms and in advance of events. It would be unrealistic to insist that every law – on pain of being held unjust – be deemed to contain or be subject to an implicit "exceptions" clause excusing noncompliance whenever the evils avoidable thereby outweigh the good effects of strict obedience.[3] But, more than that, such a proviso would so subordinate the duty to obey the law to the wider calculation of costs and benefits that the duty – so qualified – would become not a duty to obey the law, but a duty to obey the law when, but only when, the

---

[2] Neither Augustine nor Aquinas flatly stated that "lex iniusta non est lex," but this simplistic formula has become the popular stigma of natural law theories. For a fuller treatment, see John Finnis, *Natural Law and Natural Rights* 363–6 (Oxford: Clarendon Press, 1980).

[3] See Rolf Sartorius, *Individual Conduct and Norms* (Encino, Calif.: Wadsworth, 1975); Larry Alexander, "Pursuing the Good – Indirectly," 95 *Ethics* 315 (1985); Larry Alexander, "The Gap," 14 *Harvard Journal of Law and Public Policy* 695 (1991).

balance of all reasons favors doing what the law requires.[4] Hobbes seems to be expressing this view in *Leviathan,*where he states: "When therefore our refusal to obey frustrates the end for which the sovereignty was ordained; then there is no liberty to refuse: otherwise there is." – But this bears little resemblance to any duty to "obey the law as it requires to be obeyed," in Joseph Raz's phrase.[5]

Philosophers have long understood the duty to obey the law to be a prima facie duty rather than an absolute duty, or duty *sans phrase.* A prima facie duty is, one might say, a candidate duty, one that will in fact be one's duty unless a conflicting duty or other moral consideration outweighs it. When this is the case, there still will have been a reason to have done what the prima facie duty would have required, and the actor will appropriately feel compunction and an obligation to somehow make up for the omission. If, for example, I promise to tape *Seinfeld* for you but can't because my wife has gone into labor, the prima facie duty created by the promise does not simply vanish despite the fact that it was outweighed and I ought, under the circumstances, not to take the time to tape *Seinfeld.*[6] The weight a prima facie duty has may vary considerably from the very weak – as, for example, a duty not to annoy – to the very grave – for example, a duty not to take human life. But describing the duty to obey the law as a prima facie duty rather than a duty sans phrase does not eliminate the need for the qualifications mentioned already. I have no duty, not even a prima facie one, to obey the laws of Outer Mongolia. Germans had no duty, not even a prima facie one, to report the whereabouts of Jews to Nazi officials bent on annihilation.[7]

But, if there were such a thing as a prima facie duty to obey the law, shouldn't one say that the Germans in fact had a *prima facie but overridden* duty to report the whereabouts of Jews to Nazi authorities? This might at first seem to be the most natural way to employ the idea of prima facie duty. To say that there is a prima facie duty to ϕ is to say, at least, that there is a moral reason to ϕ. Sometimes to ϕ is also to ψ, and if in circumstance C there is a stronger prima facie duty

---

[4] Thomas Hobbes, *Leviathan,* J. C. A. Gaskin, ed. (XXI:15) 145 (Oxford: Oxford University Press, 1996) [hereafter, *Leviathan*].

[5] Joseph Raz, *The Authority of Law* 236 (Oxford: Clarendon Press, 1979).

[6] This account follows that of John Searle, "Prima-facie Obligations," in Zack van Straaten, ed., *Philosophical Subjects: Essays Presented to P. F. Strawson* 238 (Oxford: Clarendon Press, 1980); see also David Ross, *The Right and the Good* 16–47, 56–64 (Oxford: Clarendon Press, 1930).

[7] George Rainbolt forced me to confront this point.

not to ψ, two alternative accounts of the situation offer themselves. On one account, we say that because φ-ing in circumstance C would also be ψ-ing, the prima facie duty to φ is overridden, *although there remains a moral reason to perform a φ-ing that would have been a ψ-ing.* Alternatively, we might say that because a φ-ing is so liable to be a ψ-ing or something as bad or worse than ψ-ing, or because the ψ-ing in circumstance C would be so much worse than a not-φ-ing, *there is no residual moral reason to perform a φ-ing that would have been a ψ-ing and, hence, no unqualified prima facie duty to φ.* The latter is the better way to handle the Nazi example. Because reporting the Jews would lead to their grossly unjust torment and death, there is no moral reason to report them even though to report them would be to obey the law. Failing to report the Jews is no occasion for compunction and leaves nothing to make up to the Nazi regime; and therefore it is better to say that there is a prima facie duty to obey *sufficiently just laws*, rather than that there is a prima facie duty to obey the law, period.

A methodological observation is worth making here: The two alternative ways of describing the Nazi case present an instance of what I will call the *Redescription Problem.* It is a type of problem that recurs frequently in deontic moral philosophy, that is, that part of moral philosophy that concerns concepts like duty, obligation, and their cognates.[8] If there were no means of treating instances of the Redescription Problem, then substantive moral philosophy (of which political and legal philosophy are, in main, branches) would be to that extent afflicted with a serious degree of indeterminacy, for it would be next to impossible to determine what our prima facie duties, in fact, are. (Later on, we will encounter other instances of the Redescription Problem.) Fortunately, as the Nazi example illustrates, there is a way to determine which of the alternative descriptions of such cases best expresses our moral convictions. That way is to ascertain whether failure to perform a purported prima facie duty would leave an appropriate residue of regret or remorse, indicating the presence of moral reasons that are still operative even if, in the circumstances, they have been overridden.

Returning to our inquiry: At this juncture, we still have, intact, a prima facie duty of subjects, residents, and guests of a just state to

---

[8] See Paul M. Pietroski, "Prima Facie Obligations, Ceteris Paribus Laws in Moral Theory," 103 *Ethics* 489, 504–5 n.21 (1993); Brad Hooker, "Ross-style Pluralism versus Rule-consequentialism," 105 *Mind* 531–52 (1996).

obey the law. Though not absolute, a prima facie duty is not a triviality; for recognizing such a duty shapes not only how we evaluate options and conduct, but also how we educate the young and how we manage our feelings and opinions. But what weight can we assign this duty? Suppose I come upon a stop sign at an intersection in the middle of the desert.[9] Both intersecting roads are straight and visibility extends for miles. It is just after dawn; there is no traffic; I am rested and alert. It is my legal duty to come to a full stop before proceeding. If I don't stop, there is no real chance that any harm will come; but there is no harm in stopping either. But do I have any real reason to stop, or even any merely prima facie moral duty to do so? My first (as well as my considered) impulse is to say, Yes, there is a reason for me to stop, and more than that, there is a duty to do so, simply and only because the law to which I am subject says I must. But my (and, I trust, your) saying so opens another powerful line of attack on the idea of a duty to obey the law "as it requires to be obeyed."

The Duty Subsumed by Deeper Principles

The qualifications that have to be made to the supposed duty to obey the law are demanded by other moral principles and values. But of course sometimes the duty to obey the law outweighs such other, conflicting moral considerations, as, for example, when I would want to speed across town during rush hour to get home in time to pay the housekeeper. My prima facie duty to do what it takes to pay the housekeeper promptly is overridden. But the outcome in this example is not haphazard; there must be a sufficient set of reasons in this case that subordinate the prima facie duty to pay debts promptly to the prima facie duty to obey the law. Should the particular nature of the law-breaking action matter in this calculation? Surely it should: Speeding under most circumstances endangers the safety of myself and others. If, on the other hand, meeting an important obli-

---

[9] This example is discussed by M. B. E. Smith, "Is There a Prima Facie Obligation to Obey the Law?" 82 *Yale Law Journal* 950 (1973); Joel Feinberg, "Civil Disobedience in the Modern World," 2 *Humanities in Society* 37, reprinted in Joel Feinberg and Hyman Gross, eds., *The Philosophy of Law*, 5th ed. (Belmont, Calif.: Wadsworth, 1995); Donald H. Regan, "Law's Halo," 4 *Social Philosophy & Policy* 15 (1986); Frederick Schauer, *Playing by the Rules* 130 (New York: Oxford University Press, 1991); and Heidi Hurd, "Challenging Authority," 100 *Yale Law Journal* 1611 (1991), among others.

gation would be frustrated by stopping for a stop sign at an unpopulated intersection in the desert, the balance of reasons would seem to weigh in favor of doing what would violate the law.

At this point we have to confront two questions: (1) Is the duty to obey the law general, or is it specific to particular laws? and (2) is the duty "content-independent"[10] or is it not? If the duty to obey the law were a general one, the existence and weight of the duty should be determinable without reference to any particular law. But we have already seen reason to doubt that the duty to obey the law can be general in that sense: The legal duty not to commit murder has far greater weight than the legal duty not to jaywalk. When we speak of a general duty to obey the law we are using a shorthand for a set of more specific moral duties: for example, the duty not to commit murder, the duty not to jaywalk, the duty to comply with 26 U.S.C. §1 et seq. And if the duty to obey a specific law were content-independent, that duty's weight and importance should be determinable without reference to the character and consequences of the actions available to the actor at the time she acts. But this, as the examples show, is implausible. What determines the weight of a specific legal duty, for example, the duty not to murder or the duty not to jaywalk, is the moral quality of the type of action concerned – murder, or jaywalking – and the circumstances in which a "token" of that type of action would be performed – for example, murdering a suspected terrorist versus murdering an innocent child, jaywalking in the desert at dawn versus jaywalking on a busy street.

Because the duty to obey the law seems neither general nor content-independent, the further question arises: In a full moral evaluation of an action, is the fact that it complies with or violates the law entitled to any independent weight? Wolff, for one, has argued that it is not because, if it were, this would amount to an illegitimate double-counting of reasons.[11] If there is a safety reason to stop at a stop sign, then the fact that that reason has moved the legislature to require motorists to stop is not a further reason to stop, unless of course the public has come to rely on the practice of stopping. In that case the expectations created by the enactment may furnish a further reason to stop – but those expectations exhaust the moral significance of the enactment of the law. It may be that my not stopping is somehow unfair to those who bother to stop, but if so, the unfairness

[10]   See H. L. A. Hart, *Essays on Bentham* 254 (Oxford: Clarendon Press, 1982).
[11]   Wolff, *In Defense of Anarchism* 105.

13

is the reason to stop rather than the illegality of not stopping. To give the unfairness reason, the legitimate-expectations reason, and the safety reason a certain weight, and then to *add* illegality as a further reason is to double-count, because illegality derives whatever weight it has from those other reasons – and not vice versa.

Those who deny that there exists any general, even prima facie duty to obey the law do not deny that we often have a moral duty to do what the law happens to require; but they do deny that our moral duty derives from legality and illegality per se. We should, as Raz puts it, "comply with the law whenever there are good independent reasons for doing so,"[12] but deeper principles govern those reasons and determine what duties we have – both prima facie and sans phrase. For the skeptic, the duty to obey the law simply drops out of account.

The Duty's Clash with Autonomy and Other Values

The occurrence of conflict between a duty to obey the law and other moral values is implicit in what has already been said. The qualifications and exceptions to the duty have been necessitated by moral considerations other than the duty itself. But these points leave open the possibility that some space may be left for a duty to obey. Some philosophers have gone farther. Not content to assert that the duty to obey the law is provisional, of negligible weight, and superfluous, they argue that such a duty in any form would be incompatible with morality.

For example, in the eighteenth century William Godwin argued that notions such as the duty to obey the law amount to little more than prejudices that impair the exercise of the supreme virtues of individual judgment and benevolence. More recently, Wolff has argued that personal autonomy and legal or political authority are irreconcilable, and legal theorist Heidi Hurd has reinterpreted Godwin's and Wolff's criticisms as showing that a duty to obey the law is incompatible with rationality itself, in that the duty purports to require us sometimes to act contrary to the balance of all reasons.

A number of philosophers have responded to these challenges and have argued that authority, and the duty of obedience that political authority is thought to entail, are compatible with and practically necessary to individual autonomy. Thus, these replies typically rep-

---

[12]   Joseph Raz, "Authority and Consent," 67 *Virginia Law Review* 103, 130 (1981).

resent the duty to obey as instrumental to realizing values that include the exercise of personal autonomy. But, in order to know whether political authority is compatible with or essential to the pursuit of other moral values, we need to know what ends obedience is supposed to serve and how it serves them. This quickly leads the discussion into an arena that is the fourth source of doubt, that is, the difficulty of providing an adequate foundation for the alleged duty to obey the law.

The Duty's Lack of Adequate Foundation

In the *Crito,* Socrates' disciples urged him to flee the sentence of death Athens had imposed upon him. He refused, invoking a duty to obey that was grounded on his debt of gratitude to the city and on his consent to obey her laws. Thus began a philosophical effort that has spanned millennia: the effort to explain the grounds supporting the putative general duty to obey the law.

Express Consent. Express consent can, in the right circumstances, create a duty. Promising is a prime example. All of us have probably at one time or another recited a pledge of allegiance, or signed a loyalty oath. Some of us may have become naturalized citizens or taken an oath of office. Can such acts as these ground a general duty to obey the law? This approach leads to difficulty.

Promises generally are not binding unless the right conditions exist. I am not bound to trade you my favorite baseball card for your silver dollar if you have forced me to promise it to you by twisting my arm. Even if the baseball card is worth less than a dollar, no obligation arises – pace Hobbes[13] – because my consent was obtained by duress.

It is not within my moral power to make certain promises even freely. I cannot obligate myself to be your eternal, abject slave by promising to, no matter what I get in return.[14] I may of course be bound to return what I have received in consideration for the promise should I decide not to perform, but that is another matter. For the same reason, I cannot place myself under an obligation to do what-

---

[13] Cf. *Leviathan* (XVIII:5; XIV: 27) 92, 117.
[14] See Robert Nozick, *Anarchy, State, and Utopia* 280–92 (New York: Basic, 1974). As Paul Milich has pointed out to me, some of the less abject forms of servitude are not beyond our power to bargain into. Cf. Orlando Patterson, *Slavery and Social Death: A Comparative Study* (Cambridge, Mass.: Harvard University Press, 1982).

THE FAILURE OF POLITICAL OBLIGATION

ever you say. This makes it necessary to inquire what is the *scope* of the promise we make when we recite a pledge of allegiance.

In pledging allegiance "to the flag of the United States of America, and to the republic for which it stands," U.S. citizens could be understood to be promising a lot or only very little. At a minimum, they would seem to be promising not to take the side of foreign or domestic enemies of the United States in armed conflict. This is hardly enough to ground a general duty to obey the laws of the United States, unless it were true that every law violation is tantamount to treason – an implausible position. U.S. citizens cannot be understood to be pledging to do whatever the laws of the United States say to do – now and in all possible futures – for that would be beyond their power to promise.

Between the maximum and the minimum, it is unclear exactly what it is that people pledge when they pledge allegiance. Certain oaths of office are more explicit on this point where they speak of "upholding" the laws; the problem is that not everyone who is subject to the law has taken such an oath. Moreover, the lack of clarity of a promise normally counts against the party seeking to enforce it, especially if that party formulated it. That is the case with most oaths, pledges, and the like. In summary, those promises that are at all likely to have been made by most everybody are insufficiently clear in scope to count as binding; those that are clear enough to be binding haven't been taken by everyone who is supposed to be bound.

Hypothetical Consent. If the strategy of founding the duty to obey the law on the actual consent of its subjects falls short only because the necessary "illocutionary" acts of assent have not been performed,[15] then it is tempting to view this omission as one that might readily be corrected. It would of course be quixotic to try to correct the deficiency by asking the populace to recite a newly drawn, philosophically adequate pledge of allegiance – some people are bound to refuse, and forcing them to pledge under duress would not count as valid consent. But many philosophers have taken the position that actual consent is unnecessary in circumstances in which an adequately informed, fully rational person *would* assent (or would

---

[15] On illocutionary acts and performative utterances, see J. L. Austin, *How To Do Things with Words* (New York: Oxford University Press, 1962), and John Searle, *Speech Acts* (Cambridge: Cambridge University Press, 1969).

assent but for a wish to gain a strategic advantage over others by withholding assent). If, for example, I am found unconscious and bleeding to death, a doctor who administers life-saving measures need not fear that I may later sue him for battery – this is because the law will ask not whether I consented to be touched but whether in such an emergency a reasonable person *would* consent.[16]

Working out this suggestion requires specifying the circumstances that must exist for consent to be rationally compelled. It will be useful to distinguish between two types of specification of circumstances. One type will rely on facts about actual voluntary conduct on the part of those subject to the relevant duty; another type will not. The first type of specification is better understood as pursuing the idea of consent implied from conduct, or "implied consent," for short. But here, where the idea is hypothetical consent, we want to specify a set of conditions that makes no reference to any conduct on the part of those purportedly subject to a general duty to obey the law. For example, one might say that a perfectly just, highly beneficial scheme of mutual cooperation that depended upon mutual subjection to rules is one that a rational person *would* consent to.

But now one must ask, as David Schmidtz has done, whether the idea of hypothetical consent is doing any real work.[17] If a state of a certain description were capable of making a moral claim upon a hypothetical rational subject, it is hard to see what the idea of consent adds to the account. In other words, if some set of conditions C is capable of rationally compelling consent, and that consent in turn imposes a general duty of obedience, why not simply say that conditions C generate a duty of obedience and leave consent out of it? If actual consent is necessary to generate a duty, my even irrational refusal enables me to avoid it. To say that reason requires me to assent imputes to reason a power that it does not have – for I have the power to be obstinate. To say that in circumstance C I have a duty whether I actually consent or not is to say that consent is unnecessary – nothing is gained by going on to say that I would consent if I weren't irrational. Going on in that way simply recapitulates the grounds that are ex hypothesi sufficient to impose a duty. Hypothetical-consent accounts boil down to accounts of the conditions C that might ground a duty to obey;

---

[16] See *McGuire v Rix*, 225 N.W. 120 (Neb. 1929); cf. Jeremy Waldron, "Theoretical Foundations of Liberalism," 37 *Philosophical Quarterly* 127, 138–9 (1987).
[17] David Schmidtz, "Justifying the State," 101 *Ethics* 89, 96 (1990).

and I will treat such types of ground – such as utility and necessity – below.

Implied Consent. "Implied" consent differs from hypothetical consent in that it has reference to what a subject has in fact done, as opposed to what she would have done (though didn't) were she rational. If I am gagging on a piece of roast beef and I gesture at my throat while looking imploringly at the physician seated at the next table, my consent to her touching me can be inferred from my conduct. But notice that consent can be inferred from actual conduct even when a rational person might have withheld it. If you offer me fifty dollars to paint your house and I paint half of it, I have a duty to finish the job even though I never *said* I would,[18] and even though reason did not compel me to begin painting in the first place.

Implied consent ambiguously may refer either to conduct that is (rebuttable) evidence of actual consent or to conduct that is deemed conclusively to be the "moral equivalent" of consent whether consent was actual or not. In the former sense, implied consent includes what has been called "tacit" consent. Tacit consent, simply put, is an expression of consent manifested by silence in circumstances in which silence can reasonably be so taken, for example, when a proposal is put to me by my dentist and I fail to object, if circumstances are such that she may reasonably expect me to state that I disagree if in fact I do.[19] Implied consent in this sense, generally, and tacit consent in particular, are subject to the points made earlier about express consent.

Implied consent in the second sense mentioned above is based on conduct but is not rebuttable by evidence that the subject did not actually consent. The suggestion that there is a duty to obey the law created by implied consent in this latter sense[20] requires us to state what conduct, or combination of conduct and circumstances, must exist to generate the duty. As in the case of hypothetical consent, the real task is that of specifying the relevant conditions, and the question of actual consent is superfluous. Implied consent in this sense

---

[18]   Cf. Restatement (2d) of Contracts §50 & illus. 1 (St. Paul, Minn.: West, 1981).

[19]   See A. John Simmons, *Moral Principles and Political Obligations* 79–83 (Princeton: Princeton University Press, 1979).

[20]   This may be the sense Locke had in mind – see John Locke, *Second Treatise of Government* §119 (Cambridge: Cambridge University Press, 1960) – but a compelling case to the contrary is made in A. John Simmons, *On the Edge of Anarchy* 80–90 (Princeton: Princeton University Press, 1993).

makes a difference only where I did not, in fact, consent, but my conduct is such that I ought to be deemed to have consented.[21] What counts is the specification of conduct C that generates the duty. It is idle to add that conduct C amounts to consent and consent entails the duty. Accordingly, as in the case of hypothetical consent; what has to be looked at are the various candidates for conduct C – such as participation and receipt of benefits – and they will be discussed in turn in what follows.

Participation. Participation in a democratic process – for example, by voting, lobbying, running for or serving in office – has been thought to impose on the participant a duty to abide by the outcomes of that process. Therefore, participants have a duty to obey those laws that are outcomes – desired or not – of the democratic processes they have participated in.

One difficulty with this approach is that it fails to impose any duty on those who do not participate in democratic processes. Another is that it does not seem capable of imposing a duty with respect to laws that antedate one's participation. Saying that by participating I undertake a duty to abide by the results of the democratic process – whether past, present, or future – brings us back to the problem of scope discussed earlier. Why does my voting in the November, 1988, general election, for example, bind me to obey whatever causally flows from that event, even to executive and legislative results that I think wrongful? If, for example, I voted for Bush because I believed I could "read his lips" ("No new taxes!"), why should I be bound by a law signed by Bush that contravenes his promise? Representative democracy typically involves voting for personalities, not programs, and often for the losing personality. If an explicit pledge of allegiance cannot ground a general duty to obey, it is hard to see how the more ambiguous act of voting could, without more, do the trick.

Receipt of Benefits (Gratitude). Participation in the democratic process is not a condition that one must satisfy in order to receive its benefits.

---

21 Lawyers will recall the case of *Lucy v Zehmer,* 84 S.E.2d 516 (Va. 1954), in which the outwardly serious but (perhaps) inwardly joking defendant was held to the bargain he had let the plaintiff believe he was making. This is not properly a case of implied consent but an application of the doctrine that the law looks to "the outward expression as manifesting his intention," rather than to what remains "secret and unexpressed."

Everyone benefits from national defense, police protection, a system of civil justice to resolve private disputes, a stable currency, a modern economy supported by an infrastructure of public works, and so forth – all the fruits of a modern industrial state. Even those who refuse to vote benefit. Even those who try to opt out of society altogether benefit, for many of these benefits – "public goods," such as protection from foreign enemies – are impossible to refuse. For such benefits one owes a debt of gratitude and, as Socrates argued, such a debt is one payable by obedience.

This is one of the oldest arguments for a general duty to obey the law and therefore one of the most criticized. In the abstract, A's merely benefiting B in a way that B cannot refuse does not always and automatically impose on B any duty of gratitude. If, for example, B is idling at a traffic light and A wipes clean B's dirty windshield, it is doubtful that B is now duty-bound to be grateful, much less to gratefully compensate A.

But serious problems arise even if we assume that some debt of gratitude is owed, for it is now necessary to specify exactly what that debt is and how it may be discharged. (Let's assume that the state is the entity to whom the debt is owed – rather than, say, some set of individuals.) If there is a general duty to obey the law, then my debt of gratitude must be such as to reach each and every law, regardless of whether I (or anyone) happen to benefit from it. Why this much obedience? And why obedience at all? Why isn't it enough for me to express my gratitude in some other way, for example, by being patriotic, by voting, by volunteering for the army, by not taking every last deduction I might on my income taxes, et cetera? No satisfactory account has yet been given why obedience – rather than something else – is the debt owed and why that debt is so extensive that it encompasses every law, rather than only the beneficial ones.

This difficulty might be met if the benefits of life under government were expressly conditioned upon the beneficiaries' acknowledgment of a general duty to obey the law. Suppose that Junior's rich uncle offers to pay for Junior's education if he will abide by Uncle's extensive Code of Righteous Living, and that Junior allows Uncle to put him through college. Now, one wants to say that not only does Junior owe Uncle a debt of gratitude, but the debt can be paid only by Junior's abiding by Uncle's Code.[22] States do in fact claim – if

---

[22] Lawyers will recognize this example as a twist on the facts of *Hamer v Sidway*, 27 N.E. 256 (N.Y. 1891), where the uncle had in fact not paid, and the issue was

sometimes only implicitly – that there is a general duty to obey their laws, and living under government does in fact offer huge advantages over Hobbes's state of nature. Unfortunately, (1) the duty of obedience that states claim is claimed *unconditionally* – "opting out" is not an option; and (2) many of the benefits of living under government are public goods, that is, ones that the state cannot easily deny or that cannot justly be withheld in any event, for example, due process for outlaws. The coincidence of demand and benefit is not like that in the Rich Uncle case, and so the analogy fails.

Another problem is that many laws prohibit what is (independently) morally wrong, and it would be odd to say that I have a duty not to murder because I am indebted to a criminal justice system that punishes murder. I already have sufficient moral reason not to do what the murder statute forbids, and it is difficult to see how my refraining from what I ought not to do anyway could discharge a debt of gratitude. It would be as though I had said, "Honey, I'm so pleased with my new necktie that I won't use it to strangle the cat!" My not strangling the cat is a standing duty I have; fulfilling that duty cannot discharge a duty to show gratitude for the necktie.

Expectations. Another approach founds the duty to obey the law on the expectations we create by living among others. The argument is this: Others have a right to expect that I will obey the law, at least to the extent that they too obey it. Because rights generally impose correlative duties, the right of others to expect that I will obey the laws they do imposes a correlative duty upon me to obey those laws. Therefore (on this line of reasoning) I have a duty to obey the (generally obeyed) laws.

This line of argument echoes Socrates' claim that by failing to emigrate from the state in which we reside we subject ourselves to a duty to obey its laws. Socrates' claim about the moral effect of not emigrating can be expressed in terms of implied consent as well, but the receipt of benefits and expectations that "hanging around" likely involves largely exhaust its moral significance. More recently, Ronald Dworkin has explained political obligation as a species of what he calls "associative obligations," in terms that appear to rely at

whether the nephew's promise of clean living was adequate legal "consideration" though perhaps of no benefit to the uncle. Paul Milich suggested to me that the specification of duty difficulty might be handled this way.

least indirectly on the expectations idea.[23] This approach's points of vulnerability are evidently: (1) the premise that others have a right to expect that I will continue to do what I have done in the past and they (generally) do and (2) the premise that states generally that A's right to expect that B will φ entails that B has a duty to φ. These have to be examined in turn.

The first premise is either inadequate or flatly false. It is inadequate insofar as it fails to ground an argument that bears on the cases of the avowed anarchist, or libertarian, or notorious criminal who dispel any expectation that they will obey the law. Another intractable class of cases is that of those who secretly, or at least discreetly, disavow obedience or engage in disobedience. Not having sought to create a contrary impression, such persons cannot have conveyed to anyone any right to expect they will continue to do as they have, in fact, never done. Leaving these cases aside, there is still trouble.

Not every expectation of conformity that others have is legitimate. Even if I have served my master faithfully in the past, he has no legitimate expectation that I will continue to do so. Even slaves that have become so habituated to their slavery that they do not wish to be anything else cannot legitimately be expected to continue, because slavery is *wrongful* even if consented to.

Let us leave aside cases involving unjust institutional backgrounds or expectations that involuntary conduct will continue. The institutions most of us live under are reasonably or nearly just, or at least they are not radically unjust in the way that the antebellum South or Nazi Germany were. Moreover, most of us have conveyed, and have been happy to convey, the impression that we are generally law-abiding. We have benefited by conveying and maintaining this expectation because we are seen, to that extent, as more trustworthy to be around and to deal with.

But so what? We already have qualified the expectation we create by saying we are *generally* law-abiding. Rather few of us in Atlanta, Georgia, where I live, create the expectation that we will observe the posted speed limit. Few of us in the United States who employ domestic servants create the expectation that we will file the required quarterly report of what we pay.[24] We can't create these expectations

---

[23] See Ronald Dworkin, *Law's Empire* 195–202 (Cambridge, Mass.: Harvard University Press, 1986).

[24] Think of the Zoe Baird debacle. "Hiring of Illegal Workers by Baird Sparks Little Uproar; Senators Signal Justice Dept. Nominee Won't Be Harmed by Doing What

easily even if we in fact comply with the law, because it is well-known that the overall level of compliance is rather low.

As to the second premise, even if there were a right to expect that I would obey the law, it is not clear that that legitimate expectation, by itself, would create a general duty on my part to do so. While some rights entail correlative duties, there may be others that do not. Robert Ladenson has distinguished between "claim rights" – in the terminology of the legal philosopher Wesley Newcomb Hohfeld – and what Ladenson calls "justification rights."[25] The chief difference between the two is that claim rights entail a correlative duty on someone's part, while justification rights do not. My right to expect you to keep our dinner date is an example of the former, my right to defend myself against a lunatic attacker exemplifies the latter, if the attacker's lunacy is such that she is not subject to the usual standards of moral appraisal. Unless the putative right to expect me to obey the law is a claim right, rather than a justification right, no duty on my part to obey need follow. All that need follow is that others are justified in taking measures to promote my compliance.

Even if the supposed right to expect me to obey the law is a claim right, it needn't follow that the correlative duty I have is a duty to *obey*. In other words, my corresponding duty needn't be strictly correlative, as it would be if the verb that stands in for the "ϕ" in the formula "*A* has the right to expect that *B* will ϕ" were the only thing that could be plugged into the corresponding duty phrase: "*B* has a duty to ϕ." If it were possible for me to satisfy the corresponding duty by ϕ-ing or by *doing something else,* then the argument for the duty to obey the law would go off the tracks. But often substitute performances satisfy duties. For example, if I promise you "anything" – a trip to Paris, say – but instead give you a bottle of Arpège (an expensive French perfume), I may have done enough to honor your claim right to expect me to keep my promise.

"But surely there is no substitute for strict compliance with the law," one wants to say. "The fine for exceeding the speed limit is a *sanction* intended to put an end to speeding; it isn't meant to be a

Many Working Parents Do," *Los Angeles Times*, January 15, 1993, p. A1, col. 5; "Attorney General-Designate Baird Fined for Undocumented Workers," *The Washington Post*, January 17, 1993, p. A4; Oliphant, "Blame Clinton, not Baird," *The Boston Globe*, January 24, 1993, p. 75.

25 Robert Ladenson, "In Defense of a Hobbesian Conception of Law," 9 *Philosophy & Public Affairs* 134–59 (1980); cf. Wesley Newcomb Hohfeld, *Fundamental Legal Conceptions* (New Haven: Yale University Press, 1919).

mere means of raising revenue nor as price or fee that merely rations speeding to those willing to pay to do it."[26] This is a fine sentiment, if a bit priggish. But do we really believe that, for example, paying a parking ticket never fully satisfies our moral debt for parking in a loading zone? It may be that we are doubtful of a duty of perfect compliance just where we are doubtful that there is a general expectation of obedience.[27] The nineteenth-century sodomy laws still on the books in Georgia and other states are a probable example; we don't think we're bound by them, in part, because we don't think obedience is seriously expected.

But now the argument from expectations has to take account not only of the fact that not everyone expects us to comply, but also that there are laws to which there are varying degrees of expected compliance. Some legal rules are enacted or announced with little or no expectation that they will be observed. The decision in *Brown v Board of Education*[28] was handed down with a hope rather than an expectation that it would be implemented. The Kennesaw, Georgia, ordinance[29] requiring homeowners to possess a firearm was adopted with no intention of enforcing compliance. We might say that there was a right to expect compliance with *Brown*, because *Brown* was the right thing to do, and no right to expect anyone to comply with the Kennesaw ordinance because it wasn't (or vice versa, diverse Reader!) – but this would return us to the earlier-noticed difficulty that the mere legality of a norm seems to have no independent role in the determination of what one morally ought to do.

Respect. This argument, advanced by Philip Soper,[30] states in essence that we have a duty to respect those officials who in good faith strive to further the common good by maintaining the rule of law. The way we do that is by acknowledging a duty to obey the law. There are officials who are making a good faith effort. Therefore, we should acknowledge a duty to obey the law. Therefore, since we ought to acknowledge a duty only if we have it, we have a duty to obey the law.

---

[26] See Robert Cooter, "Prices and Sanctions," 84 *Columbia Law Review* 1523 (1984); see also Joel Feinberg, "The Expressive Function of Punishment," in *Doing and Deserving* (Princeton: Princeton University Press, 1970); but cf. Randy E. Barnett, "Restitution: A New Paradigm of Criminal Justice," 87 *Ethics* 279 (1977).

[27] Cf. Liam B. Murphy, "The Demands of Beneficence," 22 *Philosophy & Public Affairs* 267 (1993).

[28] *Brown v Board of Education of Topeka, Kansas [Brown I],* 347 U.S. 483 (1954).

[29] City of Kennesaw Code of Ordinances §8–10 (1982).

[30] Philip Soper, *A Theory of Law* (Cambridge, Mass.: Harvard University Press, 1984).

Two things are distinctive about this modern variation on the Socratic "gratitude" theme. The first is that the obligee (the person to whom the duty is owed) is not that abstract entity, the state, nor is the duty owed to our fellow citizens severally or corporately. It is owed to those of the official class who act in good faith to bring about a better world through the rule of law. No more need be said about this; it is not clear what advantage it was meant to enjoy over the Socratic version. The second distinctive point is that this variation articulates an additional step in the reasoning, from having a *duty to acknowledge* a duty to obey, to having a duty to obey. It may be that the move from gratitude to duty was too compressed in the Socratic version; here it is made plain that our duty is, in the first instance, one of acknowledging efforts of a certain kind, efforts to maintain the rule of law for everyone's benefit. That intermediate duty implies the duty to obey.

Does this additional step avoid the difficulty that the gratitude argument met at this juncture, namely, that gratitude might be manifested by means other than obedience? Making a difficulty explicit is, alas, not necessarily to remedy it. There are many ways that *B* might acknowledge *A*'s good faith effort to bring it about that, inter alia, everyone does ϕ. Some of those ways may not include ϕ-ing. A CEO might have a duty to acknowledge the good faith efforts of her Vice-President for Planning without, thereby, having a duty to follow the vice-president's plan.[31]

Utility. Utility is the ground of the duty to obey the law in Jeremy Bentham's great system of jurisprudence. For a utilitarian, it is our duty to perform that act that will, in the circumstances, produce the greatest surplus of utility over disutility – or of pleasure over displeasure, or satisfaction over dissatisfaction (depending on how we formulate the utilitarian principle). Duty is thus determined by a calculation of the utilitarian consequences of the various alternatives open to a person at a time.

But – leaving aside the "probable mischiefs"[32] of the mere act of disobedience – what assurance is there that what the law requires will be the best choice from a utilitarian perspective? Bentham saw that there was none unless the law were thoroughly reformed along

---

[31] Cf. Kent Greenawalt, *Conflicts of Law and Morality* 51–2 (New York: Oxford University Press, 1987).
[32] Jeremy Bentham, *A Fragment on Government*, J. H. Burns and H. L. A. Hart, eds., I:43 (Cambridge: Cambridge University Press, 1988).

utilitarian lines. But is even that enough? Laws are necessarily fixed antecedently to conduct, are stated in general language incapable of capturing every nuance that an actual event may exhibit, and are therefore inevitably going to forbid some acts that will be, in the circumstances, "optimific" in the utilitarian sense. This is unavoidable unless the utilitarian principle itself is made the supreme law – but that principle is a notoriously uncertain guide to conduct. (Imagine driving in a country where the only rule of the road was: Drive As You Think Best!)

One possible fix for this difficulty is to focus the utilitarian calculus on the question "What *rule* would it be best to follow in this and similar situations?" rather than on "What act would be best in this situation?" This shift in focus would take us to what is termed "rule utilitarianism" as opposed to "act utilitarianism."[33] Rule utilitarianism seems at first a likelier candidate to serve as an adequate foundation for a general duty to obey the law, because laws are rules and rule utilitarianism defines duty as the best rule, rather than the best act. But we have to ask, is what the law requires invariably the best rule to follow? The answer of course is No. Sometimes what the law requires is silly, wasteful, even harmful if not outright evil. Sometimes the law gets it right, or right enough, for it to be better that all unthinkingly obey the law rather than attempt their own individual calculations of what's best. But – unless we posit a preestablished harmony between what the law happens to require and what a complete rule-utilitarian calculation would require – there is no reason to believe that the law generally states what is, in utilitarian terms, the best rule.

But what if we take into account the effects of disobedience as well as other effects? My first act of disobedience sets a precedent for me that will make it likelier that I will discount too deeply the law's success in correcting the bias, lack of information, and coordination problems that individuals acting alone cannot as effectively cure. My disobedience sets an example to others that will, in turn, erode their confidence that the law states the best rule and is being complied with generally enough to be effective. Once these effects are included, isn't there an at least prima facie duty to obey the law?

Return now to the stop sign in the desert at dawn. I have a generally law-abiding disposition and am alone. My well-entrenched

---

[33] See, e.g., David Lyons, *Forms and Limits of Utilitarianism* (Oxford: Clarendon Press, 1965).

habit is to come to a full stop before proceeding, but I want to know *what it is like* to disobey the law. No harm can come from my going through the intersection without the full stop the law requires – of that I am as certain as I can practically be. (And, if you insist on this assurance, assume that I will take a drug that will erase any corrosive effects on my character that this act of disobedience might otherwise have.) What, other than fetishism, an abject, abstract sycophancy, could compel anyone to say that in these circumstances I nevertheless have a prima facie duty to come to a full stop?

If there being a *moral reason to* φ were all that was needed to impose *a prima facie duty to* φ, it might be sensible to insist in this case that there *is* a prima facie duty to stop. But what moral reason is there to stop, other than the fact that the law requires it? As I have described the case, there is none. Moreover, there is good reason not to count *every* moral reason to φ as imposing a prima facie duty to φ. Suppose that Susan (whom I don't know) would benefit if I bought a new copy of her book rather than a used one. Have I a prima facie duty to buy a new rather than a used copy? I would say not. But one who holds (as I do) that there is a general prima facie duty to benefit others might have to say that this moral principle, combined with the presumably morally relevant fact that Susan will benefit if, but only if, I buy a new copy of her book, generates a specific (though very weak) moral reason to buy the new copy. But if there is nothing more to having a prima facie duty to φ than having a moral reason to φ, then I would appear to have a prima facie duty to buy a new copy of Susan's book. Ways out of this apparent dilemma are available – for example, deny the general duty of beneficence, deny the moral relevance of the fact about Susan – but this is not the place to discuss them. For our purposes it is enough to note that a morally relevant reason to φ is not generally sufficient to impose a prima facie duty to φ. What is needed is an additional condition stating that the reason has significant weight (outside tie-breaking situations in which any relevant reason has "significant" weight).

Discussion of the stop sign in the desert case leads to a depressing impasse. Those who believe that there is a sufficiently significant moral reason to obey the law in all situations will intuit a prima facie duty to do so here; those who don't, won't.[34] Those who intuit a sufficiently strong moral reason will, accordingly, be inclined to think

---

[34] Cf. P. F. Strawson, "Ethical Intuitionism," 24 *Philosophy* 23 (1949).

that the actor should feel compunction and should "make it up" to society in some way for having violated the law. Those who don't, won't. Although Chaim Gans is correct that this type of case is, *in a sense*, "trivial and unimportant,"[35] a counterexample *is* a counterexample, and the thesis under discussion *is* the thesis that there is a general, prima facie duty to obey the law. Moreover, trivial as the stop-in-the-desert example may seem, the type of case it represents is a huge class. If our background morality prefers liberty to constraint, lack of a consensus intuition about the stop sign case would appear to count against the party of constraint – here, the party intuiting a duty to obey in the thin desert air.

Necessity. The duty to obey the law has been said, by Anthony Honoré,[36] to be founded on the necessity that it exist, in order that we might enjoy the fruits of civilized life. Despite the fact that even Kant resorted to the necessity explanation,[37] it essentially is a variation on the theme of utility, and many of the remarks about utility apply here. The main objection is that civilization as we know it simply does not hang in the balance every time one of us jaywalks. Civilization has survived quite a lot of lawlessness, and some have feared, perhaps with reason, that perfect law-abidingness is as ominous as the prospect of anarchy.

Fairness. A personal digression: The problem of the duty to obey the law was made vivid to me years ago when I was a graduate student in Berkeley, California. This had nothing to do with the Cambodia bombing, People's Park, or civil disobedience in the usual sense. One sunny day (most of them were sunny) I was walking on the deserted fringe of downtown and came to an intersection governed by a traffic light and "Walk/Don't Walk" signs. No car was in sight nor, it seemed, was there any other person around. I looked to my left. I looked to my right. I craned my neck to make sure that no car was entering the intersection from any direction. The "Don't Walk" sign

---

[35] Chaim Gans, *Philosophical Anarchism and Political Disobedience* 91 (Cambridge: Cambridge University Press, 1992).
[36] The Symposium in Honor of A. D. Woozley: "Law and Obedience," 67 *Virginia Law Review* 1 (1981).
[37] Immanuel Kant, *Die Metaphysik der Sitten*, translated by H. B. Nisbet as "The Metaphysics of Morals," in Hans Reiss, ed., *Kant's Political Writings* 136–8 (Cambridge: Cambridge University Press, 1970).

was illuminated but I, impatient to be about my business, walked across the street. Midway across, I noticed a man, standing on the curb that I was approaching, glowering at me. His scowl deepened as I approached. He was evidently about to cross the street himself, but not until the "Don't Walk" sign had changed to "Walk." He was middle-aged, neatly dressed, and though he was bespectacled there was nothing in the least academic about him. I assumed that he was some civilian employee of the military, or perhaps a father on a mission to rescue a wayward child, à la Mr. Robinson in "The Graduate." "Who, me, Benjamin Braddock?" I thought, withering under his gaze.

As I was about to step on the curb the man finally spoke: "Hey cancha read the sign says *Don't Walk!*" As indeed it did. I avoided eye contact and hurried on my way, certain that this was the safest way to deal with one of those cross-cultural collisions that sometimes occur in Berkeley.[38] As soon as I was safely beyond earshot I muttered *"What* a jerk!" to calm myself.

But I was troubled. *Had* I done something *wrong?* "My God!" I thought, "No cars were coming! If there were, I was the one that stood to get hurt!" But there was no question that my legal duty was to wait. I had not even given that a thought, not anyway until my *censor morum,* like the good angel in a Disney cartoon, appeared at my ear. Which of us, I began to wonder, was the (bigger) jerk?

I have not yet been able to settle myself on the issue. Even if I were remiss in failing to consider what the law required, just because it was the law, it was not necessarily his business to remind me (more of this later). I had already crossed the street, safely; what right had he to complain? What was it to him? Nowadays, as I glare at the BMWs cannonballing past me on the autobahns of Atlanta, I have greater difficulty answering: "Nothing!" I find myself thinking, "It's just *not fair* that I go 55 and everybody else goes 70 in a 55-mph zone," just as, I'm sure, Mr. Robinson thought it was just *not fair* that I could blithely ignore a "Don't Walk" sign that he was heeding. Consider the following point by H. L. A. Hart:

---

[38] Paul Milich has suggested to me that Mr. Robinson may have hailed from Seattle, where a spirit of "civic seriousness" – reaching such punctilios as waiting for the "Don't Walk" sign to change – prevails. Chuck Marvin reports that a Berliner once laid a hand upon his shoulder to discourage his crossing the Kurfürstendamm against the light. As for the special case of New York City, see "Mayor Seeks to Hobble Jaywalkers," *The N.Y. Times,* Jan. 13, 1998, at A17, col. 5; "Evading Cars, and the Law, in Dodge City," *The N.Y. Times,* Jan. 14, 1998, at C28, col.2.

> When a number of persons conduct any joint enterprise according to rules and thus restrict their liberty, those who have submitted to these restrictions when required have a right to a similar submission from those who have benefitted by their submission. . . . In social situations of this sort . . . the obligation to obey the rules is something distinct from whatever other moral reasons there may be for obedience in terms of good consequences (e.g., the prevention of suffering).[39]

Hart's idea has been taken up by John Rawls as stating a "Principle of Fairness," which gives rise to something like the duty to obey the law:

> This principle holds that a person is required to do his part as defined by the rules of an institution when two conditions are met: first, the institution is just (or fair) . . . and second, one has voluntarily accepted the benefits of the arrangement or taken advantage of the opportunities it offers to further one's interests.[40]

Rawls himself opined that "there is, I believe, no political obligation [i.e., duty to obey the law], strictly speaking, for citizens generally." He offered instead a more diffuse "natural duty" to "support and comply with just institutions" as the moral glue binding all citizens of a just state – with or without their consent. But, as noted above, there is an uncertain step that has to be taken from a "natural" duty to support (or respect) just institutions to a duty to comply with each and every one of their (applicable) laws. Moreover, the idea of a natural duty to support just institutions itself requires some sort of defense. If justice is fairness, why do I have a duty to support every fair enterprise that happens to benefit me? The floating crap game in the alley may be perfectly fair and amusing to watch, but if I choose not to support it, how can its mere fairness impose on me a duty to the contrary?

Other philosophers have tried to take the Principle of Fairness farther. What Hart and Rawls have instigated is a project of tying together a sophisticated combination of some of the ideas we have already canvassed: receipt of benefits, expectations, implied consent. Further conditions have been suggested – for example, that the "joint enterprise" or "institution" be superior in utilitarian terms to any

---

[39] H. L. A. Hart, "Are There Any Natural Rights?," 64 *Philosophical Review* 175 (1955).
[40] John Rawls, *A Theory of Justice* 111–12, 114, 115 (Cambridge, Mass.: Harvard University Press, 1971).

alternative, and that the obligor (lawyerese for the person under a duty) enjoy a net benefit in terms of her own interests from the enterprise or institution. These further amendments acknowledge that, while the fairness idea standing alone will not suffice, it can serve as a rallying point for other ideas that have seemed relevant to the issue of "political obligation," or what I have been calling the general duty to obey the law. Fully worked out, a Principle of Fairness will rest not on an appeal to fairness alone, but on a combination of factors whose joint power offers the strongest nonconsensual foundation for obedience that we are ever likely to have.

I will not explore in any further detail the question of what is the best, most unexceptionable form of the Principle of Fairness. Even in its best form, it cannot in itself answer all of the arguments against the existence of a general duty to obey. In particular, even the best attempt to provide a foundation for a general duty to obey will have no force in cases where that foundation would be unaffected by disobedience – the unshakable traffic-sign-in-the-middle-of-the-desert cases. Even Chaim Gans, an advocate of the fairness approach, confesses that "fairness doesn't require obedience to all laws on every occasion to which they apply. It [only] requires that they be obeyed . . . when disobedience might cause damage or lead either directly or indirectly to negative consequences."[41]

Returning now to the three propositions forming the inconsistent triad noted at the beginning of this chapter, we can see that the second of them – the denial that there exists a general duty to obey the law – is perhaps not so implausible after all. I don't mean to endorse each of the skeptical arguments we have canvassed along the way, but I think we have to acknowledge that, collectively, they do raise grave doubts about the existence of a general duty to obey. In fact, according to Leslie Green, there is "a significant coalescence of opinion"[42] that there is no such duty; what at the outset seemed to be the least plausible of the three turns out to be, as Philip Soper puts it, "the currently fashionable conclusion."[43] Green and Soper are not talking about the consensus of wild-eyed cranks huddled in tar-paper shacks

---

[41] Chaim Gans, *Philosophical Anarchism and Political Disobedience* 64 n.57 (Cambridge: Cambridge University Press, 1992).
[42] Leslie Green, "Who Believes in Political Obligation?" in John T. Sanders and Jan Narveson, eds. *For and Against the State* 28 (Lanham, Md.: Rowman & Littlefield, 1996).
[43] Philip Soper, "Legal Theory and the Claim of Authority," 18 *Philosophy & Public Affairs* 209, 211 (1989).

in Montana – they are referring to eminent professors at places like Oxford, Virginia, Michigan, Columbia, and Toronto. What are we to make of this?

PHILOSOPHICAL ANARCHISM

So what if there is no general duty to obey the law – no general political obligation, in other words? If the first of the triad of propositions set out at the beginning of the chapter is also true – that a state is legitimate only if it claims to impose and, in fact, does impose on its subjects a general, at least prima facie, duty to obey its laws – we are logically impelled toward the view called *philosophical anarchism*, which is the denial of the third proposition, that legitimate states are possible and actual. "There are," as John Simmons tersely puts it, "no morally legitimate states." The position is called *philosophical* anarchism to distinguish it from the more notorious *political* anarchism popularly associated with bombs and beards, Sacco and Vanzetti. Philosophical anarchists are not committed to bringing down the existing political order and even concede that "government may be necessary and that certain governments ought to be supported." But their support rests on general moral reasons that deny the state any right to rule or any presumption that there is moral reason to act as its laws require.[44]

Philosophical anarchists need not deny that "a significant body of the law's requirements, both civil and criminal, constitutes a formalization, with the backing of coercive sanctions, of independently binding moral requirements." Where what morality requires and what the law requires converge, the philosophical anarchist's practical recommendation will coincide with that of the state. But philosophical anarchism is not a "toothless doctrine," for, as Simmons points out, where "the law prohibits harmless conduct, where it imposes specifically political duties, and where disobedience has no dramatic negative consequences," these practical recommendations will diverge. Philosophical anarchism's teeth "will be found in its assertions that many distinctively political requirements – such as payment of certain taxes or military service – along with many paternalistic and moralistic laws and laws creating victimless crimes may

---

[44] A. John Simmons, "The Anarchist Position," 16 *Philosophy & Public Affairs* 268, 268 (1987).

be disobeyed without moral impropriety."[45] Nevertheless, Simmons assures us, the illegitimacy of the state – the fact that the state is nothing but a "powerful bully" – does not entail any moral duty to oppose the state or to eliminate it.

What I want to do in the following chapter is to show that the denial that a general political obligation exists, that is, the denial that there is a general duty to obey the law, does not compel us to accept the philosophical anarchist conclusion that there can be no legitimate state. But before I turn to that task, I want to remark first on the image of the convergence and nonconvergence of law and morality and, secondly, on the idea that no moral duty arises from the conclusion that the law is simply a powerful bully.

As I will explore in greater detail in later chapters, where the requirements of law and those of morality diverge is not altogether obvious. Simmons mentions taxation, paternalistic laws, laws enacting "contested moral and religious doctrines," and laws that forbid drug use or oral sex, and he suggests that without the prop supplied by political obligation there is no compelling moral reason to do what the law would have us do in these domains. Intentionally or not, Simmons encourages the thought that morality allows a more *libertarian* mode of conduct than the (nonlibertarian) state allows. But this view of the divergence is not compelled by philosophical anarchism. Morality may (or may not), for example, require acts of benevolence more stringent than what a progressive tax code requires. If law loses its presumption of moral correctness, then of course the law-abiding must also have lost any presumption of moral rectitude that they might otherwise have enjoyed. As for "contested moral and religious doctrines," in modern democracies the law enacts toleration that those doctrines themselves have not always permitted. Although philosophical anarchism may be motivated by a desire to clear the field for classical liberal or libertarian moral views, it does not, by itself, prefer them.

If one happens to hold libertarian or classical liberal views, however – and even if one does not – it is difficult to understand how we can take with equanimity the revelation that, as philosophical anarchism has it, the law is nothing but a powerful bully. Even if we happen to believe that there is a vast convergence between what the

---

[45] A. John Simmons, "Philosophical Anarchism," in John T. Sanders and Jan Narveson, eds., *For and Against the State* 28, 29, 22, 32 (Lanham, Md.: Rowman & Littlefield, 1996).

powerful bully exacts and what morality requires, we surely ought to be disturbed. In the area of divergence, we must now believe that a powerful bully enforces its will against the liberty of unconsenting people. This sounds like tyranny. In the area of convergence, we must now believe that a powerful bully illegitimately compels right-eous conduct. This sounds like a denial of autonomy and a drastic restriction of the scope of virtue. Even if the powerful bully offers compensating benefits, moral complacency does not seem to be an option here.

Chapter 2

The Correlativity Thesis

A theory of legitimacy has a three-part structure. The first part is a benchmark or *criterion* of legitimacy, such as a capacity to create political obligation, or an ability to command rational assent, or a moral permission to coerce. The criterion is a central, necessary condition of state legitimacy. The second component of a theory of legitimacy is a substantive moral one that serves to establish what does and does not satisfy the criterion component, for example, a theory of political obligation, to tell us under what conditions, if any, there is a general duty of obedience; or a theory of practical rationality, to tell us under what conditions, if any, reasonable agents would submit to state authority; or a theory of permissions, to establish the conditions, if any, under which state coercion might be morally permissible.

Unlike the first two components, the third is not normative; it describes the social facts that are the necessary background of legitimate authority. When speaking of states, it may be that the criterion is satisfied but an effort to exercise state authority fails to attain legitimacy because too few subjects recognize the authority as legitimate. This can happen where no authority has been established or a more entrenched authority occupies the field. Because our focus here is on the normative aspects of legitimacy, let us assume that there is the degree of de facto or "Weberian" acceptance sufficient to satisfy the third component. Taken together, the three components will state necessary and sufficient conditions of political legitimacy.

The first proposition of the Inconsistent Triad in Chapter 1 – that a state is legitimate only if it claims to impose and in fact does impose on its subjects a general, at least prima facie, duty to obey its laws – states a criterion of legitimacy; while the second proposition – that there is no general, even prima facie, duty to obey the laws of a state, not even those of a just state – reports the outcome of recent substantive thinking about political obligation. Philosophical anarchism simply draws the conclusion that a legitimate state is impossible. The first proposition – which I will call the "Simple Correlativity Thesis," until we have unpacked its complexities – was initially plausible. Now it is time to subject it to scrutiny as close as what has been brought to bear on the proposition that political obligation – that is, a general duty to obey the law – exists.

THE SIMPLE CORRELATIVITY THESIS

The Simple Correlativity Thesis holds that a state is legitimate only if it claims to impose and in fact does impose on its subjects a general, at least prima facie, duty to obey its laws. The Thesis is taken for granted by many writers – Wolff, most notably – and something like it often seems implicit even where not expressly avowed. Simmons, for example, tells us: "A state's (or government's) legitimacy is its moral right to impose binding duties on its subjects and to use coercion to enforce those duties. Accordingly, state legitimacy is the logical correlate of subjects' political obligations."[1] Leslie Green has written that "law is legitimate only if it justifiably claims to impose [*some sort of*] moral obligations or duties on its subjects. An adequate theory of legitimacy must therefore show how law can have this kind of force."[2] We have seen that the Simple Correlativity Thesis, taken together with the impressive contemporary critique of political obligation, undermines the initially plausible view that legitimate states are possible and actual. To the extent that it is difficult to accept the philosophical anarchist conclusion, this in itself should call the Simple Correlativity Thesis into question.

George Klosko has observed that "the fact that most citizens . . . believe that . . . their governments are legitimate indicates that their standards of legitimacy are rather low."[3] Taking this as a datum, a critic of the Simple Correlativity Thesis would argue that it states a too-exacting criterion of legitimacy, one more stringent than most speakers would be willing to impose after having digested the philo-

---

[1] A. John Simmons, "Justification and Legitimacy," 8 (unpublished MS quoted with the author's permission).

[2] Leslie Green, "Law, Legitimacy, and Consent," 62 *Southern California Law Review* 795, 797 (1989). I have interpolated Green's caution, in correspondence, that the obligations correlative to state legitimacy needn't be ones of obedience.

[3] George Klosko, *The Principle of Fairness and Political Obligation* 69 (Lanham, Md.: Rowman & Littlefield, 1992).

sophical reasons to doubt that there exists a general duty to obey. "Well, maybe my government is legitimate anyway, even if I needn't always obey," seems as likely a response as "Gosh, if it's not true that I ought always to obey, then I guess my government's not legitimate after all." We might conclude, as Rolf Sartorius and Kent Greenwalt[4] have suggested, that legitimacy and political obligation are simply two different issues.

But the defenders of Simple Correlativity are not so readily swayed. "Increasing doubt about the existence of a general duty to obey the law, coupled with unwillingness to brand general assertions of authority within ordinary legal systems as illegitimate, leads to proposals to sever the connection," Philip Soper has noticed; but, he adds, quoting Joseph Raz, "a view that denies the correlation between the assertion of authority and the assertion of a duty to obey is simply not 'faithful to the main features of the notion of political authority prevalent in our culture.'"[5] The point is a powerful one: If we reject the Simple Correlativity Thesis as a criterion of legitimacy, we have then not only to supply and defend an alternative criterion, we must also make sense of the idea that the state is not merely a powerful, legitimate enterprise, but it is also an *authority* claiming and exercising not merely a right to *be* but a right to *rule*. "Not every power amounts to an authority," Raz reminds us, for even "the justified use of coercive power is one thing and authority is another."[6]

It is easy to show that, in general, "X acts legitimately with respect to Y" does not entail that "Y has a duty to comply with X's commands." In other words, the moral permissibility of X's conduct toward Y is not conditioned upon X's having a power to bind Y in the moral sense. For example, it would be legitimate for me to threaten and to use force to repel a psychotic aggressor even though the aggressor is under no duty to desist (he might perceive me as a menacing rodent, for example). But Raz cautions:

[It is a] mistake . . . to think that since there can be political authority which is not *owed* a duty of obedience, there can also be one which does not *claim that it is owed* such a duty. To test [such a view], try to

4   See Rolf Sartorius, 67 *Virginia Law Review* 3 (1981); Kent Greenawalt, *Conflicts of Law and Morality* (New York: Oxford University Press, 1987).
5   Philip Soper, "Legal Theory and the Claim of Authority," 18 *Philosophy & Public Affairs* 209, 220 (1989), quoting Joseph Raz, "Authority and Justification," 14 *Philosophy & Public Affairs* 6 (1985). I retained Raz's emphasis throughout.
6   Joseph Raz, "Authority and Justification," 14 *Philosophy & Public Affairs* 6–7 (1985).

imagine a situation in which the political authorities of a country do not claim that the inhabitants are bound to obey them, but in which the population does acquiesce to their rule. We are to imagine courts imprisoning people without finding them guilty of any offense. Damages are ordered, but no one has a duty to pay them. The legislature never claims to impose duties of care or of contribution to common services. It merely pronounces that people who behave in certain ways will be made to suffer . . . it is unlikely that any such society ever existed . . . [and] if such a society were to exist we would not regard it as governed by authority [for] it is too unlike the political institutions we normally regard as authorities.

Although Raz's remarks may not be impeccable as argument, they do suggest that the Simple Correlativity Thesis has a complexity that we had better analyze if we are to avoid errors of oversimplification.

THE TWO CORRELATIVITY SUBTHESES AND THE WARRANTY THESIS

The Simple Correlativity Thesis combines two similar-seeming but logically quite different theses. Some of the writers on the subjects of authority and political obligation have one or the other of the theses in mind, others embrace both without distinguishing them, and still others tend to treat them as though they were interchangeable – as they are not. The two theses are these:

> *Strong Authority Thesis:* Being an authority (and, hence, being capable of legitimate authority) entails *claiming to create* in one's subjects a duty of obedience;

and the contrasting

> *Strong Legitimacy Thesis:* Being a *legitimate* authority entails *creating* in one's subjects a duty of obedience.

These two are independent, that is, with respect to any putative authority, the Strong Authority Thesis may be satisfied while the Strong Legitimacy Thesis is not. In other words, it is possible that the correct view has it that *being* an authority entails claiming to create a duty to obey but being a *legitimate* authority does not entail that there *is* a duty to obey. It may very well be true, as Raz has argued, that the best understanding of the concept of a political authority essentially involves the idea of making the claim that obedience is due. But, at the same time, it may very well be false to say, as for example Wolff and Simmons do, that an authority is legitimate only if there is a general duty to obey it.

Now, it may seem odd to suggest that, although being an authority necessarily involves claiming to be owed obedience, being a legitimate authority is consistent with not being owed any such duty. In other words, it may seem as though there is a logical link leading inexorably from the Strong Authority Thesis to the Strong Legitimacy Thesis. I suggest that this is so because we are influenced by an idea that I will formulate and call the "Warranty Thesis":

> *Warranty Thesis:* If being an *X* entails claiming to φ, then being a *legitimate X* entails *truly* claiming to φ.

If the Warranty Thesis is true, then the Strong Authority Thesis entails the Strong Legitimacy Thesis, and the distinction between the two is hardly worth making.[7] More importantly, the distinction between the two theses would not create a space in which to develop an answer to philosophical anarchism; as we have seen, if the Simple Correlativity Thesis is true, and there is no general duty to obey the law, then philosophical anarchism is an irresistible consequence.

OTHER CANDIDATE THESES

Parting company with Raz, some philosophers are uncomfortable with the idea that making moral claims is part of the essence of a legal system. H. L. A. Hart, for one, has argued that legal authority is better understood in terms of a

> theory of duty according to which committed [e.g., official] statements asserting that others have a duty do not refer to actions which they have a categorical [viz., objective] reason to do but, as the etymology of "duty" and indeed "ought" suggests, such statements refer to actions which are due from or owed by the subjects having the duty, in the sense that they may be properly demanded or exacted from them. On this footing, to say that an individual has a legal obligation to act in a certain way is to say that such an action may be properly

---

[7] As Steve Rieber has pointed out to me, the weakest logical link between the two theses would be the conditional: "If [Strong Authority Thesis] then [Strong Legitimacy Thesis]." But there does not seem to be any reason to accept this formula unless as a specification of the (admittedly stronger) Warranty Thesis.

demanded or extracted from him according to legal rules or principles regulating such demands for action.[8]

Although Hart is denying that legal officials need make any moral claims at all, what he says should also suggest to us the possibility that legal officials do make moral claims, but rather weak ones. This possibility can be given expression in the following principle:

> *Weak Authority Thesis:* Being a (political) authority entails claiming a general "justification" right forcefully to administer one's authoritative directives.

In this thesis, the "justification" right, in contrast to a claim right, involves no correlative moral duty. The political authority need not claim that the moral situation of the subject is accurately reflected by her directives. All the political authority need claim is that it is legally proper and (although Hart would not go this far) morally *permissible* to exact performance from the subject. Taken together with the Warranty Thesis, the Weak Authority Thesis would entail:

> *Weak Legitimacy Thesis:* Being a legitimate (political) authority entails having a general "justification" right forcefully to administer one's authoritative directives.

But, notice, the Weak Legitimacy Thesis, taken together with the conclusion that there is no general duty to obey the law, does not establish that no legitimate state exists. What it would take to establish philosophical anarchism, if the Weak Legitimacy Thesis is true, is this:

> *Strong Anarchist Lemma:* No authority ever has a general justification right forcefully to administer its authoritative directives.

Despite other differences in their views, Wolff and Simmons, the most prominent philosophical anarchists, do not defend and in fact seem inclined to deny the Strong Anarchist Lemma. In particular, they seem prepared to disavow the Strong Anarchist Lemma in cases in which there is a perfect convergence between moral and legal requirements, and in other cases where necessity supplies a general justification to coerce despite an imperfect convergence. This shows

---

[8] H. L. A. Hart, *Essays on Bentham* 159–60 (Oxford: Clarendon Press, 1982).

that the Strong Legitimacy Thesis is crucial to philosophical anarchism; without it, doubts about the existence of political obligation – the general duty to obey the laws of a reasonably just state – simply do not license the conclusion that legitimate states do not or cannot exist. But what support is there for the Strong Legitimacy Thesis, other than the combination of the Strong Authority and the Warranty Theses?

We may feel that the Strong Authority Thesis states an important truth about political authority that somehow has to be reflected in the criterion of legitimacy. Ronald Dworkin expresses this view:

> These two issues – whether the state is morally legitimate, in the sense that it is justified in using force against its citizens, and whether the state's decisions impose genuine obligations on them – are not identical. . . . But though obligation is not a sufficient condition for coercion, it is close to a necessary one. A state may have good grounds in some special circumstances for coercing those who have no duty to obey. But no general policy of upholding the law with steel could be justified if the law were not, in general, a source of genuine obligations.[9]

The law's requirements may happen to converge with morality's and yet fail to be legitimate, Dworkin suggests, because law is essentially coercive, and a "general policy" of enforcing moral requirements "with steel" requires a specially high level of justification – it is not enough to say, simply, that the legal and moral requirements within the state's jurisdiction largely converge. Whether law is essentially coercive is a matter to be addressed in Part Two but, in any case, Dworkin is surely correct that law is not simply a morally neutral overlay of enforcement – at a minimum it purports to be a *source* of moral requirements, as well as an enforcer of them.

In a similar spirit, Raz has argued that we must reject what he calls the "No Difference Thesis," the idea that "the exercise of authority should make no difference to what subjects ought to do."[10] Political authority alters our moral situation by ordering choices between equally rational but incompatible options where administrative reasons compel a choice, and by solving coordination problems. But, more generally, and more distinctively, law imposes an exclusive,

---

[9] Ronald Dworkin, *Law's Empire* 191–2 (Cambridge, Mass.: Harvard University Press, 1986).
[10] Joseph Raz, *The Morality of Freedom* 48 (Oxford: Clarendon Press, 1986).

explicit, and procedurally regular schedule of consequences upon the conduct that morality (in a wide sense that includes political morality) condemns. At a minimum, legal authority claims not only the justification right, or moral permission, to implement this schedule, it also claims that the state's subjects have a moral as well as a legal duty not to interfere with its forceful administration. This is consistent with the denial that there is a general duty to obey the law; it is merely to assert that the state *claims* that its subjects have a moral duty not to resist the operation of law. Call this the:

> *Modest Authority Thesis:* Being an authority entails claiming that one's authoritative directives create in one's subjects an enforceable duty not to interfere with their forceful administration.

There is a counterpart legitimacy thesis:

> *Modest Legitimacy Thesis:* Being a legitimate authority entails that one's authoritative directives create in one's subjects an enforceable duty not to interfere with their forceful administration.

Table 1 presents a summary of the discussion so far.

A satisfactory theory of the state will include an authority thesis and a legitimacy thesis. The stringency of the legitimacy thesis will determine which of the lemmas the philosophical anarchist must establish. As Table 1 shows, one who accepts the Strong Authority Thesis and the Warranty Thesis will be committed to the Strong Legitimacy Thesis. To persuade those who hold the Strong Legitimacy Thesis that philosophical anarchism is the true view, the philosophical anarchist need only establish the Weak Lemma, that is, that there is no political obligation. In Chapter 1, we saw that the Weak Lemma was more plausible than it might at first have appeared. Similarly, the Modest Authority Thesis links up, via the Warranty Thesis, with the Modest Legitimacy Thesis, which puts the philosophical anarchist to the proof of a Modest Lemma. In the same way, the Warranty Thesis translates the Weak Authority Thesis into the Weak Legitimacy Thesis, which would require the philosophical anarchist to establish the Strong Lemma.

It appears that the Warranty Thesis is instrumental in organizing the available views in this field. But the Warranty Thesis is false, as I will show in a moment. Rejection of the Warranty Thesis undoes the horizontal linkage between the authority theses and the legitimacy

Table 1. *Correlations of Authority and Legitimacy*

Authority Theses	Warranty Thesis	Legitimacy Theses	What philosophical anarchism need show
Strong Being an authority entails claiming that one's authoritative directives create in one's subjects an enforceable duty of obedience.		*Strong* Being a legitimate authority entails that one's authoritative directives create in one's subjects an enforceable duty of obedience.	*Weak Lemma* No one has any unconsented general duty to obey any authoritative directive as such.
Modest Being an authority entails claiming that one's authoritative directives create in one's subjects an enforceable duty not to interfere with their forceful administration.	If being on X entails claiming to φ, then being a *legitimate X* entails *truly* claiming to φ.	*Modest* Being a legitimate authority entails that one's authoritative directives create in one's subjects an enforceable duty not to interfere with their forceful administration.	*Modest Lemma* No one has any unconsented general duty to refrain from resisting an authoritative directive as such.
Weak Being an authority entails claiming a general (justification) right forcefully to administer one's authoritative directives.		*Weak* Being a legitimate authority entails having a general (justification) right forcefully to administer one's authoritative directives.	*Strong Lemma* No authority ever has a general (justification) right forcefully to administer its authoritative directives.

theses; with the Warranty Thesis out of the way, it becomes possible to hold, for example, a Strong Authority Thesis while rejecting the Strong Legitimacy Thesis. One might, that is, take the position that the true view combines the Strong Authority Thesis with the Modest or even the Weak Legitimacy Thesis – either combination being impervious to the Weak Lemma of the philosophical anarchist. A refutation of the Warranty Thesis opens up a logical space in which to assemble a theory, one of whose advantages would be to combine a robust conception of authority with an answer to the philosophical anarchist.

DISPROOF OF THE WARRANTY THESIS

Consider the case of theoretical authority – although there are important points of disanalogy between theoretical and practical authority, they nonetheless share, as Raz assures us, a "basic structure."[11] The key point of analogy for our present purpose is that, like practical authorities, theoretical authorities make claims that may or may not be correct. Assume that being a scientific authority entails claiming to know how the world or at least some aspect of it works. Can it follow, as the Warranty Thesis requires, that the only legitimate scientific authorities are those who *truly* know how the world works? If that is what is required, then the history of science indicates that not only were Ptolemy and Aristotle not scientific authorities, neither was Newton. Einstein, if he hasn't already, will in all likelihood turn out not to have been one either (at press time, Einstein's cosmological constant may be making a comeback, but his rejection of quantum mechanics looks more than ever to have been a mistake). The far more plausible view is that, even though later developments show a scientific authority's views to have been mistaken, that authority was nonetheless a legitimate authority at the time she held her views, if they were sufficiently well founded in the scientific understanding of her time (even though they may have been in some sense revolutionary).

One might object that the analogy fails as an objection to the Warranty Thesis if we frame the claim of the theoretical authority differ-

---

[11]   Ibid., 18. Cf. Richard B. Friedman, "On the Concept of Authority in Political Philosophy," in Richard E. Flathman, ed., *Concepts in Social and Political Philosophy* 121 (New York: Macmillan, 1973); Richard T. deGeorge, *The Nature and Limits of Authority* 12–61 (Lawrence, Kans.: University Press of Kansas, 1985). Philip Soper advocates the Warranty Thesis in the case of theoretical authority, in "Legal Theory and the Claim of Authority," 18 *Philosophy & Public Affairs* 209, 219, 225 (1989).

ently. A scientific authority might have philosophical misgivings about truth as the object of the scientific enterprise without thereby surrendering her credentials as a scientist. Accordingly, one might say that a theoretical authority need make no claim to know how things really are. She need only claim to have evidence that certain things are so. Then, according to the Warranty Thesis, she is a legitimate authority only if she truly has this evidence. Ptolemy, Aristotle, and Newton truly had the evidence they claimed to have, and so the Warranty Thesis properly counts them as theoretical authorities. The case of theoretical authority is no counterexample to the Warranty Thesis, the objection concludes, and – given the analogy between theoretical and practical authority – in fact confirms the Warranty Thesis.

The objection, so stated, fails unless the theoretical authority's claim to "have evidence" is understood to carry an at least implicit normative claim, that is, that she has evidence of such a character that one *ought to believe* that the world is so. Anyone who claimed to have evidence that the world was a certain way, but who denied that that evidence was good reason to believe the world was so, would simply not be claiming enough to be counted as an authority. One who, for example, merely inventories the evidence of the Ice Age, while denying that one ought to believe that there was an Ice Age, is no authority on the Ice Age unless she is implicitly making the further claim that the evidence she has is the best evidence available and that it is inconclusive. But, of course, if she is making this sort of claim about the character of her evidence, she has lapsed into a normative mode of speech, for she is now making the claim that the best evidence the world has afforded is the evidence she has in her account, and that claim cannot be coupled with the denial that one *ought* to base one's belief about the Ice Age on this evidence.

The objector must therefore say that one can be a scientific authority without claiming to know the truth, so long as one makes the weaker claim that others *ought to believe* what one has to say on matters within one's expertise. If scientific authority could be construed this way, what the Warranty Thesis would license is the conclusion that the legitimate scientific authority truly ought to be believed – *not* that what she would have others believe is true – and the objection to the Warranty Thesis still would dissolve. On this view of scientific authority, Ptolemy, Aristotle, and Newton truly ought to have been believed, at relevant times in history, and so they once were legitimate authorities although they are no longer.

But notice that this defense of the Warranty Thesis will not easily work for a defender of the Strong Authority Thesis. If so great a degree of humility is consistent with a claim of theoretical authority, then – insofar as practical and scientific authority are analogous – a similar humility ought not to vitiate a claim to political authority. In other words, one who defends the Warranty Thesis this way is not in a position to object to the Modest or even the Weak Authority Thesis. Defending the Warranty Thesis by toning down the claims made by theoretical authority makes it incongruous to insist on the Strong Authority Thesis when construing the claim of political authority. The Warranty Thesis may be saved, but its usefulness as a vehicle for philosophical anarchism is ruined.

At this point, a defender of the Warranty Thesis will likely point out another difficulty attending my appeal to analogy. Notice that the "you *ought* to believe" in the rendering just given of scientific authority is not obviously the equivalent of "you *have a duty* to believe" (although it at least entails "there are good prudential reasons for you to believe"). It is tempting to conclude that the counterpart practical expression to "you ought to believe" is not "you have a duty to obey" but "there are good prudential reasons for you to obey." But, in fact, political authority differs from merely prudential practical authorities in claiming more than that certain prudential reasons to obey exist. Doesn't this normatively stronger claim destroy the analogy between political and scientific authority, even if the analogy between practical and scientific authority is unaffected?

The critical point here is the relation between political authority and practical authority generally. I have assumed that political authority is a species of practical authority, but it appears that political authority is vigorously normative in a way that practical and scientific authorities may turn out not to be. Conceding that scientific authority is normative in the sense that it involves the "weakly" deontic notion of what one "ought to believe," is not yet to concede that it is "strongly" deontic in the sense that concept of duty has application, or that scientific discourse has room for locutions such as "you have a duty to believe the hypothesis best supported by the best available evidence." Similar remarks apply to prudential practical authority. From "of the options open to you, you have most reason to ϕ," it does not obviously follow that "your duty is to ϕ" (although it would seem to follow that "it would be irrational of you not to ϕ").

All of these remarks suggest that there may be hazards latent in the use of an argument from analogy. But an analogy need not be perfect to carry conviction. The question comes down to this: How does the deeper normative involvement of the concept of political authority affect the plausibility of the Warranty Thesis? As we have seen, the Warranty Thesis fails as an account of scientific and practical authority. Therefore, if there is a satisfactory alternative general account of the connection between the claims distinctive of authority and the conditions that authority must satisfy to be legitimate, the Warranty Thesis should be rejected in favor of that alternative. I now propose an account of that tie, characterized by sincerity and reasonable proximity to success:

> *Proximity Thesis:* If being an X entails claiming to φ, then being a *legitimate X* entails *sincerely* claiming to φ, and coming within tolerable limits of doing so.

Applied to theoretical authority, the Proximity Thesis, suitably interpreted, would legitimate Ptolemy, Aristotle, et al., but would not bestow legitimacy upon Nostradamus, Jeanne Dixon, or a hoaxer who accidentally points in the direction of truth. Similarly, the Proximity Thesis serves to distinguish legitimate prudential practical authorities from the illegitimate. A *separate* account of the ethics of belief or of rationality may be given, for those who are interested in pursuing the separate issue: When, if ever, do epistemic (scientific or practical) *duties* arise?

Applying the Proximity Thesis to political authority makes necessary an interpretation of the idea of "tolerable limits" that is likely to involve controversy. The Proximity Thesis, in effect, leaves one who is committed to the Strong Authority Thesis without much guidance in the choice of a legitimacy thesis. It may be that satisfying the Modest or the Weak Legitimacy Thesis is within the "tolerable limits" of the Proximity Thesis. So be it.

THE TRUE VIEW

The true view combines the Strong Authority Thesis, the Proximity Thesis, and the Modest Legitimacy Thesis. The true view does not lead to philosophical anarchism because the true view rejects the Modest Lemma. In the following chapter, I will argue for this "package" of views.

Chapter 3

Legitimate Political Authority

The central or criterion element of the correct view of political legitimacy is the Modest Legitimacy Thesis. The correct view accepts the Strong Authority Thesis but is not wedded to the Strong Legitimacy Thesis – which it rejects – because the correct view embraces the Proximity Thesis instead of the Warranty Thesis. The correct view does not lead to philosophical anarchism because the Modest Lemma needed in order to reach philosophical anarchism is false. The correct view reconciles the tension within the Inconsistent Triad of Chapter 1 by modifying its first and second propositions. The correct view replaces the Inconsistent Triad with the following, true and consistent, triad:

1. A state is legitimate only if it claims to impose on its subjects a general, at least prima facie, duty to obey its laws *and its subjects have a general prima facie duty not to interfere with their enforcement.*
2. There *may be* no general, even prima facie, duty to obey the laws of a state, not even those of a just state; *but there is a general prima facie duty not to interfere with the administration of the laws of a just state.*
3. Legitimate states are not only possible, but actual.

A defense and explanation of this view can begin with a refutation of the Modest Lemma. The Modest Lemma states that no one has any unconsented, even prima facie, general duty to refrain from resisting an authoritative directive as such. The Modest Lemma holds, in other words, that there is no general duty of noninterference with the enforcement of the laws, even those of a just state. This applies both to enforcement efforts directed at oneself and those directed at others. The Modest Lemma does not claim that there are no independent moral reasons sometimes to acquiesce in the enforcement of the law; rather, in the same tenor as the attack on the duty of obedience, the

48

Modest Lemma denies that one has a general prima facie duty not to interfere with efforts to enforce the laws of a just state.

Thus, the crucial element of my defense of legitimate political authority is the idea of a general prima facie duty not to interfere with the administration of a just (or at least reasonably just) state's laws. The argument that follows falls into two parts. In the first, I argue that such a duty exists. In the second, I argue that the notion of a legitimate political *authority* is best explained with reference to such a duty. The prima facie duty to obey the law, the often-assumed correlate of legitimate authority, is displaced but not entirely discarded for, I will argue, a political authority will normally *claim* to impose such a duty of obedience.

ADMINISTRATIVE PREROGATIVES

Notice that the duty to obey the law and the duty not to interfere with the administration of the law are quite different. The law is abstract, general, and often unknown to us although we are presumed to know it. It is addressed not to individuals directly but to classes often defined only by conduct that is forbidden or regulated – "users," "one who transports," "no one shall," and so forth. Laws speak not only abstractly but at a remove in time – some laws having been "on the books" for centuries. The *administration* of the law is what enables the dry contents of the statute books and case reporters to have a bearing on the everyday world we inhabit: the sheriff who appears at our door to tell us to "be in court," the traffic cop who signals us to "pull over," the judge who orders us to "pay her these damages." While law is the reason of the artificial creature Hobbes conceived the state to be, these are actions of its hands.[1] To have a term to use to refer to official actions of this kind, I will call them – with apologies for the barbarousness of the expression – *administrative prerogatives.*[2]

Administrative prerogatives occupy one end of a spectrum that has at its opposite end laws of the most general scope. They typically represent an effort by an official to affect the immediate conduct of an

---

[1] Thomas Hobbes, *Leviathan,* J. C. A. Gaskin, ed. (XXIII: 10) 162 (Oxford: Oxford University Press, 1996) [hereafter *Leviathan*].

[2] John Chipman Gray, in *The Nature and Sources of the Law,* 2d ed. 170 (New York: Macmillan, 1921) took the position that statutes are not law but merely "sources" yielding law only when, and to the extent that, judges' rulings drew upon them. For reasons that I will not explore here, I do not follow Gray's lead by limiting "law, *proper"* to administrative prerogatives.

individual on a particular occasion, rather than an effort of an institution to affect the conduct of classes of people throughout an indefinite futurity. I use the word "prerogative" to indicate that the official act purports to take precedence over other matters, including the question whether the official act is wise, valid, or best, all things considered, as well as to convey the claim of a right of noninterference.

Doubts about the Duty to Obey Do Not Carry Over to the Duty of Noninterference

Many of the doubts about the existence of a general duty to obey the law fail to carry over when the subject is the duty to comply with administrative prerogatives. Recall the stop sign in the desert case from Chapter 1. Several factors suggest that there is no even prima facie duty in such a case. First, it seems silly to feel remorse about violating the law here, or to try to "make up" in some way for having done so, but normally such a response would be demanded if a prima facie duty had been overridden. Second, what overrides the putative duty is not a conflicting duty, but a mere whim – even a merely prima facie duty is supposed to be sturdier than that. Third, one's response takes in both the nature of the act-type that the law forbids and the particular consequences of my token of that type. Thus the putative duty is not "content independent" in the way that some would argue a general duty should be expected to be. This list of objections to the existence of a prima facie duty to obey the law is not exhaustive, but these are major ones. Though I would not dismiss them, I do not find them conclusive; but it is an embarrassment to political philosophy that the possibility of a legitimate state is vulnerable to every worry about political obligation.

The differences between laws and administrative prerogatives are significant when we consider my claim that there is a general prima facie duty not to resist the latter even though there may be no general prima facie duty to obey the former. Failing to stop at the stop sign in the desert is one thing, failing to stop for the traffic cop in the desert is another. In general, it is harder to have an assurance of harmlessness when it is a traffic cop, rather than a traffic law, that one is disobeying. The relative directness of administrative prerogatives more firmly attaches to disobedience a train of consequences.

Another difference is epistemic. The abstractness of the law makes it difficult, if not impossible, not to be guilty of unconscious lawbreaking. Who would guess, for example, that a dealer in 1960s memorabilia might be prosecuted for sending a hookah through the mails?[3] To the extent that duty is an objective concept, it is of course possible to have a duty one has no reason to suspect one has. There are many such legal duties, and one can readily understand an unwillingness to count them wholesale as moral ones. An administrative prerogative, in contrast, is concrete, immediate, and designed to give notice to the person to whom it is directed. Moreover, extenuating circumstances are likelier to be known by, or be readily discoverable by, the official on the spot, and so it is to that extent more presumptuous to dismiss or pretermit the official's assessment. Administrative prerogatives often serve a channeling function; they direct behavioral traffic into the legal avenues for examination and assessment and, as such, are not punitive.

But can it make any sense to say, for example, that Junior may have no duty to obey the rule that he is to clean up his room, but he has a duty not to resist my administrative prerogative requiring that he now clean up his room? Surely it does. Normally, every reason for Junior to follow the rule is a reason to comply with my order, but the reverse is not true. My requiring that Junior clean up his room now may rest on reasons having little to do with the reasons for the rule. It may be, for example, that on this occasion I am too tired to pick up after Junior and Aunt Louise is about to visit. Children generally regard rules with suspicion. When the rule isn't enforced, they infer that compliance isn't expected; then, when it is enforced, they feel (or affect) surprise and even indignation at what they claim is arbitrary parental conduct. (Appeals to fairness are next in line: If Little Sister's room is a mess, why should Junior be singled out?)

Children of tender years are too young to be subject to duties at all. As they grow, moral assessment of their conduct becomes appropriate as their intellectual ability to abstract and generalize (not to mention other powers, such as empathy) improves. Rule following is a fairly sophisticated, even mysterious,[4] accomplishment, especially given the inattention, forgetfulness, self-absorption, impulsiveness, and susceptibility to temptation that children are prey to in characteristically greater degree. Parents sooner expect and observe a child's compliance with specific commands; these are then supple-

---

[3] See *Casbah, Inc. v Thone*, 512 F. Supp. 474 (D.C. Neb. 1980).
[4] See Ludwig Wittgenstein, *Philosophical Investigations*, G. E. M. Anscombe trans., ¶¶160–201 (New York: Macmillan, 1951); Saul Kripke, *Wittgenstein on Rules and Private Language* (Cambridge, Mass.: Harvard University Press, 1982); Frederick Schauer, *Playing by the Rules* (New York: Oxford University Press, 1991).

mented with explanations and, finally, generalized into rulelike formulae. A parent is likely to treat even conscious rule breaking as less serious a delict than disobedience of a direct order. Contumacious refusal to "Stop that!" or to "Do it now!" has the power to drive parents to despair because they feel that – even if the reasons for rules are hard for the child to grasp – it ought at least to be possible for the child to appreciate that domestic order depends on the child's ready compliance with straightforward demands, without prior or full explanation. Of course the reason for the latter may be just as difficult to convey as the reasons for a rule, but what is important to observe is that we would be less ready to excuse "direct" disobedience than rule breaking. I suspect that the reason for this is that we appreciate that a child's moral development is such that rule breaking may not yet be wrongful in the way that resisting the parent's administrative prerogative is.

The duty not to interfere with the administrative prerogatives of a just state is of course subject to many of the same qualifications and exceptions as the general duty to obey the law, but it is, as I said, better supported by appeals to utility and necessity. Moreover, an individual's act of resistance to an administrative prerogative to enforce law L is likely to betoken a much wider estrangement from civil society than simply breaking law L. One who runs the stop sign in the desert may do so in circumstances that approach perfect isolation from society. Not so one who ignores the traffic cop's effort to enforce the law requiring a full stop at the stop sign. A scofflaw who has accumulated hundreds of unpaid parking tickets may excite no alarm whatever until he resists the officer who has come to execute a warrant for his arrest.

Notice also that the duty not to resist a just state's administrative prerogatives is relatively "content independent," compared to the duty to obey the law. If a duty to ϕ is content independent, that duty's existence and weight should be determinable without reference to the character and consequences of the actions available to the actor at the time she acts. Examples showed that it is implausible that the duty to obey the law is content independent in this way, because the weight of a specific legal duty depends on the moral quality of the type of action the law forbids or commands and the circumstances in which a "token" of that type of action would be performed.

Reconsider now the examples of the murderer and the jaywalker. Although the duty not to murder is far weightier than the duty not to jaywalk, the respective duties of the murderer and of the jay-walker to submit peaceably to lawful arrest are of equal weight. The variability of the gravity of the underlying offense simply does not register here. Of course, the officer may use deadly force if necessary to capture a *fleeing* murder suspect, yet not to capture a fleeing jay-walker, but this reflects the far greater degree of prospective danger to society that the murder suspect is presumed to present.[5] The offi-cer's duty with respect to either suspect is to "push forward and make the arrest," and she is privileged to pursue either, to forcefully detain either, and to forcefully overcome the resistance of either. If either's resistance threatens to kill or to seriously wound her, the offi-cer is privileged to use "extreme force when extreme resistance is offered."[6] The suspect's duty is in either case to submit without resis-tance – or so says received legal doctrine, whose practical wisdom we should not lightly disparage.

Circumstances favoring resistance also must be much more extreme to outweigh the duty not to resist an administrative prerog-ative than they need be to overcome the duty to obey the law. Morally, I may permissibly run a stop light to rush my wife to the hospital, but I may not permissibly try to outrun the squad car giv-ing chase. This is for two reasons: (1) Resistance normally creates additional risks of harm, and (2) resistance is normally unnecessary to achieve morally proper ends. But suppose that my wife's condi-tion is so dire that I ought not, all things considered, stop for the offi-cer. The reasons to stop are outweighed, but my conduct is none-theless an occasion for compunction, and surely I ought if possible to "make up" to the officer by explaining the extreme situation I

---

[5]   Compare *Tennessee v Garner,* 471 U.S. 1 (1985) (disapproving the use of deadly force to detain a fleeing nonviolent felony suspect) with *Ricci v Arlington Heights,* 116 F.3d 288 (7th Cir. 1997) (approving full custodial arrest of a violator of a "fine-only" licensing ordinance) *cert. dismissed* – S.Ct. – (May 4, 1998).

[6]   See *Durham v State,* 159 N.E. 145 (Ind. 1927), where the defendant, a deputy game warden, used deadly force to effect an arrest for illegal fishing. The suspect had attempted to paddle away, the deputy grabbed the boat, and the suspect began to whack the deputy over the head with an oar. The deputy was charged for batter-ing the suspect by shooting him in the arm. The appellate court, unwilling to hin-der "the strong arm of the law," counseled the suspect not to "measure strength with the arresting officer." The distinctiveness of the duty not to resist administra-tive prerogatives is seen also in the law of citizen's arrest and the demise of the common-law privilege to resist unlawful arrest. See *United States v Hillsman,* 522 F.2d 454 (7th Cir. 1975) and compare *Galvin v State,* 46 Tenn. 283 (1869) with Model Penal Code §3.04(2)(a)(1) (Philadelphia: American Law Institute, 1962).

faced – but these are precisely the indicia of prima facie obligation noted in Chapter 1. Of course, hypothetical circumstances can be concocted to avoid these indicia – for example, the cop is known to me to be arbitrary and vindictive – but now the bona fides of the officer's exercise of authority are in question.

Is it a mistake to think that compunction is appropriate in all such cases? Suppose that, while visiting New York City, I am innocently and fortuitously surrounded by a group of strangers who have just jaywalked. A police officer, acting in all good faith, places the group, including me, under arrest. Remaining would be a serious inconvenience, and I notice an opportunity to slip away undetected by anyone. Circumstances are such that no bad effects of any kind can reasonably be expected. Isn't it silly to say that I should feel any more compunction, or any more of an obligation to "make it up" to someone, here than at the stop sign in the desert?

It seems natural to me to view the slinking-away-from-the-crowd case as relevantly different from the stop sign case. I would be a little bit ashamed to say that I had ignored the officer, while being rather more at ease in discussing my having run the stop sign in the desert. But I am willing to entertain the possibility that reasonable, morally mature others would respond to the two cases as being equally inappropriate occasions for even the mildest remorse. I am sure that my upbringing has shaped my likely response, and other upbringings may very well lead to different susceptibilities. One way of deflecting the point would be to say that the slipping-away-from-the-crowd case is not a case of resisting or interfering at all, but is rather merely a case of avoiding an administrative prerogative. But to put such weight on the distinction between interference and evasion would, itself, be an evasion – a point to which I will return later. Does it all simply come down to a question of how one was raised? Substantive moral philosophy does not offer much in the way of resources to resolve such clashes of intuition. Here, I can only say that if your intuitions don't match mine at this point, they may yet after you have had a chance to digest my overall position.

A different response to the view I am advocating is to point out that circumstances may endow a private individual with a similar kind of authority. If, for example, a power failure disables a stop light, drivers may have a prima facie duty not to interfere with the efforts of a pedestrian who undertakes to direct traffic through the intersection. Here, the person first to undertake such a chore seems to acquire an entitlement to complete it, that is, a claim against interference by others who would like to perform the same service. But the state's agents claim priority over earlier-comers, and to that extent the state's exercise of administrative prerogatives is unlike similar measures undertaken by civilians. The justification of this monopoly of the prerogative is a subject to which we will return later; what has to be explained here is the connection between the alleged duty of noninterference and the overall legitimacy of the state claiming such a prerogative. If the two are unconnected, then to that extent it seems unlikely that I have succeeded in showing that a global judgment of institutional legitimacy cashes out as a general duty to respect administrative prerogatives. If you will forgive my resorting once again to what Daniel Dennett disparaging calls the "intuition pump," consider the following example.

You are standing in the middle of an open field somewhere in Germany in early 1945. In the distance, a figure is racing in your direction. He is wild-eyed and desperate to make progress. He takes no note of you as he veers to the right and disappears into the woods. You then notice another figure approaching. He is evidently giving chase to the desperate character who has just passed. By the latter's uniform, you can tell that he is an Allied military policeman, an MP It is obvious to you that if you look to your right, the MP will take this as a cue that the fugitive has gone in that direction and the MP will catch him. Likewise, if you look to the left, the MP will be misled and the fugitive will escape. For all you know, the fugitive may be a political prisoner, a Jew or a Gentile, a murderer or a rapist. Assume that you will suffer no consequences whatever you do.

An hour later, an almost identical situation arises, but this time the pursuer is not an Allied MP but a German policeman. And then, after another hour, the same scenario recurs, only this time the pursuer is a civilian. What may you do in these three cases (assuming they are otherwise unconnected)? I hope I have sufficiently primed the response that there is a prima facie duty not to mislead the MP, but no prima facie duty not to mislead the German policeman or the civilian. That is because the MP is acting on behalf of legitimate states (by and large), while the German policeman and the civilian are not.

For this purpose, it doesn't matter what the fugitive has done. What matters is that the fugitive will undergo something not to his liking if he is caught. If you mislead the MP, you will have interfered with an administrative prerogative of a legitimate state; if you mislead the German policeman, you will have interfered with an administrative prerogative of an illegitimate state; if you mislead the civilian, you will simply have led to one private person's frustration rather than another's. If you mislead the German policeman or the civilian, you have nothing to feel remorse for having done even if the fugitive turns out to be a murderer (regret is another matter). If you mislead the MP, you have something to feel compunction about, even if the fugitive is entirely innocent.

If I have given you reason to think that there *is* a prima facie duty not to interfere with the administrative prerogatives of a just state, what more can be said about the duty's weight? A further indication of its weight is given by the fact that the duty is not dissolved merely because the law the official is seeking to implement is a nullity. In other words, there may be no legal *or* moral reason to comply with defective law *L*, and yet, at the same time, there may be a compelling reason to comply with the administrative prerogative of an official relying on *L*. This was the issue in *Walker v City of Birmingham*,[7] a landmark case arising from the civil rights movement in the American South. In *Walker*, an Alabama court had, on the city's petition, enjoined Dr. King and his associates from violating a Birmingham ordinance that would require them to get the City Public Safety Commissioner's (i.e., Eugene "Bull" Connor's) permission to demonstrate against racial segregation. Dr. King then led a march in violation of the ordinance and the injunction. The city applied to the court for a contempt order, which was granted despite the defendants' argument that the ordinance was unconstitutional. Dr. King and his associates were fined fifty dollars and sentenced to jail for five days. Ultimately, the Supreme Court of the United States affirmed the contempt order despite the fact that a *prosecution* for violating the constitutionally infirm ordinance would certainly have failed.[8]

The result in *Walker* may strike us (as it struck the dissenters) as paradoxical: Alabama could not punish Dr. King by prosecuting and convicting him of violating the ordinance, but it could and did punish his conduct as contempt of an injunction against violating the ordinance. The view I am offering makes sense of this result: Dr. King had no moral duty to obey the ordinance, perhaps not even prima facie, but he did have an at least prima facie duty not to resist the court's administrative prerogative. Insofar as the result in *Walker* is grounded on moral reasoning, it was understandable (and, in my

[7] 388 U.S. 307 (1967); see also Howell Raines, *My Soul Is Rested* 148–204 (New York: Bantam, 1978); David J. Garrow, *Bearing the Cross* 231–86 (New York: Morrow, 1986).

[8] See *Shuttlesworth v Birmingham*, 394 U.S. 147 (1969).

view, correct) for the Court to require those in Dr. King's position to direct their legal arguments against the injunction to the issuing authority even though, absent the injunction, Dr. King could legally and morally have ignored the ordinance altogether. This is not to say that Dr. King's all-things-considered duty was to obey the injunction; it is simply to point out that when a bona fide administrative prerogative is at issue, rather than a bare legal rule, we are far more inclined to accept Bentham's direction, to "obey punctually, censure freely."[9]

The distinctiveness of administrative prerogatives also helps to explain, in part, the peculiar nature of indirect civil disobedience (CD for short). Direct CD is disobedience of some law *L* on the ground of the injustice of *L*, while indirect CD is disobedience of some law *M*, other than *L*, undertaken to protest the injustice of *L*. I engage in direct CD if, for example, I am required to register for the military draft and refuse to do so; I engage in indirect CD if I trespass and impede traffic in order to protest or sabotage the draft. Some believe that indirect CD presents a special problem. If, like John Rawls, we think CD is a "mode of address," and that CD generally is troublesome because it involves a conflict of duties, we can better understand our special attitude toward indirect CD if we posit a law-regarding duty – other than the duty to obey – capable of coming into conflict with pro-disobedience considerations like a duty to resist injustice or a right to defend liberty.[10]

I suggest that in certain types of case indirect CD is intelligible as a "mode of address" only if there is a prima facie duty not to resist administrative prerogatives. Think of a case in which an unjust law *L* cannot easily be violated directly (e.g., it appropriates funds to support an insurgency against a just foreign government), and a group chooses to protest by nonviolently disobeying *M*, a trespassing ordinance. Suppose that the trespass is harmless, and law enforcement officials choose not to take action. Their inaction cannot of course absolve the protestors should a prosecution later be initiated. But,

---

[9] Jeremy Bentham, *Fragment on Government*, J. H. Burns and H. L. A. Hart, eds., 10 (Cambridge: Cambridge University Press, 1988).

[10] See John Rawls, *A Theory of Justice* 363–8 (Cambridge, Mass.: Harvard University Press, 1971); Abraham Fortas, *Concerning Dissent and Civil Disobedience* (New York: New American Library, 1968); Howard Zinn, *Disobedience and Democracy: Nine Fallacies on Law and Order* (New York: Vintage, 1968); cf. Ronald Dworkin, *A Matter of Principle* 106–9 (Cambridge, Mass.: Harvard University Press, 1985). See also *United States v Schoon*, 971 F.2d 193 (9th Cir. 1992) (no necessity defense available in cases of indirect CD).

absent some official action, there is a sense in which the protest has been defused, "co-opted," neutralized, by adroit official tolerance.[11] The protesters have been denied the opportunity to express their conviction that the evil of L is a grave one. The protesters' only real option is to protest L by disobeying M, but officials have deflated the protestors' attempted declaration by refusing to take note of their disobedience of M. (Perhaps only those who have tried unsuccessfully to get arrested can know how frustrating this tactic can be!) Upping the ante by, for example, engaging in Weatherman-style property crime, may yet provoke an official response. But this would both violate important rights of others (the right not to have one's property trashed being generally more important than the right to be free of minor trespasses), and likely alienate the wider public.

The situation can be described as follows. The protestors hope to show the seriousness of the evil of L by violating M. Officials counter by expressing – by inaction – the view that violating M, at least *these* people's violating M, is no big deal. If, on the other hand, officials made an effort to enforce M through the usual administrative prerogatives ("Move along!" "Come with me!" etc.) this would offer the protestors the opportunity to resist (nonviolently, typically) and exhibit their conviction that the evil of L is grave enough to overbalance not only the duty to obey M but also the duty not to resist the state's administrative prerogatives. This semiotic tango makes no sense as a mode of address unless there is something at stake besides the duty to obey M, which, in the circumstances, is officially deemed to be (literally) negligible.

Failure to appreciate the difference between authoritative directives in general and administrative prerogatives leads to the kind of dissonance exhibited in the Berkeley street corner example in Chapter 1. Mr. Robinson responded to my conduct as though I were flouting an administrative prerogative. In fact, a "Don't Walk" sign is an automated substitute for a traffic cop, hence Mr. Robinson's pique. I suspect that midblock jaywalking might have struck even Mr. Robinson as more a matter of carelessness than contumacy. Does this mean that the view I am defending exalts submission to the person of another, at the expense of an equal and general subjection to impersonal rules? If so, this would be at a troubling variance from the tradition of Rousseau and Kant, who stressed the difference between

[11] Cf. Herbert Marcuse, "Repressive Tolerance," in R. P. Wolff, Barrington Moore, Jr., and Herbert Marcuse, *Critique of Pure Tolerance* (Boston: Beacon Press, 1965).

subordination to the general and impersonal, as against the personal and idiosyncratic, will of others. Fortunately, my view has no such consequence because the administrative prerogatives of a *just state*, and the officials who dispense them, are themselves governed by general rules.[12]

The correct view, I am arguing, is "fallibilistic" about a general duty to obey the law – that is, it admits that there is good reason to doubt that there is such a duty – but it insists that there is a general, prima facie duty not to resist the administrative prerogatives of a just state. This is close to the reverse of Hobbes's view. According to Hobbes, all subjects have a duty to obey the laws of the sovereign. This duty is the consequence of the compact by which all have surrendered rights to the sovereign in order to escape the state of nature and its insecurity. But according to Hobbes this compact cannot have included the surrender of certain rights, namely:

> A covenant not to defend myself from force, by force, is always void. For . . . no man can transfer, or lay down his right to save himself from death, wounds, and imprisonment, (the avoiding whereof is the only end of laying down any right;) and therefore the promise of not resisting force, in no covenant transferreth any right; nor is obliging. . . . [a]nd this is granted to be true by all men, in that they lead criminals to execution, and prison, with armed men, notwithstanding that such criminals have consented to the law, by which they are condemned.

Hobbes does not go so far as to say that subjects cannot have consented not to resist more commonplace administrative prerogatives, but he is clear that

> [I]f a man be held in prison, or bonds, or is not trusted with the liberty of his body; he cannot be understood to be bound by covenant to subjection; and therefore may, if he can, make his escape by any means whatsoever.

Curiously, Hobbes admits that there is a general duty not to interfere with administrative prerogatives directed at others:

> To resist the sword of the commonwealth, in defence of another man, guilty, or innocent, no man hath liberty; because such liberty, takes away from the sovereign, the means of protecting us; and is therefore destructive of the very essence of government.

---

[12] Gerald Postema pointed out to me the need to address this concern.

But even here Hobbes's principles lead him to confess that a group of outlaws may without injustice engage in mutual aid in defense against execution or imprisonment by the sovereign.[13]

Leaving aside Hobbes's account of the matter, does the condemned man example show that there is no general prima facie duty not to resist the administrative prerogatives of a just state? No. I will assume (what I believe to be contrary to fact) that capital punishment is morally permissible. Hobbes's example may show that we regard the desire for life and liberty to be so profound that escape attempts are excusable, so long as not harmful – let the condemned slip free and run away if he can, but he is not morally free to, for example, use force, take hostages, et cetera. Or, at most, the condemned man's case may show that there is no general all-things-considered duty not to *avoid* long imprisonment or execution. Avoidance, like resistance, is contrary to law, but it differs from resistance in being nonconfrontational and relatively harmless.

The case is more troublesome still if we stipulate that the condemned man is innocent. Resistance may be the only option, and it must strike us as not merely excusable but possibly justified. But, again, that is why the general duty insisted on here is prima facie, that is, important and typically decisive but defeasible by compelling countervailing moral reasons. In the final, all-things-considered analysis, our duties may well be transparent to the existence of states and the authority of their agents. But prima facie duties are not something that we can toss aside after use, like a ladder we have climbed and no longer need. Prima facie duties are important because moral education is important, and because they are enduring elements of our adult dispositions and moral character. Perhaps in order to accommodate this point, the writers for *The Fugitive*, the long-running television series about the wrongly accused Dr. Richard Kimball, made sure that he was always able to peaceably elude his pursuers and was himself sedulously pursuing his wife's real killer. Success in solving the crime was the best as well as the only safe way for Dr. Kimball to make up for his outlawry.

Hobbes's example also makes vivid the limiting case in which *not resisting* an administrative prerogative means *obeying* it. Often, it is possible to comply with an administrative prerogative without obeying it, for example, if I am ordered to pay damages but instead bargain with the plaintiff to pay a lesser amount in return for waiving an

---

[13]   *Leviathan* (XIV:29) 93, (XXI:22) 147; (XXI:17) 145.

appeal. Or if I am ordered to be in court on a certain day but send my attorney instead to ask for a continuance. But sometimes the only way not to resist the executioner's order to "Put your head on the block" is to put your head on the block, which is to obey. Thus, the view I am defending is committed to saying that there are prima facie duties to obey applicable administrative prerogatives whenever in the circumstances they are entailed by the general prima facie duty not to interfere with their enforcement. Even so, the scope of the duties to which this view is committed is drastically narrower and less objectionable than that of political obligation as traditionally conceived.

Doubts about the Strong Lemma Count against the Modest

Anyone who doubts the philosophical anarchist's Strong Lemma – no authority ever has a general (justification) right forcefully to administer its authoritative directives – should also doubt the Modest Lemma. This is because there is reason to believe that the state's having a justification right must entail at the very least a "claim right" of noninterference. If one takes a strict view of rights as moral constraints on others,[14] it is impossible to maintain, as Ladenson does, that in enforcing the law the state "does not press a claim against others but rather responds to demands for justification."[15] Nor can one maintain, as Christopher Wellman has, that "the true correlative" of the state's right to rule "is merely a citizen's lack of right to not be coerced."[16] In a strict Hohfeldian matrix, nothing is properly called a right to ϕ unless it involves not merely a liberty to ϕ (that is, no duty not to ϕ) but also a duty incumbent upon others not to interfere with one's ϕ-ing, as George Rainbolt has argued. Thus, either Ladenson's and Wellman's conceptions of the right to rule resolve into bundles including a liberty to enforce, a liberty not to enforce, and a claim against interference (but without any immunity against extinction of the whole package) or they do not amount to a right properly so-called. If it is a right, properly so-called, then it is inconsistent with the Modest Lemma, which denies that a general duty of nonresistance exists.

---

[14] George Rainbolt, "Rights as Normative Constraints on Others," 53 *Philosophy and Phenomenological Research* 93–112 (1993).
[15] Robert Ladenson, "In Defense of a Hobbesian Conception of Law," 9 *Philosophy & Public Affairs* 134, 138 (1980).
[16] Christopher Wellman, "Liberalism, Samaritanism, and Political Legitimacy," 25 *Philosophy & Public Affairs* 211, 212 n. 1 (1996).

Even if one is not taken by a structural argument along Rainbolt's lines, there remains something irreducibly odd about conceiving a state that is justified in enforcing its laws while its citizens have not only no duty to obey the law but also no duty not to interfere with the administrative prerogatives by which the law is executed. One wants to say that whatever justifies forceful administrative prerogatives has also to impose on citizens a duty of noninterference. As much is true for the privilege of self-defense: To say that I have a right to defend myself is to say that morally competent others have a duty not to interfere with my exercise of that right. They may make factual mistakes that persuade them otherwise (and the duty is a prima facie one that may be outweighed), but in the objective idiom of duty that's what their duty is. Similarly, one who admits that the balance of all reasons justifies the just state generally in forcefully pursuing its administrative prerogatives cannot intelligibly deny that that very balance imposes a general prima facie duty of noninterference.

WHY THIS VIEW IS ALL THE AUTHORITY WE NEED

Law changes our moral situation in at least three ways: (1) Legal judgments and enactments can alter the balance of reasons and thereby create new moral duties; (2) legal judgments and enactments provide a mechanism for enforcing moral duties, whether preexisting or flowing from legal acts; and (3) sufficiently just states impose a general duty not to interfere with their administrative prerogatives. These powers are enough to constitute a robust conception of legitimate political authority. This is the only sense in which political obligation and legitimacy need to be correlated.

Someone will object that a robust conception of political authority has to include an account of how the state can claim that its subjects have a duty to obey the law "as it requires to be obeyed." We must ask how, precisely, the law requires that it be obeyed. Upon reflection, it appears that the law is indifferent to how it is obeyed. No legal system requires us to pay our taxes cheerfully, or out of a sense of public spiritedness, or out of a sense of duty. We are simply required to pay. True, some criminal laws penalize only those violations committed with the knowledge that the law requires otherwise, but that is not at all the same as to penalize conduct for having been motivated by reasons other than a desire to comply with the law. We are generally free to obey "under protest," that is, for reasons that do not include any wish to discharge a contested duty to obey.

A political authority is, necessarily, one that makes (or is at least ready to defend its fitness to make) general claims about certain aspects of the moral situation of its subjects. But the legitimacy of that authority does not require that those claims be true, in addition to being sincere and sufficiently well-founded. Political authorities normally claim (at least implicitly) that there is a general duty to obey the law. It would be difficult to understand them as authorities otherwise. But their legitimacy as authorities does not hang on the correctness of this moral claim. We may consistently adopt an attitude of "conscientious watchfulness"[17] toward the just state without contesting its legitimacy, namely, its right to "order us around" by the issuance of administrative prerogatives and our coordinate duty not to interfere with them.

This answer may not satisfy those who believe that authority necessarily involves some sort of "surrender of judgment,"[18] and that therefore the exercise of political authority must either reflect moral truth or be illegitimately presumptuous. Contrast the following expressions:

Do it.
Please do it.
Do it because I say so.
Do it because it's good.
Do it because I say it's good.
Do it because I say it's good and there's no time to explain.
Do it because I say it's good and I should know better than you.
Do it because I say it's good and it's better that you take my word
    for it.

Given the right context, any of these might be chosen to make an authoritative pronouncement, but each differs from every other at least in the nuances normally conveyed. "Do it" is too peremptory

---

[17] The phrase is Joseph Raz's; see "Authority and Consent," 67 *Virginia Law Review* 103, 130 (1981).

[18] See, e.g., Richard Flathman, *The Practice of Political Authority* 90 (Chicago: University of Chicago Press, 1980); Richard B. Friedman, "On the Concept of Authority in Political Philosophy," in Richard E. Flathman, ed., *Concepts in Social and Political Philosophy* 121 (New York: Macmillan, 1973) at 29; Joseph Raz, *Practical Reason and Norms*, 2d ed. (Princeton: Princeton University Press, 1990).

and "Please do it" too precatory to serve as paradigm expressions of authority. Authorities don't simply demand, they command. That is to say they speak from a certain position that gives what they say a character unlike the mere demand that anyone might make. Authorities don't just ask, either, pretty please.

"Do it because I say so" doesn't well express authority because it is too much a mere ipse dixit, and it obscures rather than evinces the standing that an authority at least pretends to. "Do it because it's good" is too reticent; it, as it were, introduces the hearer to what is to be done, then retires, leaving the two to get better acquainted. "Do it because I say it's good" comes closer, but it merely insinuates that there are circumstances that make the speaker an authority whose opinion of the good is worthy of deference.

Saying "Do it because I say it's good" with the addition "there's no time to explain" is a paradigmatic expression of at least special-purpose authority. The speaker asks her hearer to surrender judgment because the speaker has been alerted to the combined circumstance that (1) it would be good to ϕ and ϕ quickly, and (2) persuading the listener that this is true would greatly reduce the good of doing ϕ. This expression is suited to an emergency, but the general idea carries over to other situations involving transaction costs to bring the hearer or hearers into agreement with the speaker. The implied promise "I'll explain later" could be replaced by "We've been over that." The idea is, again, that the speaker claims that circumstances are such that a great good will fail to be gotten if consensus has to be waited on.

The speaker implicitly also claims that he is in a better position to correctly balance the value of the good to be gotten by doing ϕ against the value of first obtaining consensus that ϕ is the thing to do. This is what "Do it because I say it's good and I should know better than you" claims. The disadvantage of this way of paraphrasing the claim of political authority is its epistemic pretension. A medical authority might use this locution, but we regard doctors as experts in a way that we don't regard legislators. Therefore the best way of paraphrasing the claim of political authority is with the last expression. "Do it because I say it's good and it's better that you take my word for it." This way of putting it makes clearer the fact that the superior position claimed by political authority is not essentially or even chiefly epistemic. The balance of competing interests, claims, and reasons struck in the legislative bargain is one that rather few would claim to represent a privileged knowledge of the matters concerned; yet it is one that political authority can plausibly claim to be better for each citizen to follow than his or her own assessment of what the best balance would be.[19]

Although political authority is closely related to epistemic authority, it is not reducible to it. It is not that legislation can never represent what we might call moral discovery, that is, convey fresh evidence of what Heidi Hurd calls "antecedently existing" reasons and moral obligations, but I think such instances are relatively rare.[20] An example might be a "statutory" rape enactment that, in part, pronounces the wrongfulness of what otherwise might seem innocently mistaken conduct. Far more common is the case of legislation that represents moral improvisation, that is, a rule that is morally obligatory only because a rule offers important benefits not securable otherwise, for example, by making salient one of many possible solutions to a coordination problem.[21] Think of driving on the right (or left) side of the highway – absent any prior custom, surely nobody had a moral obligation to drive on either particular side before the law declared which it was to be. Moreover, the salient solution to a coordination problem need not be the optimal one, in terms of the parties' preferences, much less the one that is morally best. Think of the tax code. It is very hard to believe, with Hurd, that the governmental scheme of levies and expenditures – whether as a whole or in any part – is any clue to what we would independently and antecedently have a duty to do with our money.

But this is not to say that political authority carries no epistemic

---

19 See Joseph Raz, *The Morality of Freedom* 46–53 (Oxford: Clarendon Press, 1986). With regard to coordination problems, Anthony Honoré claims that "there is often no possibility of doing the right thing apart from law since there is, apart from law, *no right thing* to do." See his "The Dependence of Morality on Law," 13 *Oxford Journal of Legal Studies* 1, 12 (1993); emphasis added. His claim is less controversial if understood epistemically ("no knowably right thing") rather than ontologically ("no right thing").

20 See Heidi Hurd, "Sovereignty in Silence," 99 *Yale Law Journal* 945 (1990), "Challenging Authority," 100 *Yale Law Journal* 1611 (1991); and cf. Larry Alexander, "Law and Exclusionary Reasons," 18 *Philosophical Topics* 5 (1990); Don Regan, "Authority and Value: Reflections on Raz's Morality of Freedom," 62 *Southern California Law Review* 995 (1989).

21 See Thomas C. Schelling, *The Strategy of Conflict* 57–8 (New York: Oxford University Press, 1960); David K. Lewis, *Convention: A Philosophical Study* 35 (Cambridge, Mass.: Harvard University Press, 1969); Edna Ullmann-Margalit, *The Emergence of Norms* 83–4 (Oxford: Clarendon Press, 1977); Gerald J. Postema, "Coordination and Convention at the Foundations of Law, 11 *Journal of Legal Studies* 165 (1982); Leslie Green, "Law, Co-ordination, and the Common Good," 3 *Oxford Journal of Legal Studies* 299 (1982).

freight. In fact, because there is a degree of parallelism between political and epistemic authority, a legitimate political authority gives citizens *good reasons to believe they ought to obey its laws,* just as legitimate scientific authorities give the laity good reasons to believe what they say about the workings of the world. Notice, though, the gap that remains between *giving good reasons to believe one's duty is to* φ, and *there being* a duty to φ. Good reasons needn't be sufficient or conclusive reasons, whether the issue is scientific or political authority. What those good reasons *are*, in the case of political authority, is not always made vividly clear. In many instances, the best that can be said of a law that is a legislative compromise (as most are) is that important but conflicting ends and interests were weighed and balanced, and general conformity with the means specified by the law in question is better than the alternatives (including the alternative of doing nothing).

This is why the better analysis reflects, somehow, the "second-order" nature of the reasons authorities distinctively give. In the case of political authority, its exercise gives us stronger reason to believe that our best course is not to follow our uncoordinated inclinations, than to believe that the specific solution enacted into law – and thus made "salient" – independently reflects the optimal solution. The exercise of political authority, in other words, gives us better reasons to think the matter is one that is "better decided, than decided rightly," than it does to believe that the matter has, in fact, *been* "decided rightly," especially if commanding universal assent is one's ideal of rightness.[22]

FURTHER OBJECTIONS CONSIDERED

To combine the Strong Authority Thesis and the Modest Legitimacy Thesis in a single view may seem to represent a political authority as deceitfully making moral claims that it does not warrant to be true. Or the combination might seem to be sustainable only if esoteric, because, if it were promulgated generally, popular support for the law would weaken and the state itself would be destabilized. I will conclude this chapter by trying to show that these worries are misplaced.

---

[22] Joseph Raz's writings on this difficult subject have shaped my way of looking at them. See my "Rethinking Exclusionary Reasons: A Second Edition of Joseph Raz's *Practical Reason and Norms*," 12 *Law and Philosophy* 329–43 (1993).

The claim stated by the Strong Authority Thesis is not one that each and every state will need or want to make explicitly. In ideal circumstances, citizens would be sufficiently disposed to heed political authority without having to be reminded of its moral claim. Similarly, in awful circumstances, an embattled state might rely so heavily on the threat of sanctions that its moral claim comes close to being abandoned. And again, before a cynical polity, authority might choose for forensic reasons not to press the moral claim. Each of these circumstances is consistent with the truth of the Strong Authority Thesis. The point is that no person or persons can be a political authority by the mere accident of being respected, deferred to, and obeyed. Any political authority must satisfy this subjunctive condition: If the issue of obedience is raised, the authority must be prepared to defend the claim that morality, in the wide sense that includes political morality, requires it. This doesn't mean that authority must make the silly claim that what it says to do is ipso facto morally obligatory – as Jeffrey Reiman has pointed out, there are no moral authorities in that sense[23] – but it does, at a minimum, require that an authority be prepared to defend the position that its directives are ones that, having been promulgated, (political) morality requires to be obeyed. (A political authority is of course capable of issuing directives that are not authoritative, for example, the declaration that May is Peanut Month.)

The Modest Authority Thesis fails to capture this essential posture of political authority. If a putative authority claimed no more than a duty of noninterference with its administrative prerogatives – conceding its subjects' moral liberty otherwise to ignore its authoritative directives – the face it would present would be incoherent indeed, unless it happened not to issue any general authoritative directives at all. This last would be something like a state of martial law, ordinary civil authority having been suspended, in conditions too chaotic even to allow the framing of general decrees, for example, a curfew. Admittedly, such a regime might be an authority, but it would be a martial, not a political authority. Political authority entails the issuance and maintenance of norms, that is, general directives. "There is a rule against ϕ-ing, but – except on those occasions when ϕ-ing would amount to resisting an administrative prerogative – you may have no moral duty to obey it" is a message that can

---

[23]   Jeffrey H. Reiman, *In Defense of Political Philosophy* 1–16 (New York: Harper & Row, 1972).

convey little other than confusion. But this is the only message that the Modest Authority Thesis can send.

The view I am defending leaves no objectionable room for hypocrisy because an authority that cynically claimed that its subjects had a moral duty to obey its laws – that is, made the claim while disbelieving it – would violate the Proximity Thesis and thus forfeit its claim to legitimacy. Such a state might nonetheless be an authority in the de facto sense. Seemingly more difficult is the case of the authority that is fallibilistic (that is, ready to confess the possibility of error) about the duty to obey, while making the claim that obedience is due. Sincerely claiming that p, while harboring serious doubts whether p, is of course possible. You and I both do it all the time. For example, I know that my statement of many matters of fact is overly concise and therefore, on strict view, false; and yet I make such statements day in and day out in perfect sincerity. Similarly, a scientific authority may in all sincerity use an analogy, in a popular exposition of a difficult concept, knowing that it is at best an approximation of the truth and is literally false. Such a writer is no less a legitimate scientific authority.

Some theories are criticized as self-defeating, in the sense that, if applied, they defeat their own ends. For example, the utilitarian's "greatest happiness" principle has been criticized (rightly or wrongly) on the ground that a person or society that directly pursues the greatest happiness will be more miserable for the effort.[24] Insofar as the view I am defending has the legitimacy of states as an end, one might object that it too is self-defeating, in the sense that if the theory were widely known it would weaken political authority. Put another way, one might object that the view I am defending would be self-defeating unless knowledge of it were restricted in a way that would offend what Larry Alexander has called the "Publicity Principle," which "rejects the legitimacy of any moral principle that cannot be publicly advocated without undermining itself."[25]

The objection will go like this: Combining the Strong Authority Thesis, the Modest Legitimacy Thesis, and the Proximity Thesis leaves a gap between what the state claims as an authority and what must be true for the state to be legitimate. If this gap is recognized by everybody, the law will be less likely to be heeded because even loyal

[24] Cf. Derek Parfit, *Reasons and Persons* 5–7 (Oxford: Clarendon Press, 1984).
[25] Larry Alexander, "Law and Exclusionary Reasons," 18 *Philosophical Topics* 5, 11 (1990).

citizens – those who accept the legitimacy of the state – will know that all they are morally bound to do (above and beyond what morality already requires) is to avoid interfering with law enforcement. Believing this, citizens will cease to consult the law on the issue of what morality requires and will rely exclusively on their own moral notions and calculations of the likelihood of being caught and punished. This will begin a downward spiral: As more and more citizens see others disregarding the law everywhere but at the point of enforcement, they too will adopt that attitude. Eventually, the state will degenerate into a condition not unlike a relaxed, proceduralized martial law – increasingly inhabited only by Holmesian "bad men" and saints – in which no one takes the law seriously except when it happens to coincide with his or her personal moral conclusions or is in the process of being enforced.

This objection is cogent, but not particularly troublesome. The objector envisages the state weakened, perhaps, but not to the point of collapse. Weakening the state, without inviting anarchy, has ironically been the very aim of mainstream political theory at least since Madison. But even the weakening the objector contemplates would not be a necessary consequence of the widespread acceptance of the view espoused here (hope of which the author modestly disavows!). The state is a "bully pulpit," as Theodore Roosevelt put it, but it is a contingent matter whether anyone preaches from it, and whether persuasively. The acts of the state themselves are capable of changing the moral situation of citizens, for example, by solving coordination problems and prisoners' dilemmas, by adjusting expectations, and by providing remedies for private and public grievances. The enfeeblement of the state the objector portrays presupposes a picture of morality standing aloof from the law, rather than being entwined with it. This picture is not sustainable, as I have indicated and as Parts Two and Three will further show.

SUMMARY

I have not offered a complete theory of the legitimacy of the state – to echo Rousseau, "Do not read my book if you expect me to tell you everything" – but I hope to have clarified what such a theory must look like and to have cleared away some misunderstandings that have seemed to foreclose the possibility of a legitimate state. I have not discussed the role of justice in the theory of legitimacy, except to suggest that only a nearly just state is capable of being legitimate.

Obviously, the task of characterizing the just and the nearly just state would in itself occupy a book longer than this one. My task here has been to allay the fashionable doubt that even a just state can be legitimate.

The "anarchical fallacy" I have been concerned with in this first part arises from the combination of the idea of the state as an authority and the idea of a correlativity between authority and a duty to obey. The "Inconsistent Triad" of Chapter 1 exhibited the anarchical tendency of a certain conception of legitimacy. If legitimacy depends upon there being a general duty of obedience, then the legitimacy of the state is vulnerable to every worry about political obligation. Given that the worry about political obligation has not gone away after over two millennia of treatment, it is tempting to conclude that the legitimacy of the state must remain likewise doubtful or else be boldly cut away from any condition involving a duty to the state. This temptation must be resisted – otherwise, no sense can be made of the idea of the state as a political *authority*.

The view I have argued for combines what I have termed the Strong Authority Thesis, the Modest Legitimacy Thesis, and the Proximity Thesis. This combination has the advantage that it exhibits the nature of the citizen's obligation to a legitimate state while at the same time preserving a vigorous conception of the nature of political authority. There is an evident gap between what the state claims and what, to be legitimate, it must deliver; its reach exceeds its grasp, as it were. Properly understood, though, this gap is not troublesome. Rather, it is a reflection of the gap that must ever exist between legitimacy and infallibility.

Part Two

The "Law Is Coercive" Fallacy

"The idea of coercion shall in their minds have become inseparably connected with that of a law."

Bentham, *Of Laws in General* XI: 8

Chapter 4

The Concept of Coercion

That law *is* coercive is something we all more or less take for granted. It is an assumption so rooted in our ways of thinking that it is taken as a given of social reality, an uncontroversial datum. Because it is so regarded, it is infrequently stated, and when it is, it is stated without any hint of possible complications or any need of qualifications. I will call this the "pre-reflective view," and I want to examine it with the care it deserves.

To call the view that law is coercive a pre-reflective view is not to say that it is not held by thoughtful people. On the contrary, the pre-reflective view is a pervasive assumption of modern legal and political theory. It is an assumption made by many Marxists, as well as those in the political center and on the right. It is not an idle assumption: What we regard as coercive we regard as prima facie illegitimate and we hold it to an accounting; what is not coercive, in contrast, is presumed to be in order. To be able to cast the law, or the free market, as a coercive force is to be able to cast upon its defenders a burden of persuasion, which, even if carried, leaves what has to be defended under a cloud. Where, as in morality and politics, so much is uncertain, claiming the benefit of a presumption may be the decisive rhetorical advantage – the beneficiary of the presumption winning, as it were, by default.

In the last two and a half decades various attempts have been made to subject the concept of coercion to rigorous analysis. These attempts have not generated a consensus, but they do serve to sharpen and deepen our understanding of what is involved in the idea of coercion. In what follows, I will apply this analytical work to the question: Is law coercive? The answer that we will get is not a reassuring "Of course," but a surprising – one might even say repugnant – "No; except in extraordinary circumstances, law is not coercive."

The significance of this result lies in its bearing upon issues of the legitimacy of the state as a whole and of its particular functions, such as adjudication. State power must still be justified, of course, as always. But, without the taint of coerciveness, its exercise is no more presumptively illegitimate than its nonexercise and no more presumptively illegitimate than nonstate power. Abandoning the prereflective view does not mean adopting any sort of presumption favoring the legitimacy of law. What it does do is to force us to rethink the theory of the state from the ground up.

THE CONTEXTS OF COERCION CLAIMS

What, exactly, *is* coercion? It will be helpful to focus our thinking on characterizing the circumstances that are involved in accepting or rejecting a *coercion claim*. A coercion claim is simply any statement roughly equivalent to one of the form "By ϕ-ing, person(s) A coerce(s) or attempt(s) to coerce person(s) B into ψ-ing."[1] A's action X will typically involve a declaration or threat, which I will refer to as A's *coercive proposal.*[2] The action ψ of B that A seeks to bring about will frequently be an omission or forbearance.

Discussing coercion is complicated by the fact that coercion claims are made in various contexts. Fortunately, a rough but usable division of these contexts into three distinct types can be made. I call these types *justification supplying, justification defeating,* and *justification demanding.* I will now try to characterize these types.

What I call the justification-supplying context of a coercion claim can best be explained by illustration:

CASE 1. *State v Toscano*

Toscano is charged with the crime of conspiracy to commit fraud. Toscano defends by proving that Leonardo threatened Toscano and his family with bodily harm if Toscano did not participate. Toscano

---

[1] See Alan Wertheimer, *Coercion* 5–6 (Princeton: Princeton University Press, 1987) [hereafter, Wertheimer].

[2] Some have insisted that there exists such an animal as a "coercive offer," memorably (if perhaps inaccurately) exemplified in the following passage:

"This guy is a personal friend of J. Edgar Hoover," Johnny said. "You can't even raise your voice to him."

"He's a businessman," the Don said blandly, "I'll make him an offer he can't refuse." (Mario Puzo, *The Godfather* 39 [New York: Putnam, 1969])

There has been extensive controversy about this point, and in an effort to avoid it I have chosen to use the neutral, generic term "proposal."

summarizes his defense by saying that Leonardo *coerced* his participation.[3]

CASE 2. *Austin Instrument v Loral Corp.*

Loral contracts to buy gears from Austin. Austin delivers some of the gears but refuses to ship the rest unless Loral pays more for the entire shipment and agrees to order still more gears. Loral, unable to meet its other obligations any other way, grudgingly agrees. Loral's shareholders demand an explanation of its knuckling under. Loral's management claims that Austin *coerced* the concessions.[4]

In Cases 1 and 2, an actor makes a coercion claim in order to *justify* her behavior. Some would prefer to say that at best the actor's behavior is *excused* in Case 1, but I will not pursue that issue here. In any event, the point of the actor's coercion claim in these contexts is to avoid responsibility and the attendant blame for her challenged conduct.

Coercion claims also occur in justification-defeating contexts, in which the claimant introduces the issue of coercion not directly to justify her own conduct, but to defeat another actor's putative justification for his. Two examples:

CASE 3. *State v Rusk*

Rusk, a male, asks Pat, a female, for a ride home. When Pat stops in front of Rusk's apartment, Rusk takes Pat's keys and says, "Now, will you come up?" Pat goes up to Rusk's apartment. Rusk refuses to return Pat's keys and begins to undress her. Pat removes the rest of her clothes. Pat asks "If I do what you want, will you let me go without killing me?" Rusk responds by putting his hands on Pat's throat and lightly squeezing. Pat and Rusk have intercourse, and Pat leaves. At Rusk's trial for rape, the state claims that Rusk *coerced* Pat's assent to his advances.[5]

CASE 4. More of *Austin v Loral*

Same as Case 2. After taking delivery of the remainder of the gears originally ordered, Loral refuses to pay more than the price originally agreed to, and refuses to accept delivery of any additional gears. Austin sues Loral to enforce the agreement as modified. In defense, Loral claims that Austin *coerced* its acceptance of the modified terms.

[3] 378 A.2d 755 (1977).
[4] 29 N.Y.2d 124 (1971).
[5] 289 Md. 230, 424 A.2d 720 (1981).

75

In Cases 3 and 4, a coercion claim is made not to supply a justification but to defeat another actor's proffered justification of his conduct.[6] As Cases 2 and 4 illustrate, however, the two contexts may be linked. In those cases, Loral points to the same coercive conduct on Austin's part to achieve the end – in Case 2 – of absolving itself of responsibility for its own conduct and – in Case 4 – of defeating Austin's claim that it is justified in seeking damages from Loral.

The third context, which I call justification-demanding coercion, is the one I want to single out for extended discussion. In this type of context, a coercion claim is made not to supply or to defeat a justification, but rather it is made by way of *demanding* an explanation of an instance or kind of conduct. Some examples will help define this context in which coercion claims are found.

Case 5. Highway Robbery

Gunman stops Traveler on the highway and demands "Your money or your life!" Gunman's proposal is *coercive*.[7] Traveler surrenders his money. Gunman has *coerced* Traveler.

Case 6. Robbery Statute

A state enacts a statute that provides that anyone convicted of highway robbery shall be punished for a term of not less than five and not more than twenty years. It is popularly thought that the state *coerces* its citizens not to engage in highway robbery.

Our normal response to Case 5 is to condemn Gunman's behavior unless some further facts in *justification* of his conduct are provided, for example, that Traveler is bankrolling a terrorist organization, and Gunman is acting to frustrate a terrorist plot that can be checked in no other way. In Case 5, the coercion claim occurs in a justification-*demanding* context. Whether that claim must be modified or with-

---

[6] I ignore the point that in Case 3 the issue, properly speaking, is not "justification" in the technical legal sense, but whether the state can prove that Rusk performed the *actus reus* of rape. For a provocative argument that coerced agreements can occur and can be binding, see Margaret Gilbert, "Agreements, Coercion, and Obligation," 103 *Ethics* 679 (1993).

[7] A proposal may be coercive even if it fails to achieve its purpose. See Peter Western, "'Freedom' and 'Coercion' – Virtue Words and Vice Words," 1985 *Duke Law Journal* 541, 562–3 (1985), who explains the error of the contrary view, that "coercion" is essentially a "success" word, which is held by many, see, e.g., Michael Bayles, "The Concept of Coercion," in J. Roland Pennock and John W. Chapman, eds., *Coercion: Nomos XIV* (Chicago: Atherton-Aldine, 1972).

drawn if a sufficiently strong justification is provided is a *further* question, upon which we feel the Gunman bears some sort of burden of proof. Hans Oberdiek has expressed the rhetorical significance of coercion claims this way:

> Coercion is a *moral notion*. That is, like deception, wantonness, bribery and countless other concepts, coercion embodies a moral assessment: *insofar as* an act or institution is coercive, it is morally unjustified and therefore stands in need of a moral defense or excuse. At the same time, coercion is an incomplete moral notion, since truly describing an act or institution as coercive does not conclusively settle its moral unjustifiablity, though it does place a definite *onus probandi* on anyone who wishes to defend or excuse the act or institution.[8]

Case 6 has seemed to many to be sufficiently analogous to Case 5 to support the analogous coercion claim. State stands to citizen as Gunman stands to Traveler; that is to say, the state *coerces* its citizens and therefore a justification is demanded. Or, I should say, a *special* justification is demanded, which would not be the case if, for example, the state failed to enact such a statute or repealed it.

THE ANALYSIS OF COERCION CLAIMS

We notice that justification-supplying, justification-defeating, and justification-demanding contexts can overlap. In Case 5, for example, the coercion claim might supply a justification for Traveler's submission, even as it demands a justification for Gunman's conduct. Furthermore, in Case 5, the coercion claim would serve to defeat an attempt by Gunman to justify his conduct by asserting that Traveler had made him a gift.

The fact that coercion claims can occur in very different types of context, even overlapping types of context, might seem to be an obstacle to any attempt to give a univocal account of the truth-conditions of the concept of coercion. Just as the meaning of the word "bank" varies radically if we vary the context of its occurrence from, say, watercourses to finances, so also we might reasonably fear the

---

[8]   Hans Oberdiek, "The Role of Sanctions and Coercion in Understanding Law and Legal Systems," 1975 *American Journal of Jurisprudence* 71, 80. Assigning the burden of proof to an opponent is a key move in what has been termed the "argument from ignorance." See Richard H. Gaskins, *Burdens of Proof in Modern Discourse* (New Haven: Yale University Press, 1992).

concept of coercion to exhibit a similar radical variation from context to context.

In what follows I will defend the position that a univocal account of the truth conditions of coercion claims is possible. Disagreements about the proper statement of those truth conditions will be found, but these disagreements will not turn out to be the product of inattention to different contexts of use. To put the point differently, the "pragmatic" considerations that govern the *idiomatically proper* use of the word "coercion" and its cognates are separable from the *semantic* issues I want to pursue, namely: (1) What must be true for it to be true to say that "*A* coerces *B*," and (2) on the best account of these truth conditions, is it true to say that law is coercive?[9] As we shall see, there are sharp differences between the accounts of the truth conditions of coercion claims that have been proposed, but these differences are not to be explained by pointing out unappreciated pragmatic differences. The significance of this assumption is that it allows us to make use of extensive work to clarify the meaning of coercion and to apply that work to the question of whether law is coercive.

What if this assumption is false? What if, in fact, coercion claims *do* occur in different contexts in such a way that no univocal account of their truth conditions is possible? If that is the case, then the risk of committing fallacies of equivocation in reasoning about coercion must be constantly guarded against. Consider the following:

Premise:	Law is coercive.
Premise:	Whatever is coercive bears a burden of specially justifying itself.
Conclusion:	Law bears a special burden of justifying itself.

If coercion is an equivocal concept then the above inference may be as fallacious as:

Premise:	First National is a bank.
Premise:	A bank channels a flow of water.
Conclusion:	First National channels a flow of water.

---

[9]   The distinction between pragmatics and semantics is set out in Paul Grice's seminal article "The Causal Theory of Perception," 35 *Aristotelian Society Supplement* (1961), reprinted in *Studies in the Ways of Words* 224 (Cambridge, Mass.: Harvard University Press, 1989), and was developed further in his 1967 William James lectures, titled "Logic and Conversation," reprinted in *Studies in the Ways of Words*.

If coercion is not univocal then the popular view that law is coercive may be guilty of equivocation if it is intended to have justification-demanding force, as normally it is. The popular view, therefore, tacitly makes the same assumption that I am making explicitly. Now let us see where this assumption takes us.

Wertheimer's "Two-Prong" Analysis

Political philosopher Alan Wertheimer has made an extensive survey of legal opinions dealing with coercion and has extracted from them what he calls a "two-prong" theory of coercion:

> *A* coerces *B* to ψ if and only if (1) *A*'s proposal creates a choice situation for *B* such that *B* has no reasonable alternative but to ψ and (2) it is *wrong*[10] for *A* to make such a proposal to *B*.

Wertheimer calls condition (1) the "choice" prong and condition (2) the "proposal" prong. The choice and proposal conditions are individually necessary and jointly sufficient. If we review the cases discussed above we can appreciate how Wertheimer's conception works.

In Case 1, Toscano's defense will invoke the wrongfulness of Leonardo's proposal, but it will fail unless Toscano can carry whatever burden he will bear on the issue of whether he was left with a reasonable alternative, such as alerting the police. In Case 2, Loral's management will argue that market conditions left it no reasonable alternative to agreeing to Austin's terms, but it must also show that Austin's proposal was a wrongful one, one that Austin had no right to make. And so with the other cases.

I will assume that Wertheimer has correctly identified the structure of the concept of coercion as it operates in the law, postponing for a moment the further question of whether it can serve as a general account of the concept. Notice that Wertheimer's analysis has important consequences *within* the law. For example, consider plea bargains:

CASE 7. Plea Bargain

District Attorney has offered not to seek the death penalty in return for Defendant's plea of guilty to a homicide charge. Defendant insists that

---

[10] Wertheimer at 172 (emphasis in original). I will later refine Wertheimer's formulation so that "wrongful" here is understood to mean *prima facie* wrongful rather than wrongful, all things considered.

he is innocent but is aware that the State has a strong case. Defendant enters the guilty plea but later seeks to have his conviction overturned on the ground that his plea was *coerced.*[11]

Here, we may safely assume that the Defendant really has no reasonable alternative to accepting the District Attorney's offer, any more than the Traveler has, in Case 5, to accepting the Gunman's proposal. Is the guilty plea then coerced? On Wertheimer's analysis the issue turns upon whether the District Attorney acted wrongfully in making her proposal. Unlike the Gunman, the District Attorney does not act wrongfully (from the standpoint of law) if she pursues her *"declared unilateral plan,"*[12] that is, if she pursues what she has stated she will do if her proposal is not accepted – seek the death penalty. (Assume, for the present, that a proposal is wrongful only if what is proposed would be wrongful to carry out.) If our focus is the legality of the proposal, Wertheimer's analysis can be applied in a way that supports the U.S. Supreme Court's doctrine that plea bargains are not inherently coercive and, hence, are voluntary and enforceable. But one who believes (as I do) that capital punishment is *morally* wrongful (despite the Supreme Court's opinion) will conclude that the proposal *is* coercive. In either case, our view of the wrongfulness of the District Attorney's declared unilateral plan shapes our view of its coerciveness.

Identifying the "Baseline"

The Plea Bargain case brings out an important feature of the proposal prong of Wertheimer's analysis. Establishing whether *A* acts wrongly in making a proposal to *B* requires that we first establish *B*'s moral *baseline*, that is, the moral rights and entitlements against which we must judge *A*'s proposal. Consider the following pair of cases:

CASE 8. Hard Bargain

A learns that *B*, whose train has derailed, is about to miss a steamship connection that is essential to *B*'s avoiding a huge loss. *A* proposes to

---

[11] This example is based on *North Carolina v Alford*, 400 U.S. 25 (1970).
[12] The term is Vinit Haksar's. See Vinit Haksar, "Coercive Proposals," 4 *Political Theory* 65, 68 (1976) [hereafter Haksar, "Coercive Proposals"].

help B by carrying B to port on A's elephant, but only on condition that B buy the elephant for a large sum. B accepts.[13]

CASE 9. Sea Rescue

A, while sailing, discovers B drowning in the middle of the sea. A offers to rescue B, but only on condition that B pay him a huge sum of money. B agrees, and is saved.

Most of us would agree that Case 8 is not a case of coercion but rather of hard bargaining. B is no worse off for A's appearance on the scene – just the contrary – even though B has no real alternative to going along with A's proposal. But what may be unclear is whether A acts wrongfully in taking advantage of B's predicament. Contrast Case 2, in which Austin threatens to stop delivery under its contract unless Loral agrees to a higher price. Austin acts coercively because Austin's "declared unilateral plan" makes Loral *worse off* relative to the baseline supplied by their prior dealings and contract law. In Case 8, however, B has no entitlement to or legitimate expectation of A's services. Therefore, relative to B's baseline in Case 8, A's carrying out A's declared unilateral plan will leave B no worse off than B had a moral right to be; and therefore A has not coerced B.

The Sea Rescue case, Case 9, is a difficult one. It brings into relief the crucial role of the baseline. Different people have conflicting, but equally vivid, intuitions about how Case 9 should be classified. All will agree that B has no reasonable alternative to accepting A's proposal. But against what baseline should the effect of A's declared unilateral plan be judged? If we ask whether A's declared unilateral plan makes B worse off against a moral baseline that includes a positive duty to aid those in distress, then A's proposal is wrongful and coercive. If, on the other hand, the baseline we consider includes no duty to be the "Good Samaritan," then A's proposal makes B no worse off and is not coercive. Robert Nozick points out that people will disagree whether cases such as Case 9 are cases of coercion "because they disagree about what the normal and expected course of events is, which is to be used as a baseline."[14] Consequently, one's classifi-

---

[13] This example is drawn from Jules Verne, *Around the World in Eighty Days*, George Makepeace Towle, trans., 40–1 (New York: Bantam, 1984).

[14] Robert Nozick, "Coercion," in Sidney Morgenbesser, Patrick Suppes, and Morton White, eds., *Philosophy, Science, and Method* 444, 449–50 (New York: St. Martin's, 1969), reprinted in Robert Nozick, *Socratic Puzzles* (Cambridge, Mass: Harvard University Press, 1997).

cation of Case 9 will depend not only on the "plain facts" it presents but also on one's wider moral convictions.

IS LAW COERCIVE? A REPUGNANT CONCLUSION

Let us set aside for a moment the question of how to go about specifying the proper baseline for evaluating coercion claims. What can we say about Case 6, in which the state that punishes highway robbery is said to coerce its citizens not to engage in such conduct? We have provisionally accepted the idea that a proposal is not coercive unless, in Vinit Haksar's words, "the proposer's declared unilateral plan [is] an immoral one, i.e., if the proposer carried out his declared unilateral plan he would be violating a moral duty."[15] But can anyone seriously argue that the state acts immorally, or contrary to a moral duty, by punishing the highway robber? The answer must be, No. But this in turn seems to commit us to saying that Case 6 is *not* a case of coercion after all! Haksar, for one, embraces precisely this conclusion: "The state is not making a coercive proposal when it proposes fairly and justly that it will not put [anyone] in jail if he is law abiding . . . [p]enal laws, when fair and just, do not involve coercion."[16]

To make the point another way, consider the following variation on Case 5:

CASE 10. Tables Turned on the Gunman

As in Case 5 but, rather than comply with Gunman's demand, Traveler states that he, too, is armed and that he is prepared to defend himself and his wallet, with deadly force if necessary.

Has Traveler made a coercive proposal to Gunman? Most of us would answer, No. Those who disagree might consider the following:

CASE 11. 98-Pound Weakling

A person of modest physique, Weakling, is subjected to humiliating taunts when he takes off his shirt at the beach. In particular, Nemesis, a more muscular person, kicks sand in Weakling's face. Weakling therefore undertakes a strenuous muscle-building regime and, months later, suitably enlarged, returns to the beach. As Weakling hopes and intends, Nemesis refrains from further provocation.

---

[15]   Haksar, "Coercive Proposals" at 68.   [16]   Ibid. at 73 and 74 n. 11.

Many, if not most, of us would say that Weakling has not coerced Nemesis and that Weakling's implicit threat to measure his strength against Nemesis's does not constitute a coercive proposal. If this is our response to Case 11, I cannot see how our response to Case 10 can differ. (To say that Traveler's threat is not wrongful is not necessarily to say that his shooting Gunman to defend his possession would be permissible, for sometimes it is permissible, even laudatory, to threaten to do what would be wrong to do.[17]) But if our considered judgment is that Traveler does not coerce in Case 10, shouldn't we likewise deny that the state acts coercively in Case 6, when it promulgates legislation threatening to punish highway robbers?

One might suggest that Case 6 is distinguishable from Cases 10 and 11 insofar as, in the latter pair, coercion is absent only because the putative coercee has *initiated* the use of force. But both cases can readily be redescribed to remove that feature, yet without disturbing the intuition that the relevant actor (Traveler, in Case 10; Weakling, in Case 11) has not engaged in coercion. In both cases, replace the putative coercee's threatening conduct with the putative coercer's generalized anxiety about the possibility of its occurring, and let Traveler and Weakling display their general preparedness to use force not to a manifest threat but to a world supposed to harbor such threats. Coercion? Again, most would answer, No. But if not in these cases, not in Case 6 (Robbery Statute) either. We are impelled toward what many will see as the "repugnant conclusion" (if I may hijack Derek Parfit's vivid term) that law is *not* coercive, contrary to our prereflective consensus.

---

[17] Of this, more later. Cf. Wertheimer at 102 (calling for a "morality of proposals" to supplement the "morality of actions"). Cf. also Model Penal Code §3.06(3)(d)(ii) (Philadelphia: American Law Institute, 1962) (appearing to allow the Traveler's use of deadly force in situations like Case 10).

Chapter 5

Political Theory without Coercion

There are many ways to avoid Haksar's argument to the repugnant conclusion that law isn't coercive. There are, for example, different conceptions of the proper moral baseline to use in Case 6, the Robbery Statute case, just as there was disagreement about the proper moral baseline to use in Case 9, the Sea Rescue case. But the standard view, that law is coercive, is already badly embarrassed if it has to deal with the Robbery Statute case by taking a stand on what the right moral baseline is. Wertheimer asks, "How do we *set* B's moral baseline? . . . a full answer to this question would require nothing less than a complete moral and political theory." But if that's so, then classical liberalism, "an entire political theory [that] may rest on a theory of coercion" (and an unexamined one at that), leads us right into "a theory of coercion [that] rests on a moral and political theory – in particular, on a theory which allows us to set moral baselines."[1]

That the state is an utterer of coercive proposals and a coercive agent is an *assumption* of liberal political theory which has served it by enabling it to cast an *onus probandi* upon those who argue for a more active state. The slogan "law is coercive" is supposed to tell us why state action stands in *special* need of justification while, at the same time, stating a truth as nearly "value-free" as any that social science is capable of locating. Yet, now having explored the conceptual terrain, we seem to find that the position that "law is coercive" can only be the conclusion of a full-blown moral/political/legal theory, and cannot therefore serve as a datum, much less as a foundation stone.

Political liberalism, libertarianism, and anarchism are not the only ideologies that have a stake here. Marxists have to defend them-

---

[1]   Alan Wertheimer, *Coercion* 217, 220–1 (Princeton: Princeton University Press, 1987) [hereafter, Wertheimer].

selves against the charge that their ideology is less hospitable to liberty than any of various forms of market capitalism. Marxists would like to challenge the assumption that "free" markets are in fact free, at least as far as workers are concerned. If such a challenge were successful it would tend to "even the score" between Marxism and capitalism in the liberty sweepstakes: Capitalism would lose points because of the coercive behavior of capitalists vis-à-vis workers.

Marxists would like to show that the typical capitalist wage proposal is a *coercive* proposal. Moreover, Marxists would like to show that this is an "objective" fact about economic relations under capitalism. This strategy would be derailed, however, if the Marxists' coercion claim presupposes an appeal to a favored *moral baseline*, because then the appeal would not be a direct one to an objective, social datum, but to some prior, controversial (and difficult) *moral* argument against capitalism.[2]

COERCION AND MAKING UNFREE

One possible skeptical response to the repugnant conclusion is to shrug it off as inconsequential. A skeptic might deny that the concept of coercion is of any particular interest and insist that *making unfree* is really the important idea or, to put the point in J. L. Austin's quaintly sexist phrase, making unfree – not coercing – is the "trouser" concept. On this skeptical view, law makes us unfree, to some extent, and the only issue is whether it compensates for this making unfree by freeing us in other ways that are of a greater extent, or are more valuable. The semantic niceties of "coercion" are neither here nor there because what people really mean when they say that law is coercive is that law necessarily makes us unfree to do certain things that we would otherwise be free to do – and only a lunatic would deny this.

There is a reply to this skeptic. The skeptic must either say, or deny, that whenever person A's doing ϕ makes person B unfree to do ψ, A is normally expected to justify her having ϕ-ed. If the skeptic denies that a "making unfree" claim generally creates a justification-demanding context, then she will have admitted that there is an important difference between coercion and making unfree. This is so because coercion claims generally create a justification-demanding

---

[2] See David Zimmerman, "Coercive Wage Offers," 10 *Philosophy & Public Affairs* 121, 122–3 (1981).

context, even when their main point is to supply or to defeat a justification. When people assume or assert that law is coercive, they generally mean to be invoking some feature of law that demands (and,
usually, has) a justification. If "making unfree" does not force the
issue of justification, it cannot by itself do the work that coercion has
done in political theory.

If, on the other hand, the skeptic asserts that "making unfree"
claims *do* generally occur in justification-demanding contexts, she
faces the embarrassing fact that many uses of the locution do not fit
the mold. Natural circumstances, for example, make us unfree in
many ways that no one thinks demand any sort of justification. For
example, the gravitational pull of the Earth makes us unfree to fly
about like birds, but this doesn't call for any sort of justification. People, to the extent that they are bodies and have lives of their own to
live, make us unfree in myriad ways. Your standing where you do
makes me unfree simultaneously to occupy that space – but ordinarily no justification for this is needed. Similarly, if I depart from my
usual habit of lunching at the school cafeteria, I thus make you
unfree to speak to me there about your pressing concerns. I make you
unfree, but my action doesn't need special justifying; thus, a making
unfree may be entirely unobjectionable even though it is entirely
effective. In contrast, a coercive proposal is an affront to the recipient
even if it is rejected.

Coercion, I will note in passing, is also a more focused concept
than making unfree. Coercion marks the involvement of one person's (or group's) will with another's by means of a communication
to the coercee that an otherwise absent consequence will be attached
to the coercee's conduct in case the coercee does not comply. It presupposes certain psychological conditions; what coercer *A* must
intend to change is not simply coercee *B*'s situation, but specifically
B's *choice* situation. The schlimazl, who thoughtlessly leaves his feet
in the aisle of the bus, makes the schlemiel, who trips over them,
unfree to pass, but the schlimazl has not tried to get or gotten the
schlemiel to do his bidding in any way.[3]

---

[3] A number of other idiomatic nuances are consistent with, though not entailed by,
Wertheimer's analysis. For example, the consequence attached by a coercive proposal is, properly speaking, something other than the mere frustration of the
coerced's desire in acting. Thus, (1) "If you put up that fence, I will tear it down,"
is not coercive, whereas (2) "If you put up that fence, I will break your arms," is
coercive. A coercive proposal also differs from a warning, which is a prediction of
a consequence rather than its threatened imposition. Thus, (3) "If you put up that
fence, my cattle will knock it down," is a warning, not a coercive proposal, while

COERCION AND THE BURDEN OF JUSTIFYING LAW

One wants to say, "But surely the state coerces the prisoner it confines behind bars and within walls guarded by guns! And surely the prisoner is no less coerced for the fact that his punishment may be merited!" There is no question that the prisoner is *made unfree,* and there is no question that this making unfree *must be justified.* But what of the rest of us?[4] We are not in jail, and yet we are, all of us, threatened with jail, that is, faced with the state's proposal to confine us if we once (or persistently) flout its laws.

The pre-reflective view that law is coercive is a view that reaches far beyond the case of the prisoner languishing in her cell. It is a view that takes in the entire institution of law and places upon it a burden of justifying itself as its proposals affect each and every one of us, all the time, wherever we are and whatever we are doing. Neil MacCormick has well paraphrased this aspect of the pre-reflective view:

> The very existence of a standing body of law defining offenses and appointing penalties to offenders marks in itself an intrinsic coercive feature of state societies. To have penalties of any kind is to subject ourselves all and sundry to standing threats aimed at securing our compliance with law for fear of the consequences of non-compliance.[5]

The pre-reflective view, in other words, expresses something about the condition of all people living under the rule of law, and it places

---

(2) is. See Robert Nozick, "Coercion," in Sidney Morgenbesser, Patrick Suppes, and Morton White, eds., *Philosophy, Science, and Method* 444 (New York: St. Martin's, 1969) reprinted in Robert Nozick, *Socratic Puzzles* (Cambridge, Mass: Harvard University Press, 1997). [hereafter, Nozick, "Coercion"]. Nor does A coerce B by simply forcing B's hand, or by throwing him off of a building, for in these cases we would rather say that A *compelled* B, to mark the difference between B's acting and not acting. Compare Nozick "Coercion" (taking this position) with Neil MacCormick, *Legal Right and Social Democracy* 233 (Oxford: Clarendon Press, 1982) (contesting it). Nothing of substance turns on these niceties. For fuller exploration of the psychological conditions presupposed by a coercion claim, see Nozick, "Coercion," and Joseph Raz, "Liberalism, Autonomy, and the Politics of Neutral Concern," in Peter French, ed., *Social and Political Philosophy,* vol. 7 of *Midwest Studies in Philosophy* 108 (Minneapolis: University of Minnesota Press, 1982). Following Wertheimer, I pass over these details. See Wertheimer at 203.
4   I realize that the "we" I address here may exclude many readers. It has been reported that the United States incarcerates a higher percentage of its population than any other country on Earth. See "American Imprisonment Rates Are World's Highest," 2 *Overcrowded Times* 1 (1991).
5   Neil MacCormick, *Legal Right and Social Democracy* 243 (Oxford: Clarendon Press, 1982); see also H. L. A. Hart, *Law, Liberty, and Morality* 21 (Stanford: Stanford University Press, 1963).

upon law the burden of justifying itself – a burden from which human conduct *by and large* is excused. The legitimacy of each and every law, and every action taken under its color, is thus automatically and always suspect, unlike the run of human activities, which are presumptively innocent.

Not all political philosophies are committed to the idea that everyday human behavior is presumptively justified, that is, innocent and legitimate absent special reason to think the contrary. Those who accept the doctrine of original sin may, for example, believe that all human conduct, however ordinary, is ultimately tainted and in need of redemption. Similarly, unqualified versions of consequentialism measure every human action against a duty to optimize outcomes. The very strenuousness of these regimes has led some philosophers to question their correctness.[6] Bruce Ackerman, perhaps alone among recent political philosophers, has not relied on the idea that the state is peculiarly subject to a presumption of illegitimacy. Rather, Ackerman states a "Principle of Rationality" according to which *all* power – state power and otherwise – is presumptively illegitimate, that is, it is to be considered illegitimate unless and until the powerholder gives a reason for having the power while another does not. Ackerman's "Principle of Rationality" thus serves essentially the same rhetorical function that the pre-reflective view has performed for other theorists: It establishes that power is presumptively illegitimate. (Being powerless, on the other hand, is presumptively okay!)

The pre-reflective view does more than simply demand a justification. One might demand a justification without suggesting anything about what should happen pending delivery of an adequate justification in proper form. But the pre-reflective view subjects the law not only to a demand for justification – a denial of any presumptive legitimacy – but also to a presumption of *il*legitimacy, which means that its status is suspect and that doubts and controversy about its legitimacy count against it. The "risk of non-persuasion" as to the ultimate adequacy of justification falls, by default, upon the apologist for the state, its existence, and its policies.[7]

---

[6] On original sin, see Romans 5:12–19; on consequentialism see, e.g., Shelly Kagan, *The Limits of Morality* (Oxford: Clarendon Press, 1989); Samuel Scheffler, ed., *Consequentialism and Its Critics* (Oxford: Oxford University Press, 1988); Peter Unger, *Living High and Letting Die: Our Illusion of Innocence* (New York: Oxford University Press, 1996); but see Bruce A. Ackerman, *Social Justice in the Liberal State* 4–5 (New Haven: Yale University Press, 1980).

[7] The phrase is Richard H. Gaskins's, taken from his *Burdens of Proof in Modern Discourse* (New Haven: Yale University Press, 1992).

Such is the import of the popular, pre-reflective view that law is coercive. Arguments for the pre-reflective view are rare. Here is one offered by the late Michael Bayles: "Before a penal law is passed, a person can perform an action without probable punishment by the state; afterwards he cannot. Hence, an alternative choice has been made less desirable and penal law is coercive."[8] It is a very quick one, but it is an argument. (It is a bad argument because it assumes that whatever makes an alternative less desirable is coercive.)

The popular understanding has been taken up by philosophers and legal theorists too numerous to mention and is evident in the work of H. L. A. Hart, Rawls, Nozick, and Ronald Dworkin. Nozick's seminal article on coercion was, as he put it, intended to be "a preliminary to a longer study of liberty, whose major concerns will be the reasons which justify making someone unfree to perform an action, and the reason *why making someone unfree to perform an action needs justifying.*"[9] But the "longer study," which ultimately appeared as *Anarchy, State, and Utopia,* does not, by Nozick's own admission, "present a precise theory of the moral basis of individual rights," but it does take seriously "the anarchist claim that in the course of maintaining its monopoly on the use of force and protecting everyone within a territory, the state must violate individuals' rights and hence is intrinsically immoral."[10] In other words, Nozick capitalizes on the popular view that law is coercive, hoping to tame its anarchistic tendencies while, at the same time, using it as a fulcrum to unseat John Rawls's centrist theory and other theories farther to the egalitarian left.

Rawls's recent writings have emphasized the inherently coercive nature of law. He writes, for example that

> political power is always coercive power backed by the government's use of sanctions, for government alone has the authority to use force

---

[8] Michael Bayles, "Coercive Offers and Public Benefits," 55 *The Personalist* 139, 141 (1974). Other expressions of the pre-reflective view are cited in Neil MacCormick, *Legal Right and Social Democracy* 236 (Oxford: Clarendon Press, 1982) (counting Aquinas, Austin, Bentham, Kelsen, the early Raz, sociologist Max Weber, and anthropologist E. A. Hoebel as adherents), in Hans Oberdiek, "The Role of Sanctions and Coercion in Understanding Law and Legal Systems," 1975 *American Journal of Jurisprudence* 71–2 (naming Hobbes, Bentham, Austin, von Jhering, Kelsen, Aquinas, Kant, Hart, and Raz), and in Peter Westen, "'Freedom' and 'Coercion' – Virtue Words and Vice Words," 1985 *Duke Law Journal* 541, 575–6 and n. 110 (listing Plato, Bentham, Kelsen, Harold Laski, and Weber).

[9] Nozick, "Coercion," 440 (emphasis added).

[10] Robert Nozick, *Anarchy, State, and Utopia* xiv, xi (New York: Basic, 1974). Nozick later disavowed this approach without proposing an alternative. Robert Nozick, *The Examined Life* 286–7 (New York: Simon & Schuster, 1989).

in upholding its laws. . . . This power is regularly imposed on citizens . . . , some of whom may not accept the reasons widely said to justify the general structure of political authority . . . or . . . they may not regard as justified many of the statutes enacted by the legislature to which they are subject. . . . *This raises the question of the legitimacy of the general structure of authority.*

It is on this basis that Rawls derives what he terms "the liberal principle of legitimacy," namely: "Our exercise of political power is fully proper only when it is exercised in accordance with a constitution the essentials of which all citizens as free and equal may reasonably be expected to endorse in the light of principles and ideals acceptable to their common human reason."[11] Thomas Nagel writes to the same effect: "In view of the coercive character of the state, the requirement [of unanimity, at least as to some "higher-order principle" authorizing nonunanimous decisions] becomes a condition of political legitimacy."[12] The coercive nature of law not only renders the state presumptively illegitimate, it sets the bar of legitimacy at a higher level than is normally necessary for the legitimacy of individual or concerted private activity: What state legitimacy requires is unanimous assent, at least at some level of generality, and if not actual assent, at least hypothetical.

When is political power exercised "in accordance with" the constitution demanded by Rawls's principle? That has been the central problem of the philosophy of law at least since Ronald Dworkin's "general attack" on positivism in 1967. Theories of adjudication like Dworkin's are best understood as elaborate attempts to forge a logical tie between controversial outcomes in "hard" cases and antecedent legitimating foundations about which no reasonable controversy is possible. Lacking such a tie, the judicial act offends the losing party's presumptive entitlement to be free of the coercive interference of the state.[13]

Because the power of the state is coercive, it is presumptively

[11] John Rawls, *Political Liberalism* 136–7 (New York: Columbia University Press, 1993) (emphasis added) [hereafter, *Political Liberalism*].
[12] Thomas Nagel, *Equality and Partiality* 150–1 (New York: Oxford University Press, 1991).
[13] Ronald Dworkin, "The Model of Rules," 35 *University of Chicago Law Review* 14, 22 (1967), reprinted in *The Philosophy of Law*, Ronald Dworkin, ed., 38, 43 (New York: Oxford University Press, 1977), and in Ronald Dworkin, *Taking Rights Seriously* 22 (Cambridge, Mass.: Harvard University Press, 1977). I borrow the phrase "legitimating foundations" from Stephen Burton, *An Introduction to Law and Legal Reasoning* 168 (Boston: Little, Brown, 1985).

unjustified, that is, it must be considered unjustified until it has met its burden of justification. State inaction, on the other hand, is subject to no such burden, just as the run-of-the-mill human action is not subject. The popular and the philosophical understandings of the pre-reflective view are at bottom in accord in their rhetorical purpose of shifting to the state and its apologists the burden of persuasion as to every last detail of the legal edifice. As H. L. A. Hart has put it:

> We are committed . . . to the general critical principle that the use of legal coercion by any society calls for justification as something *prima facie* objectionable . . . for where there is no prima facie objection, wrong, or evil, men do not ask for or give *justifications* of social practices, though they may ask for and give *explanations* or may attempt to demonstrate their value.[14]

The pre-reflective view not only lends itself to the suggestion that law's burden of justification is especially weighty, it also lends credence to the view that it is necessary to keep a constant vigil against the law even if it carries its burden of justification. As Douglas Husak has noted: "The objectionable feature that attaches to each instance of coercion persists even after a demonstration that the particular deprivation of freedom is justified. The objectionable feature that attaches to each instance of coercion is simply *outweighed* in such cases by whatever considerations ultimately justify the given deprivation."[15] It is hardly surprising, then, to find the coercive nature of law invoked to justify state inaction where that has been subjected to legal or moral challenge.[16]

THE PRESUMPTION OF LIBERTY

The pre-reflective view is thus indistinguishable in its rhetorical role from its better-known cousin, the presumption of liberty. But, unlike

---

[14] H. L. A. Hart, *Law, Liberty, and Morality* 20–1 (Stanford: Stanford University Press, 1963).

[15] Douglas Husak, "The Presumption of Freedom," 17 *Nous* 345, 355 (1983) (emphasis in original). See also Gerald Dworkin, "Compulsion and Moral Concepts," 78 *Ethics* 227, 229 (1968). In lawyers' terms, the pre-reflective view creates a presumption that does not "burst" like a bubble as soon as some evidence on the state's behalf is adduced. See Charles McCormick, *Handbook of the Law of Evidence*, 2d ed., §342 (St. Paul, Minn.: West, 1972).

[16] For a striking judicial instance, see *DeShaney v Winnebago County Dept. of Social Services*, 489 U.S. 189, 203 (1989)("The most that can be said of the functionaries in this case is that they stood by and did nothing when suspicious circumstances dictated a more active role for them."); see also *Heckler v Chaney*, 470 U.S. 821, 832 (1985) ("when [the state] refuses to act it generally does not exercise its *coercive* power over an individual's liberty" – emphasis in original).

the presumption of liberty, the popular view that law is coercive has not been subjected to sustained critical scrutiny. It is worth noting that the presumption of liberty has been disavowed by Rawls, the preeminent liberal theorist of our day. Rawls writes:

> No priority is assigned to liberty as such, as if the exercise of something called "liberty" has a pre-eminent value and is the main if not the sole end of political and social justice. There is, to be sure, a general presumption against imposing legal and other restrictions on conduct without sufficient reason. But this presumption creates no special priority for any particular liberty . . . [and] although in *A Theory of Justice* I sometimes used arguments . . . which suggest that the priority of liberty as such is meant . . . this is not the correct interpretation.[17]

Notice that Rawls clings to a presumption against legal restrictions even as he jettisons a presumption favoring liberty, and that the presumption is against imposing legal restrictions "without sufficient reason." The implication is that the nonimposition of legal restrictions enjoys some sort of presumption of correctness; and that reason "sufficient" to justify legal restrictions may mean more than "some" or even "good" reason. If there were a presumption favoring liberty, it would have precisely this character. Joel Feinberg has expressed their relation this way: "If a strong general presumption of freedom has been established, the burden of proof rests on the shoulders of the advocate of coercion."[18] Despairing of the antecedent, Rawls seems to have disowned the connection while affirming the consequent.

Why has the presumption of liberty vanished from serious political philosophy? This may readily be seen by pursuing the question Why should there be such a presumption? If the answer is: "Because liberty is good," Stephen pointed out the initial difficulty over a century ago: "The question whether liberty is a good or bad thing appears as irrational as the question whether fire is a good or bad thing. It is both good and bad according to time, place, and circum-

---

[17] John Rawls, "The Basic Liberties and Their Priority," in III *The Tanner Lectures on Human Values,* S. McMurrin, ed., 5–6 (Salt Lake City: University of Utah Press, 1982), reprinted in *Political Liberalism* at 291–2. See also H. L. A. Hart, "Rawls on Liberty and Its Priority," 40 *University of Chicago Law Review* 534, 537–55 (1973) reprinted in Norman Daniels, ed., *Reading Rawls,* 230, 233–52 (New York: Basic, 1975) and in H. L. A. Hart, *Essays in Jurisprudence and Philosophy* 223, 226–47 (Oxford: Clarendon Press, 1983).

[18] Joel Feinberg, *Social Philosophy* 22 (Englewood Cliffs, N.J.: Prentice-Hall, 1973) (emphasis mine); cf. Richard T. deGeorge, *The Nature and Limits of Authority* 116 (Lawrence, Kans.: University Press of Kansas, 1985).

stance."[19] Furthermore, liberty qua good is but one good among many. Security is a good, happiness is a good, a good night's sleep is a good. Are there presumptions in favor of these as well? Let us say that X's being a good suffices to create a presumption in favor of X, in the weak sense that, if X is a good then, all else being equal, X should be preferred to not-X. But if goods are many and each generates a presumption in its favor, conflicts between presumptions can be expected to be rife – and if we have to resolve a conflict between, for example, a presumption favoring liberty and a presumption favoring security, then the presumption has ceased to do its work, which is to tell us what to prefer in situations of conflict, disagreement, or imperfect information.

Or is there a hierarchy of goods, with liberty at the top? If that were so, then sense could be made of the idea that liberty enjoys a presumption in its favor while other goods do not. But not since the heyday of G. E. Moore's *Principia Ethica* have philosophers felt at ease ranking the goods. If it were possible to do so, why not simply found our political philosophy on the true doctrine of the good? But that would be to follow intuition toward the abyss of religious warfare that Rawlsian liberalism takes its greatest pains to avoid. May we, instead, put intuition aside and derive the priority of liberty from a wider philosophical theory of the person? Again, pitching the tent there would expose liberalism to the charge that it is just another comprehensive, and controversial, philosophical view masquerading as neutral and *au-dessus de la meleé*.

How very appealing it must be, then, to be able to turn away from the presumption of liberty – and the misty metaphysics of the good that inspires it – and to find just as useful a tool at hand amongst the plain, hard, flinders of sociological fact: the fact that law is coercive. Unfortunately, reflection seems to show that the truistic formula "law is coercive" is no more serviceable for the special purposes of political philosophy than is the discredited idea of a presumption of liberty. Unless the repugnant conclusion can somehow be avoided, the popular, pre-reflective view that law is coercive will similarly have to be retired from the argumentative repertoire of legal and political philosophers.

---

[19] James Fitzjames Stephen, *Liberty, Equality, Fraternity* 85 (Cambridge: Cambridge University Press, 1967). See also Shelly Kagan, "The Argument from Liberty," in Jules L. Coleman and Allen Buchanan, eds., *In Harm's Way: Essays in Honor of Joel Feinberg* 16–41 (Cambridge: Cambridge University Press, 1994).

Chapter 6

Coercion Redivivus

We have now called into doubt what so many have assumed to be obviously true, that law is coercive. Let's retrace the path that led to this doubt, to make certain that we have not gone astray. I had provisionally adopted Alan Wertheimer's two-prong analysis of the concept of coercion, and it is time to consider objections to it. A striking feature of the two-prong analysis is that it is "thoroughly moralized,"[1] that is, both its choice prong and (more obviously) its proposal prong involve moral judgments. A number of theorists have made general objections to "moralized" accounts of coercion.

I will now explore these objections and also enquire whether any nonmoralized alternative analyses can save our pre-reflective intuition that law is coercive. I will also reconsider the possibility that the repugnant conclusion can be avoided by attending to contextual aspects of coercion claims. Finally, I will explore the possibility that the repugnant conclusion can be avoided within a moralized account of coercion.

OBJECTIONS TO MORALIZED ANALYSES

One objection to a moralized account of coercion goes this way: If the assertability of a coercion claim depends upon an assessment of the morality of the proposal made to the putative coercee, and the normative reasonableness of the options left to her, then to assert the coercion claim is to have judged that the coercer's act was morally

---

[1] Alan Wertheimer, *Coercion* 173 (Princeton: Princeton University Press, 1987) ("*both* prongs are thoroughly moralized" – my emphasis) [hereafter Wertheimer]. See also Cheyney C. Ryan, "The Normative Concept of Coercion," 89 *Mind* 481 (1980); Jeffrey Murphy, "Consent, Coercion, and Hard Choices," 67 *Virginia Law Review* 79 (1981); Larry Alexander, "Zimmerman on Coercive Wage Offers," 12 *Philosophy & Public Affairs* 160 (1983); Robert Hale, "Coercion and Distribution in a Supposedly Non-coercive State," 38 *Political Science Quarterly* 470–77 (1923).

defective. If that is so, then the phrase "justified coercion" is oxymoronic, because if conduct is coercive it is ipso facto *un*justified. But there is nothing oxymoronic about the phrase "justified coercion," as can be seen by the fact that most people view most of the law, most of the time, as justified coercion. Ergo, any moralized account must be rejected.

This objection fails because it falsely assumes that on a moralized account coercion claims function, as Wertheimer puts it, "as mere linguistic placeholders for general moral disapproval of the relevant proposals."[2] Coercive conduct is not, on a moralized account, ipso facto unjustified; it is, rather, ipso facto in need of some special justification. This point could be expressed (using even more Latin) by saying that coercion is not ipso facto but *pro tanto* unjustified; that is, it is unjustified insofar as it is mere coercion and nothing more. Therefore, on a moralized account, there is nothing oxymoronic about the classification "justified coercion."

Recall the Highway Robbery case, Case 5. The Gunman's proposal is prima facie wrongful, and his conduct is therefore coercive. If the Traveler is unwittingly aiding a terrorist group, and the Gunman is acting to frustrate a terrorist plot that can be checked in no other way, then it makes perfectly good sense on a moralized account to say that the prima facie wrongfulness of the Gunman's proposal made it coercive and thus in need of the justification supplied by the fact that it is instrumental to the frustration of the terrorist plot. It is of course true that a moralized account *could* be construed to require that the proposal prong be read as referring to proposals wrongful *all things considered*, but there is no necessity for this. A moralized account of coercion need not insist on collapsing all levels of moral complexity, and the better reading of Wertheimer is to take "wrong" to mean "prima facie wrong."[3]

Of course, as noted in Part One, we will sometimes be faced with instances of the Redescription Problem, for example, whether to say that, because of Nazi law's evil nature, Germans had no even prima facie duty to obey it, or to say that they had a prima facie duty to obey that was overridden by Nazi law's evil nature. In our present context, the question pertains to prima facie wrongs rather than prima facie duties, but the parallel between the two is plain. In Case 5, should we say that Gunman should feel remorse if we factor in the

---

[2] Wertheimer at 243.   [3] David Blumenfeld brought this point home to me.

95

further hypothesis that Traveler is unwittingly aiding terrorists? I should think so. (Consider the World War II commandos who blew up a ferry that happened to be carrying the Nazi's supply of heavy water, killing innocents in the process – had they no cause for remorse?) As I noted earlier, our best clue as to how to resolve redescription problems is our considered judgment whether there would be a residue of remorse or some duty to "make it up" to the party to whom the duty was owed. In Case 5, as redescribed, there is, and thus it is better classified as a case of justified coercion. But in Case 10 (Tables Turned) and Case 11 (98-Pound Weakling), remorse would not be appropriate and, under a moralized analysis, the cases not ones of coercion; so also, I think plain, with our crucial Case 6 (Robbery Statute). We want officers of the law to be considerate as they go about their business, but we don't expect – nor would we encourage – *anguish* on their part.

Another point worth noting is that the objection we are considering *assumes* that law is an instance of justified coercion, that is, of coercion which is justified. The objection could be understood, then, as trading upon the pre-reflective obviousness of the coercive character of law. In other words, the objection could be interpreted as charging that moralized accounts of coercion have to be rejected *because* they misclassify law as "not coercive," rather than as "coercive but justified." Now, we have not yet pursued the possibility that law, or some significant portion of the law, is coercive by reference to some suitable moral baseline; so it is not yet altogether certain that moralized accounts are open to the general objection that they misclassify law, a paradigm case of coercion. Note, however, that any objection to a moralized account that rests exclusively on an appeal to the presumed coerciveness of law will not merit much consideration in our present inquiry, in which we have called the pre-reflective view into question.[4]

NONMORALIZED ANALYSES

Do nonmoralized accounts of coercion have anything else to offer? Even if they cannot be established by any knockout punch against moralized accounts, we may still find them to be more attractive on

---

[4] G. A. Cohen argues that the fact that a moralized account tends toward the repugnant conclusion serves as a reductio ad absurdum of moralized accounts of coercion (or of "being forced"). *See* G. A. Cohen, "The Structure of Proletarian Unfreedom," 12 *Philosophy & Public Affairs* 3, 4 and n.2 (1983).

their own merits. In particular, they hold out the promise that the concept of coercion might figure in the value-free social science that Mill and Weber called for.[5]

"Pressure" Theory

One simple type of nonmoralized account of coercion rests on the idea that coercion is a matter of psychological pressure, pure and simple. Thus, a pressure theory might render "A coerces B" as "A, by ϕ-ing, puts very great psychological pressure on B to ψ." Looking back to our cases, we would expect this pressure theory to count Case 9, the Sea Rescue case, as one of coercion, because by offering to rescue B on condition that B pay a huge sum, A has brought great pressure on B to accept these terms. The issue of whether A has a background duty to rescue B does not arise, as it would on a moralized account.

Similarly Case 5, the Highway Robbery case, will count as one of coercion because, by threatening B, A has put very great pressure on B to surrender his money. And, likewise, Case 10, in which Traveler turns the tables on Gunman, counts as coercion; the fact that Traveler's conduct is not wrongful, while Gunman's was, is not a difference that registers on the pressure theory, in contrast to moralized accounts. And, likewise, Case 7, the Plea Bargain case, turns out to be one of coercion, legal doctrine to the contrary notwithstanding and regardless of the moral merits of capital punishment.

It appears that a pressure theory will classify many more types of case as coercive than a moralized analysis will. Even Case 8, the Hard Bargain case, comes out as a case of coercion if the degree of psychological pressure brought to bear is "very great." Even ordinary increases in the price of essential commodities in competitive markets and routine conditions attached to charitable donations may have to be classified as coercive.[6] Unless the pressure theory sets its "pressure threshold" at a very high level, it will count as coercive significantly many more cases than, say, Wertheimer's moralized account. Pressure theory tends, in other words, to overinclusiveness.

Pressure theory may turn out to be underinclusive at the same

---

[5] See John Stuart Mill, *Essays on Some Unsettled Questions of Political Economy* (London, 1874); Max Weber, *The Methodology of the Social Sciences*, Edward A. Shils and Henry A. Finch, trans. (Glencoe, Ill.: Free Press, 1948).

[6] See Harry Frankfurt, "Coercion and Moral Responsibility," in Ted Honderich, ed., *Essays on Freedom of Action* 66 (London: Routledge and Kegan Paul, 1973).

time. Reconsider Case 6, the Robbery Statute case. On the pressure theory, law is not coercive as to honest folk, for the simple reason that the statute brings no pressure to bear on them at all – their consciences sufficiently curb any impulse they might have to rob. Nor is law coercive as to the shrewdly dishonest, either, for their confidence in their ability to escape detection insulates them from any very great psychological pressure. Thus, on the pressure theory, the coerciveness of law is an individualized question, and where legal sanctions are slight or rarely applied, or are consistent with independently sufficient pressure from other sources – such as society or conscience – they fail to count as coercive at all. A simple pressure theory, then, is on reflection unlikely to satisfy anyone, and in particular it is unlikely to save very much of the pre-reflective belief that law is coercive.

Nonmoralized Baseline Accounts

The chief weakness of the pressure theory, as a bulwark of the coerciveness of law, derives from the fact that it measures pressure against an individualized index. Only the susceptible are coerced on this view, but this contradicts our intuition that at least a coercive proposal, that is, attempt, can be made upon a steadfast person, and that the making of such a proposal demands a justification even if it is rejected. It may be that the pressure theory is better interpreted as implicitly making reference to an objective standard of pressure. Thus, on a properly developed pressure theory, Toscano, in Case 1, is coerced by a threat of serious bodily harm, but could not be properly said to be coerced by any threat of *being thought a weenie*,[7] no matter how susceptible Toscano may in fact be to Leonardo's thinking him a weenie, and perhaps not even if Leonardo intends to exploit Toscano's special susceptibility.

The simple pressure theory thus gives way to any of a variety of *nonmoralized baseline* accounts. Pressure counts only insofar as it nudges the coercee away from some "normal and expected" base-

---

[7] The following illustrates the importance of this idea: "After I visited Yale in 1970, I was trying to explain to a classmate how the place had changed, and he said, 'What's their word for weenie?' That was the point, I told him: they were so tolerant that they didn't have a word for weenie. He mulled that over for a few moments. 'In that case,' he finally said, 'They're *all* weenies.'" (Calvin Trillin, *Remembering Denny* 64 [New York: Farrar, Straus & Giroux, 1993] [emphasis in original]). The law of duress speaks of a "person of reasonable firmness." See Model Penal Code §2.09 (Philadelphia: American Law Institute, 1962).

line, which is not to be furnished by any appeal to the wrongfulness of *A*'s proposal, but in some other way. Our inquiry now turns to the two types of nonmoralized baseline accounts that have in fact been proposed: *predictive* baseline accounts, and *preference* baseline accounts.

Predictive Baselines. A "predictive" baseline account identifies coercive proposals as those that make *B* worse off relative to where *B* would be had the proposal not been made. In other words, *A*'s proposal makes *B* worse off if *B* complies and also makes *B* worse off if *B* does not comply but suffers *A*'s "declared unilateral plan," where "worse off" means "worse off than *B* would otherwise have been." For example, in Case 9, the Sea Rescue case, if in most similar instances the person in *A*'s position rescues the person in *B*'s then *B*'s predictive baseline is rescue by *A* without *A*'s extracting a promise of payment. Gauged this way, *A*'s proposal is coercive. If, on the other hand, in most similar instances no gratuitous rescue occurs, the predictive baseline involves no rescue, and *A*'s proposal is not coercive. Unlike a moralized account, the predictive baseline is intended to avoid any appeal to what *B* has a *right* to expect, or to what *A* has a *right* to propose, or to any other moral notion.[8]

In most societies the predictive and the moral baselines will largely coincide, and so a given proposal will be classified identically against either. But the moral and predictive baselines sometimes diverge; Nozick describes such a case:

CASE 12. Nozick's Slave Case

A owns slaves, including *B*. As a matter of sound plantation management, *A* flogs *B* every morning, and has done so for years. One morning, *A* proposes not to flog *B* if but only if *B* will ψ.[9]

[8] Wertheimer would distinguish between statistical and phenomenological baselines, within the category of predictive baselines, as follows: The statistical baseline looks only to what can be predicted to occur as a matter of social statistics, the phenomenological looks only to what *B* in fact (and perhaps wistfully) expects. See Wertheimer at 207. It could be argued that any baseline account is inescapably moralized insofar as it rests on the notion of "making *worse off.*" The preference baseline, which I discuss in the following section, would not necessarily be exposed to this objection, and so I do not pursue it here.

[9] Robert Nozick, "Coercion," in Sidney Morgenbesser, Patrick Suppes, and Morton White, eds., *Philosophy, Science, and Method* 447–8, 450 (New York: St. Martin's, 1969), reprinted in Robert Nozick, *Socratic Puzzles* (Cambridge, Mass: Harvard University Press, 1997) [hereinafter, Nozick, "Coercion"].

Measured against a moral baseline, A's proposal is coercive because the morally expected course of events includes no beatings and A's proposal – "Do ψ or be beaten" – makes B worse off relative to this baseline. But measured against the predictive baseline, which includes a daily beating, A's proposal makes B better off, for B at least now has an option – ψ-ing to avoid being beaten – that B did not have before.

As Nozick points out, most of us would say that the Slave Owner's proposal is coercive, and that fact would seem to show that the moralized baseline account, which classifies the slave case as coercive, is superior. But Nozick resists this conclusion and appeals to the following example:

CASE 13. Nozick's Drug Dealer Case

Drug dealer A regularly supplies drugs to addict B. One day, A announces that he will not sell to B at the going price, but will give B what he needs that day just in case B beats up B's friend C.

Nozick classifies this as a case of coercion despite the fact that B's moralized baseline includes no drugs. This result is obtainable by choosing the predicted course of events as the baseline. This case shows, Nozick says, that in assessing coercion claims it is not true that "the (morally) expected course of events always takes precedence over the normal or usual course of events, where these diverge."[10]

The correct classification, in Nozick's view, has both the Slave Owner's and the Drug Dealer's proposals tagged as coercive. But to arrive at this result, we have to use the moral baseline in Slave Owner but the predictive baseline in Drug Dealer. Why the difference? This is Nozick's diagnosis:

The relevant difference between these cases seems to be that the slave himself would prefer the morally expected to the normal course of events whereas the addict prefers the normal to the morally expected. . . . It may be that when the normal and morally expected courses of events diverge, the one of these which is to be used in deciding whether a conditional announcement of an action constitutes a [coercive] threat or an offer [noncoercive] is the course of events that the recipient of the action *prefers*.[11]

[10] Nozick, "Coercion," at 450.
[11] Ibid., at 451 (emphasis added). This expedient may lead to odd results. The addict who hates his addiction is not coerced, but the addict who had no such distance from it (either having sunk so low, or having not yet realized the consequences of

Let us examine the possibility of generalizing Nozick's preference tiebreaker to arrive at a nonmoralized account of coercion that, perhaps, is more sophisticated than a simplistic pressure theory.

Preference Baselines. Nozick's account could be described as a "dual baseline account with a preference tiebreaker." That is to say, where the moral and predictive baselines coincide, Nozick's account is deliberately indifferent between them; where they diverge, the coercee's preference dictates which baseline is to apply. Several writers have taken Nozick's view a step further and have located the relevant baseline as set by the coercee's preferences, which are not restricted to a choice between a moral and a predictive baseline.

Thus, on Keith Gunderson's and Michael Gorr's analyses, A coerces B just in case B would prefer that A's proposal had never been made.[12] This takes us beyond the pressure theory because it focuses on how the coercee (perhaps coolly) regards what the coercer has done to the coercee's choice situation. On this proposal, Cases 1 (*Toscano*), 2 and 4 (*Austin v Loral*), 3 (*Rusk*), 5 (Highway Robbery), 10 (Tables Turned), and 11 (98-Pound Weakling) all count as cases of coercion; while Cases 7 (Plea Bargain), 8 (Hard Bargain), 9 (Sea Rescue), and 12 (Nozick's Slave) do not. The wrongfulness of the proposals in these cases is neither here nor there; what counts is whether the coercee welcomes them.

What then of Case 6 (Robbery Statute)? On this preference baseline analysis, as with the pressure theory, discerning the coerciveness of a proposal becomes largely a subjective, individualized inquiry. Honest folk welcome what the statute proposes, especially if it is understood as involving a coordinate promise to punish *only* the guilty. Moreover, even not-so-honest folk might prefer law to anarchy. Nozick puts the problem this way: "Who knows what the world would be like if there were no punishment for crimes? It might well be that the institution of punishing crimes would improve the consequences of almost all actions, and hence count . . . as making [noncoercive] offers to people."[13] Although Nozick suggests an alterna-

addiction, or being self-deceived) is. Attitudes so remote from the issue at hand – for the addict, "Do I beat this guy up or not?" – don't seem to be entitled to count for this much.

12 See Michael Gorr, "Toward a Theory of Coercion," 16 *Canadian Journal of Philosophy* 383, 388–91 (1986); Keith Gunderson, "Threats and Coercion," 9 *Canadian Journal of Philosophy* 247, 253–4 (1989).

13 Nozick, "Coercion," at 451. The "biconditional" nature of the law's proposals is noted by Nozick as a problem for the view that law is coercive. *Id.* at 469 n.33. The

tive escape from the repugnant conclusion, which I will discuss farther along, it should now be clear that moralized accounts of coercion aren't alone in getting into difficulty when it comes to saving the
pre-reflective view that law is coercive.

David Zimmerman has proposed a different nonmoralized, pref-
erence-baseline account. On his analysis, *A* coerces *B* if *A* actively
prevents *B*'s preferred, feasible, preproposal situation. Zimmerman's
aim is to give empirical substance to the Marxist view that the capitalist's wage proposal to workers is coercive even if the workers prefer the capitalist's proposal to starvation. This proposal would certainly count Case 12 (Nozick's Slave) as coercive; it would almost as
certainly count Case 7 (Plea Bargain) as coercive; and, depending on
how it is worked out, it might also count Case 8 (Hard Bargain) as
coercive. What of Case 6 (Robbery Statute)? Again, much as with
Gunderson's and Gorr's preference baseline proposals, we must ask
whether the withering away of the state is in fact a preferred (not
preferable, given Zimmerman's rejection of moralized accounts) and
feasible alternative to the rule of law.

In summary, the "pressure" theory and the nonmoral-baseline
accounts do not obviously present a superior alternative to
Wertheimer's "thoroughly moralized" two-prong analysis. Moreover, it is far from clear that any of these nonmoralized accounts offer
any greater resistance to the repugnant conclusion, and they may
turn out to offer less. The fault, if fault there be, is not peculiar to the
moralized analysis of coercion. Salvation for the pre-reflective view,
if it is to be found, must be looked for elsewhere.

ATTENDING TO CONTEXT

I now want to explore a range of moves available to both moralized
and nonmoralized accounts to avoid the "repugnant conclusion"
that law is, after all, not coercive. We reaped the benefit of Alan Wertheimer's careful survey of the concept of coercion as it operates
within the law, and simply applied that analysis to the case of the law
itself, much in the way we might have applied the analysis to a new
situation arising *within* the law, such as the Plea Bargain case, Case 7.

---

law proposes to punish all, but *only,* the guilty. One tactic might be to adopt a rule
that all proposals containing a coercive component are to count as coercive. Thus,
"I will break your arms if, but only if, you fail to pay me by Wednesday," counts
as coercive even though the component subproposal, no breakage if debt timely
paid, may be welcome.

One could characterize this approach as taking an *internal* conception of coercion and making an *external* application of it. Is this objectionable? Note here that if it is, that will not depend on whether the internal conception is moralized or nonmoralized. Let me consider two likely objections.

Improper External Use of an Internal Concept?

One objection goes as follows. To the extent that an analysis of coercion is drawn, like Wertheimer's, primarily from legal examples and is adjusted to fit legal doctrines, then it at best captures a *legal* conception of coercion. It is to that extent a conception of coercion that is internal to law, and it is therefore not a suitable yardstick to apply to the external question of the coerciveness of law itself. The use of an internal standard to make an external judgment is no more proper here than it would be if, for example, one were to employ the concept of duty found in our legal system to answer the question "Is there a duty to obey the law?" The latter question isn't the trivial question "Is there an internal, *legal* duty to obey the law?" but an *external* question, paraphrasable as "Is there an external, *moral* duty to obey the law?"[14] Likewise, here, the question isn't "Is law coercive, as judged by the criteria internal to legal doctrine?" but, rather, "Is law coercive, as judged from an external perspective (taking no position on the troubled issue whether this perspective is moral or nonmoral)?"

This objection has two flaws. First, it assumes that a philosophically adequate conception of coercion cannot be drawn from legal examples or adjusted to conform to legal doctrines. As Wertheimer points out:

> The typical and perfectly reasonable strategy for developing a theory of coercion is to engage in the traditional forms of philosophical analysis, testing our theories for coherence, consistency and compatibility with our linguistic and moral intuitions in a variety of hypothetical examples. We then try to abstract from our intuitions to a more general account of coercion.

But, as Wertheimer goes on to argue, there are compelling reasons to supplement the typical analytical methodology. Because "our moral

[14] H. L. A. Hart warned against such a fallacy in his celebrated exchange with Lon Fuller. See Hart, "Positivism and the Separation of Law and Morals," 71 *Harvard Law Review* 593, 615–21 (1958).

views about coercion are somewhat inchoate," unless we attend to cases and examples we are apt to lose ourselves among slogans and imponderables. Law, it happens, furnishes a rich and vivid fund of concrete cases in which issues of coercion have been argued before and decided by judges who, in turn, have endeavored to *explain* the grounds for their decisions. True, in some sense judges decide legal, rather than straightforwardly moral, issues, but this is not to say that the law's concerns are divergent from those of morality, for "the law's interest in coercion reflects our moral views." Moreover, legal decisions carry consequences for the parties involved and, to that extent, counsel for the parties, and judges, are motivated to reason and argue with extraordinary thoroughness and care. In sum:

> There are few philosophical problems about which we can find a practical literature so extensive, so deep, so rich in philosophical concepts at home in philosophical discourse, and so much of the kind of dialogue and argumentation characteristic of the best philosophy. A philosopher interested in [the analysis of] coercion ignores the law at his peril.[15]

The second flaw that weakens the objection becomes plain once we ask where, exactly, do the legal (internal) and the ordinary language (external) conceptions of coercion diverge? The objection is empty unless the objector points to some instance that Wertheimer's two-prong analysis (or any other) misclassifies and is misclassified because the analysis has been warped by the influence of legal examples and doctrines. Notice that Wertheimer's approach does not dispense with any of the typical stages of conceptual analysis; it is distinctive only in that it prefaces the usual technique with an extensive mining and sifting of legal examples.

It is therefore simply question-begging to assert that a conception of coercion that is internal to law can have no proper external application. But suppose this were true nonetheless. Even if it were, it would be of no help to those who would like to maintain the pre-reflective view that law is coercive. For in that case a defender of the pre-reflective view would have to explain the connection between coercion as she conceives it and the internal conception of coercion, which ex hypothesi she cannot properly use to express herself? What content can an external conception of coercion have, if it is discon-

---

[15] Wertheimer at 10, 13, 14; and see P. F. Strawson, "Ethical Intuitionism," 24 *Philosophy* 23 (1949).

tinuous with a conception that is internal to law and consistent with the substantial bulk of our ordinary, nonlegal, linguistic and moral intuitions?

The External As a Special Context

At this point I think we should return to a possibility considered and set aside earlier: that the claim that law is coercive is couched in its own special context, a context that is immune to the application of any general analysis of the concept of coercion. There is ample reason to revisit this suggestion because it is implicit in the thinking of two of the most acute students of coercion, Robert Nozick and Wertheimer himself.

Wertheimer offers his two-prong analysis of coercion with this disclaimer: "The truth conditions of a coercion claim can vary with context," and he goes on to argue that, in fact, "coercion claims are emphatically and technically [*sic*] contextual." By this he means that coercion claims typically have either a normative or a descriptive point and that the point determines the applicable truth (or assertability) conditions. Among various contexts Wertheimer identifies, he includes the following:

> A frequently invoked and important type of coercion claim captures the fact that the state has required some behavior as a matter of *law*. Whereas coercion claims often indicate moral disapproval, that is not so here, where we may only want to distinguish between actions undertaken in response to legal prohibitions and those that are not or to distinguish between legal processes which involve punishment and those that do not (as in the distinction between coercion, regulation, and taxation).

What Wertheimer seems to be suggesting here is that the claim that law is coercive can be understood in a way that is not undermined by the two-pronged analysis or by Haksar's argument to the "repugnant conclusion." In this special context, the point of saying, for example, that a would-be cocaine abuser desisted because of a coercive threat is simply to say that, as a matter of fact, there is a statute in the jurisdiction penalizing such use. We needn't even conclude that the would-be user had "no choice" if the risk of prosecution was slight, and we needn't express disapproval of the threat of legal punishment. In my view, this can be a serviceable stipulation, but is it satisfactory to say that characterizing law as coercive has *no* normative force? Wertheimer, in a footnote to the passage quoted above, adds:

One might say that characterizing the law as coercive is not completely neutral, for we would not identify the use of legal prohibitions in this way unless we thought there was some moral significance in doing so. I think that is true. But this does not entail that we make moral judgments of approval and disapproval in characterizing the use of law as coercive.[16]

Wertheimer is of course correct in saying that in characterizing law as coercive we don't *necessarily* condemn it; but he overlooks the fact the "moral significance" of such a characterization is to cast a burden of justification upon the law. What is coercive may be, but *had better be*, justified because, in default of an adequate justification, it is illegitimate. So understood, the claim that law is coercive is not only "not completely neutral," it is decidedly partial. Neutrality would consist in suspending judgment about the legitimacy of law, rather than counting ignorance of a justification as a sufficient reason to condemn law as illegitimate.

Wertheimer suggests another way in which the claim that law is coercive occurs in a special context:

> In most coercion contexts, [what the coercee] does would change his moral or legal status – were it not for the coercion. He would, for example, be obligated to do something he was otherwise not obligated to do. By contrast, the state's coercive threats typically give [the citizen] prudential reasons to do what he is morally obligated to do in any case (not kill, not steal, pay his taxes, and so forth). Because the coercion does not change [the citizen's] moral status, whether the state is exercising coercion is not problematic. Put slightly differently, the moral considerations that (help) determine whether someone is coerced (in the sorts of responsibility-affecting contexts on which I have focussed) are importantly distinct from the sorts of moral considerations that figure in the justification of state coercion.[17]

Wertheimer is not altogether plain here, in part because he is wrestling with an objection to his "thoroughly moralized" account that we considered earlier: namely, that a moralized account has to be rejected *because* it misclassifies law as noncoercive. In conducting our examination, the coercive character of law is not to be presumed. Wertheimer, on the other hand, wants to bring his analysis into line with the pre-reflective view that law is coercive and even to represent that view as, in some sense, correct.

---

[16] Wertheimer at 182, 184, 186 (emphasis in original), 187 n. 17, and 186 n. 16.
[17] Ibid. at 256.

Wertheimer seeks to achieve these ends in the following way. He distinguishes "responsibility-affecting" contexts – which correspond to the justification-supplying and justification-defeating contexts I identified earlier – from the contexts in which the claim that law is coercive occurs, which are of two types: Type 1 is a descriptive context in which phrases like "the law coerces shopkeepers into closing on Sunday" operate as a paraphrase of something like "there are legal sanctions against opening a shop for business on Sunday," and Type 2 is the context in which the justification of the state is at issue. Neither of these types of coercion claim is problematic for a moralized account of "responsibility-affecting" contexts, for neither of these two types normally occurs in a responsibility-affecting context. This, in essence, is Wertheimer's answer to the objection that his analysis must count law itself as normally noncoercive.

The problem with Wertheimer's position is plain from our earlier discussion of the objection he is seeking to avoid: He has advanced no basis whatever for distinguishing the Type 2 "law is coercive" context from other justification-demanding contexts, and he has given no reason to think that the analysis for "responsibility-affecting" contexts is any different from what would be appropriate for justification-demanding contexts generally. In any event, carving out a special context or crafting a special analysis to save the pre-reflective view would simply have the effect of cutting it loose from all semantic moorings, as we noted before.

Token Subtraction or Type Subtraction?

Nozick poses the question whether law coerces anyone not to steal, if the empirical and moral norm is that people don't steal. Nozick is evidently unwilling to allow the badness of a Hobbesian state of nature automatically to make the utterances of the law count as offers, rather than threats, and the law itself noncoercive. To avoid such a conclusion, Nozick proposes

> to consider the normal and expected course of events, if B steals, without . . . the particular act the State will bring about [namely, punishing B's stealing], and against this background assess whether the State's statement that if B steals, it will punish B constitutes a [coercive] threat (i.e. whether the State's statement, if carried out, makes B's stealing worse than it would have been in this new course of events). There remain some problems about knowing what the course of events would be without this act, but these seem manageable. On this

view, even though in the normal and expected course of events B gets punished for theft, the statement that he will be punished for theft counts as a [coercive] threat since the act of punishment, if B steals, unfavorably affects the consequences of one act of B's (stealing) against the background of the normal and expected course of events minus *this* act of punishment.[18]

Nozick's proposal is ingenious but unsatisfactory. If we are generally free to use this "token subtractive" technique, then *any* morally permissible proposal can be rendered as coercive. For example, if in the Tables Turned on the Gunman case (Case 10), we look not at the morally expected and predictable course of events, in which the Traveler uses his gun to ward off the Gunman, but at how unfavorably the warding-off "affects the consequences of one act of [the Gunman's] stealing against the background of the normal and expected course of events minus *this* act of [warding off]," then we come out with the equally repugnant conclusion that the Traveler coerces the Gunman not to rob him.

By repeated application of the "token subtractive" maneuver, we reach the extremely repugnant conclusion that everyone who unfavorably affects the consequences of anyone else's doing anything, acts coercively. Nozick therefore has to confine the suggestion to the case of law, but he states no principled basis for doing so. Nozick's motive is evidently to somehow save the pre-reflective view that law is coercive; but the need to resort to such ad hoc jiggery perhaps is our best clue that the pre-reflective view should be given up.

SAVING THE COERCIVENESS OF LAW ON A MORALIZED ACCOUNT

So far we have proceeded on the assumption that the law's proposals are not wrongful. This assumption, when plugged into a moralized account of coercion, propelled us toward the repugnant conclu-

---

[18]   Nozick, "Coercion," at 451–2 (emphasis in original, but for ease of comprehension I have taken the liberty of replacing Nozick's variables). For a proposal to save the pre-reflective view that relies on a similar mechanism, see Peter Westen, "'Freedom' and 'Coercion' – Virtue Words and Vice Words," 1985 *Duke Law Journal* 541, 581. David Zimmerman endorses Nozick's token-subtractive approach to "some proposals," including (presumably) any of the form "if you do that, I will punish you," but Zimmerman is not sure "whether Nozick is making a general theoretical point here, or simply handling a single case in the most plausible way." David Zimmerman, "Coercive Wage Offers," 10 *Philosophy & Public Affairs* 121, 142 (1981).

sion that law is *not* coercive. Now that we appear to have exhausted other possibilities of avoiding the repugnant conclusion, it is time to examine this assumption.

The assumption that the law's proposals are not wrongful seems eminently reasonable in many cases. Insofar as the criminal law proposes to punish those who harm others bodily and those who, like the Gunman in Case 5, violently threaten others and their property, its proposals seem just the reverse of wrongful. They are certainly not wrongful on balance; nor are they proper occasions for the residual remorse and compensatory duties that are the phenomenological mark of the prima facie wrongful. There is irony here, since these areas of the criminal law are often thought to be a paradigm of coerciveness.

Yet it may be that the assumption that the law's proposals are not wrongful is unrepresentatively plausible in precisely these cases. We have been discussing "the law" and its coerciveness as though the law is a homogeneous whole. Only a moment's reflection is needed to call this assumption into doubt.

Punishment, Regulation, and Taxation

The types of law are myriad, and the classifications of these types are too numerous for any list to be attempted here. There is, for example, civil law as well as criminal. Within each of these divisions there are various kinds of legal burden: arrest, fine, probation, imprisonment for varying durations, work-release, parole, as well as execution, on the criminal side; compensatory and punitive damages, restitution, injunction, and sanctions, on the civil.[19]

The human activities targeted by legal action are also of various sorts. While much of criminal and civil law is intended to discourage conduct that is itself wrongful – "malum in se" – each division also burdens conduct that is not in itself wrongful but merely "malum prohibitum," that is, wrongful only because prohibited. Even within the category of malum in se, the law may threaten and impose burdens far in excess of what any private person would be morally permitted in self-help.

These distinctions suggest that the repugnant conclusion may be

---

[19] For analyses that erode the monolithic appearance of law, see *The Concept of Law* at 26–48; Joseph Raz, *Practical Reason and Norms* 154–62, 2d ed. (Princeton: Princeton University Press, 1990); and Neil MacCormick, *Legal Right and Social Democracy* 237–240 (Oxford: Clarendon Press, 1982).

avoidable on a moralized account of coercion in at least two broad types of case: those in which the law punishes conduct that is not malum in se, and those in which the law exceeds the bounds of morally permissible self-help. By "moral" self-help I mean those measures that individuals have a right to pursue to defend themselves and their interests against unjustified encroachments by others. It also includes those remedial means one has a right to pursue against others. Moral self-help is thus independent of, if tolerated by, legal procedures.[20]

The Malum Prohibitum Cases

In the first type of case, the law burdens conduct that is not wrongful itself, but wrongful only because illegal. When the law proposes to punish what is itself wrongful, as in the Robbery Statute case (Case 6), its proposal seems not wrongful for two reasons: (1) The putative coercee has no moral right to engage in the forbidden conduct, and (2) the law makes a coordinate promise to make the putative coercee better off than she would be in a world of moral self-help. But when the law proposes to punish conduct that is, considered by itself, morally innocent, neither of these reasons obtain. In these cases the law's proposal leaves the coercee worse off than she would be in a world without this *specific* law, for the law now attaches a consequence to her innocent conduct, and the law's coordinate promise to protect her from the defects of self-help is of no value.

Call these cases the malum prohibitum cases. These cases make up the bulk of the law in any modern, industrialized state. Within this category we find the transaction-facilitating provisions of commercial law, the market-failure-fixing devices of administrative, regulatory, and environmental law, and, generally, the "rules of the road" that are essential to coordinating the otherwise clashing impulses and interests of a diverse citizenry. In these malum prohibitum cases, citizens don't appear to be under any extralegal moral duty to conform to the dictates of the law, and therefore it seems natural to say that the law's proposals are coercive; they are coercive and, until the state carries its burden of justifying them, they are presumptively illegitimate.

If the malum prohibitum cases can be classified as coercive under

---

[20] Cf. *Flagg Bros. v Brooks*, 436 U.S. 149 (1978) (distinguishing 14th amendment "state action" from legally tolerated self-help).

a moralized account, this would mollify (if not satisfy) those on the political right who view the growth of the administrative, regulatory, and taxing functions of the state with special suspicion. Those on the political right tend to be more upset by, say, bureaucratic interference in the marketplace than they are by excessive police zeal in dealing with "street" crime. This may reflect their view that the state's burdening conduct, which is wrongful (if at all) only because the state says so, is especially offensive to the cherished value of liberty.

Nevertheless, there are good grounds to doubt this way of viewing the malum prohibitum cases. In particular, there is no guarantee that conduct that appears innocent viewed in isolation is in fact innocent when taken in context. Reconsider now the Principle of Fairness first advanced by H. L. A. Hart and elaborated by Rawls, Klosko, and others, and discussed in Chapter 1 as a basis for a general duty to obey the law. By the operation of the Principle of Fairness what might otherwise have been a perfectly innocent act or omission becomes morally wrongful simply by virtue of the fact that others have limited their liberty in beneficial ways. For example, even though it might not be wrongful in a state of nature to fail to contribute a certain sum to the defense of one's neighbors, it is wrongful to fail to contribute if one's neighbors have done so and one has thereby benefited. In such a case, failing to contribute, a malum prohibitum, *is* morally wrongful.

"But wait!" someone will say, "to use the Principle of Fairness in this way is to concede that forcing contributions is prima facie wrongful – hence, coercive, on the moralized analysis – even if forcing the contributions is ultimately justified by the Principle!" This is an important point because it exposes yet another instance of the Redescription Problem. Shall we say that fairness justifies a prima facie wrongful forcing of another to contribute, or shall we say that forcing contributions from those who benefit from a fair scheme of cooperation is not (even) prima facie wrongful? As before, the only tool available to resolve the issue is to ask whether a moral residue of compunction and compensation would be appropriate on the part of those doing the compelling. The dynamics of the present case are basically the same as in the case of deciding whether Germans had (a) a prima facie duty to obey the law that was overridden by the injustice of the Third Reich, or (b) a prima facie duty to obey the laws of a just state, which the Third Reich was not. In that case, the issue was resolved by pointing out the impropriety of a German's feeling a residue of remorse in case circumstances dictated disobedience –

THE "LAW IS COERCIVE" FALLACY

thus one could conclude with as much confidence as is possible in such matters that the proper description of the duty involved was a prima facie duty to obey the law *of a sufficiently just state*, and not, tout court, a prima facie duty to obey the law.[21]

What does intuition tell us here? Should those who force contributions feel compunction even though fairness justifies what they do? Or ought they feel nothing of the sort because what they do is essentially fair? If they should "make it up" to the unwilling contributor, how should they go about doing that (and don't say "by keeping those benefits flowing!")? A defender of the qualified view that law is coercive in the malum prohibitum cases would like not to be drawn into this battle of intuitions (in which she seems to come off rather poorly) and to be able instead to appeal to the *principle* that forcing is prima facie wrong – but, as argued above, this kind of appeal to principle (now plainly functioning as a sort of *ur*-intuition, rather than a dry social datum) is simply to beg the question.

The Principle of Fairness can be disputed, of course, and – as we saw in Chapter 1 – has been, particularly by those of the libertarian persuasion.[22] But there is no knockdown argument showing the Principle of Fairness is false. Moreover, its limitations as a foundation of a general duty to obey the law do not affect its use here, where the issue is whether it is prima facie wrongful to exact contributions in circumstances satisfying the Principle of Fairness, rather than whether there is a prima facie duty to volunteer them. Therefore the qualified view, that law is coercive in the malum prohibitum cases, fails to avoid the mire of controversy. This qualified view, just as much as the pre-reflective view, cannot sustain the position that the coerciveness of law or some part of law is a given, for which political and legal philosophies must account, rather than a conclusion, which they may reach or reject.

---

[21] Jack Sanders pointed out the difficulty discussed here.

[22] See Robert Nozick's notorious "classical music" counterexample, in *Anarchy, State, and Utopia* 90–6 (New York: Basic, 1974) [hereafter, *Anarchy, State, and Utopia*]. Nozick argues that – contrary to the Fairness Principle – I can't be enforceably obliged to dedicate one day a year to playing classical music over a community public address system, even if everyone else does, and even if I enjoy the music they play. Nozick's counterexample would be less compelling if it were to involve, say, a day's labor at the community sanitation plant to monitor the level of toxic bacteria in the water supply. This suggests that the Principle of Fairness, suitably modified, can escape Nozickian counterexamples. See George Klosko, *The Principle of Fairness and Political Obligation* (Lanham, Md.: Rowman & Littlefield, 1991).

Does Law Manipulatively Threaten the Free Rider?

Up to this point, I have assumed that it is morally permissible to propose to do just those things that it is morally permissible to do. But this equivalence is not generally true. Sometimes it is wrongful to do what one has a right to propose to do, as, for example, when I threaten to shoot a nonviolent trespasser. And sometimes it is wrongful to propose to do what one has a right to do, as in the case of blackmail. Just because I have a right to tell the police that you are a drug abuser it does not follow that I have a right to propose that you buy my silence. Explaining the wrongfulness of blackmail has posed something of a difficulty for the reason that, in most cases, we do have a right to propose to do or not do whatever we have a right to do or not do. Consider the two following cases, the first proposed by Kent Greenawalt, the second by Wertheimer.[23]

> CASE 14. Greenawalt's Moralistic Informer
>
> *A* learns that *B* is abusing drugs. *A* believes that *B*'s drug abuse is wrongful and therefore proposes to *B* that *A* will tell *B*'s parents unless *B* stops.

> CASE 15. Wertheimer's Greedy Informer
>
> *A* learns that *B* is abusing drugs. Drug abuse doesn't matter to *A*, but making money does. *A* therefore proposes to *B* that *A* will tell *B*'s parents unless *B* pays *A* $100.

Many would agree that the Greedy Informer's proposal is coercive, while the Moralistic Informer's is not. Wertheimer suggests that this result can be reconstructed by including the Moralistic Informer's declared unilateral plan (telling *B*'s parents) in *B*'s moral baseline, while *excluding* the Greedy Informer's identical declared unilateral plan from *B*'s moral baseline.

But on what basis can we make the discrimination? One salient feature of the Greedy Informer's proposal is that it is a *manipulative threat*, whereas the Moralistic Informer's proposal is a *warning*. That is to say, the Moralistic Informer's informing is an already impending consequence of *B*'s conduct; while the Greedy Informer has no such "natural" impulse to inform, but, rather, *invents* an intention to

[23] See Kent Greenawalt, "Criminal Coercion and Freedom of Speech," 78 *Northwestern University Law Review* 1081, 1096–7 (1983); Wertheimer at 220.

inform and does so for a reason that responds to no feature of B's conduct other than the vulnerability it exposes.

Greenawalt's and Wertheimer's work thus suggests a principled way of choosing whether or not to include a specific proposal in B's baseline. Roughly speaking, a proposer's declared unilateral plan belongs in the moral baseline just in case the proposer is disposed to pursue the plan apart from the proposal situation. In other words, if the proposer had no disposition to carry out the plan in the prepro-posal situation, then, but only then, the plan should be excluded from the proposee's baseline.

Consider how this works out. In the Greedy Informer case, although the Drug Abuser has no moral right secretly to abuse drugs, the Informer's declared unilateral plan is excluded from the moral baseline because the Informer has no disposition, apart from the pro-posal situation, to carry it out. Because the Informer's proposal makes the Abuser worse off as compared to the *corrected* moral base-line, it counts as coercive. In contrast, in Moralistic Informer, the declared unilateral plan is one that the Informer is disposed to carry out anyway. The plan therefore is part of the Abuser's baseline. The proposal makes the Abuser no worse off, with respect to this cor-rected baseline, and so it is not coercive.

Now consider a typical "Principle of Fairness" case:

CASE 16. Free Rider

A group of people agree to spend a day each, each year, maintaining the water quality in their area. Everyone will benefit, and all (but one, the Free Rider) agree to contribute, but only on the condition that all others contribute as well. The group proposes to punish the Free Rider if she fails to contribute when her turn comes. Emigration is not a rea-sonable option.

Even if we believe that the Free Rider would act wrongfully by not contributing, *and even if we believe that her being punished would not be wrongful,* we may not be so sure that she is not being coerced.

The Greenawalt/Wertheimer suggestion imports a degree of sophistication into the two-prong analysis. A proposal may be wrongful in two ways: The plan it announces may be *wrongful,* or the proposal may be wrongful even though the plan it announces is not. The suggestion can be expressed in terms of the moral baseline: The proposee's moral baseline includes a plan just in case the proposer is disposed to carry it out regardless of the proposal situation. In Case 16, the coercion question ultimately turns on whether the group in fact had a preproposal disposition to punish failures to contribute. This is made doubtful by the conditional nature of the agreement. If, apart from the proposal to punish the Free Rider, the group had no disposition to punish noncontribution, then the plan to punish must be excluded from her baseline and the proposal counted as coercive. On the other hand, if there was a disposition to punish noncontribution, the Free Rider's baseline should reflect that, and the proposal should not count as coercive. Obviously, large-scale, ongoing cooperative schemes – like the state – are not conditioned on getting any particular holdout to join in. Therefore, if Case 16 is to stand for the world as we find it, the Free Rider's baseline should include the group's disposition to punish, and its proposal – like the state's – as noncoercive.

Now consider another case:

CASE 17. Sodomy Statute

Hardwick double-parks on a residential street while he goes into an apartment to have sex with another man. An officer investigating the double-parking finds Hardwick and his partner in flagrante delicto. Hardwick is arrested and charged with two counts: a misdemeanor parking violation and a felony violation under the following statute: "A person convicted of the offense of sodomy shall be punished by imprisonment for not less than one nor more than twenty years." Prosecutions under the statute, which was enacted in 1833, are exceedingly rare, and the District Attorney views it as an anachronism. The District Attorney offers to drop the sodomy charge in exchange for a plea of guilty to the parking violation.[24]

This case is unlike the ordinary Plea Bargain case, Case 7, in that the District Attorney has no independent intention to press the sodomy charge. It approximates the case of Wertheimer's Greedy Informer, Case 15, rather than Case 14, the Moralistic Informer. It is, I think, a genuine case of a coercive use of the law, and a case whose coercive character does not depend either on the wrongful character of the law or on the law's bringing disproportionate sanctions to bear.

Cases like Case 17 do little, however, to deflect the repugnant conclusion. Case 17 is better described as a coercive *use* of the law, rather

---

[24] The statute is based on OCGA §16-6-2 (1982). See *Bowers v Hardwick,* 478 U.S. 186 (1986). I do not want to suggest that the Georgia Sodomy statute, on which Case 17 is based, is not both wrongful and disproportionate to any wrong it might conceivably relate to. For those readers who find it impossible to ignore these aspects, I suggest substituting any other statute that has fallen into desuetude.

than a case of law's inherent coerciveness. Classifying Case 17 as coercive depends on the fact that in the normal and expected course of things, Hardwick is not charged with sodomy. To see this, let's reverse the earlier assumption that the sodomy statute is neither wrongful nor disproportionate – assume now that it wrongfully proposes to burden individual autonomy, or it proposes a grossly disproportionate range of penalties. Is this *statute* coercive?

The statute, we now suppose, satisfies the proposal prong, but does it satisfy the *choice* prong, about which we have had so far so little to say? It appears not. The choice prong is satisfied only if the proposal leaves no reasonable alternative to compliance, but in this case the sodomy statute has fallen into desuetude. To the extent that legal enforcement is only a remote possibility, or its sanctions are mild, it becomes less plausible to suggest that the citizen has no reasonable alternative to complying with the law's commands. The setting that made the use of the statute in Case 17 coercive tends to defeat the claim that the statute itself constitutes a coercive proposal.

Many philosophers seem to regard emigration as the only alternative to compliance with the law of the jurisdiction. Of these, many, like Rawls, reject this alternative as unreasonable; some will reject it, in the highest Socratic tradition, as dishonorable.[25] What these philosophers overlook is the range of less drastic, and more reasonable, alternatives to compliance that any but the most Orwellian regime leaves open. For most of us, most of the time, there are reasonable alternatives to complying with the law. Unless, that is, we view disobeying the law as unreasonable per se . . . which, of course (as we saw in Part One), we don't.

To summarize, we looked to the malum prohibitum cases to

---

[25] Rawls writes: "Political society is closed: we come to be within it and we do not, and indeed *cannot*, enter or leave it voluntarily." *Political Liberalism* 136 (New York: Columbia University Press, 1993) (emphasis added). He explains, further: "The government's authority cannot . . . be freely accepted in the sense that the bonds of society and culture, of history and social place of origin, begin so early to shape our life and are normally so strong that the right of emigration . . . does not suffice to make accepting its authority free, politically speaking, in the way that liberty of conscience suffices to make accepting ecclesiastical authority free, politically speaking" (*id.* at 222). Here, Rawls is invoking what he takes to be the fact that "political power is always coercive power," *id.* at 136, in a way typical of a justification-defeating context of coercion claims. The pre-reflective view of law does double duty for liberal political theory, in this sense: it casts a burden of justification upon the state *and* it rebuts any appeal to implied consent that might be offered to justify the state's inevitable coercion.

replace the lost paradigm case of legal coercion, the criminal statute. A move in this direction might please those on the political right, but we found that it quickly became ensnared in difficulty. Hart's and Rawls's Principle of Fairness reminded us that there is moral malum in malum prohibitum. We then considered the morality of proposals, as distinct from the morality of actions generally, in the hope that we could secure a sense in which the malum prohibitum cases are coercive despite the Principle of Fairness. Unfortunately, the only convincing case of coercion we found, the Sodomy Statute case (Case 17), depended on the special feature that the statute was not generally enforced. This, in turn, suggested that the choice prong of Wertheimer's two-prong analysis may not be generally satisfied, either.

Finding ever more difficulty on this path around the repugnant conclusion, I suggest that we abandon it, and return to the second of the two possibilities outlined earlier. We should explore the possibility that law is coercive because its sanctions are generally disproportionate to those that are allowable under a regime of moral self-help.

The Disproportionality Cases

The Tables Turned on the Gunman case, Case 10, involved what I have been calling moral self-help. Moral self-help can lose its morally permissible quality if it is excessive, and the same applies to proposals to use self-help. Consider the following:

CASE 18. Bad Check Self-Help

Rummel promises to repair Doe's air conditioner and, in return, accepts her check for $120.75. Rummel cashes the check but does not repair the air conditioner. Doe, armed, confronts Rummel. Rummel admits that he had no intention of fixing the air conditioner. Doe tells Rummel that he will now march to her basement, where he will be locked up for from two to ten years.[26]

Doe's proposal is coercive because it is wrongful. But how can it be wrongful, if the Traveler's proposal in Case 10 was not? The answer is that Doe's declared unilateral plan in Case 18 is a disproportionately severe response to Rummel's conduct; while the Traveler's declared unilateral plan in Case 10 is not. This may seem unintuitive,

[26] This scenario is loosely based on the facts of *Rummel v Estelle*, 445 U.S. 262 (1980).

since in both cases the ultimate threat is shooting: in Case 10: "Leave me with my money or I'll shoot," and in Case 18: "Get in my basement for two to ten years or I'll shoot." What is crucially different is that Doe, in Case 18, does not give Rummel the option of evening the score by either returning the $120.75 or repairing the air conditioner.

Compare now this case:

CASE 19.   Bad Check Prosecution

Same as Case 18, but Doe does not confront Rummel. Rather, Doe complains to the District Attorney, who prosecutes Rummel for theft by false pretenses, which is punishable by imprisonment for from two to ten years. The District Attorney will also seek to prove that Rummel had committed two prior crimes in order to have Rummel sentenced to prison for life, under a recidivist statute.

How can Doe's proposal in Case 18 be coercive, and the legal machinery involved in Case 19 not be? Neither case leaves it open to Rummel to even the score by returning Doe's money or doing the promised work; so the proposals should count as wrongful in both instances, shouldn't they? If they do, we could generalize the argument and conclude that law is coercive wherever its sanctions exceed the limits that compensatory justice sets to moral self-help.

Generalizing in this way will involve reliance on two assumptions. The first is that the limits of compensatory justice *are* the limits of moral self-help. The second is that the limits of moral self-help set the limits of morally permissible sanctions generally. There are good reasons to doubt each of these assumptions, however.

Suppose people could not propose self-help measures that did any more than threaten wrongdoers with being made to compensate their victims. It would follow that people could legitimately do nothing to deter those wrongdoers who were prepared to pay the required compensation – assuming (unrealistically) that all wrongs are compensable and all wrongdoers able to compensate. Even if a premium were to be added to the allowable compensation to cause the wrongdoer to "internalize" the cost of detecting and apprehending him, the idea that our rights and peace of mind may be peremptorily "rented" by wrongdoers is obnoxious to our wider moral ideas.[27]

---

[27]   My argument here follows Nozick's in *Anarchy, State, and Utopia* at 57–71.

Reconsider Case 10, the Tables Turned on the Gunman case. Is it really plausible to say that the Traveler has no moral right to do anything beyond disarming the Gunman and recovering some monetary premium? Can the Gunman justly claim a right to be free to rearm and try his luck with this Traveler again and with other travelers to follow, at a time and place of his choosing? The more plausible view is that the Traveler does not act wrongly in taking *some* measures to incapacitate and deter the Gunman and those similarly disposed. It cannot be maintained, then, that permissible self-help cannot go beyond the boundaries of compensation.

The lingering worry we have about permitting self-help to go beyond compensation has to do with the abuses of self-help that will inevitably result. What self-help lacks is sufficient regularity to avoid clouded or biased judgment of the facts and excessive zeal in punishing. If Traveler, in Case 10, and Doe, in Case 18, are permitted to do more than exact compensation, what *is* the limit? This worry should call into doubt the second assumption questioned above, that the limits of moral *self*-help set a general limit to morally permissible measures.

One reason to doubt that the limits of moral self-help can be a sure guide to the limits of morally permissible *public interest* measures is that public measures may be significantly less risky than private ones directed toward the same ends. As at least one or two movies opening this summer at a theater near you will make vivid, the niceties of due process are rarely the vigilante's forte. Therefore, a severer but regularly imposed public penalty may be less an affront to the wrongdoer's undeniable dignity than a milder but more arbitrary private remedy. (Of this, more, in Part Three.) This, of course, does not even point the way toward an answer to the question "When *do* state sanctions become so disproportionate as to be coercive?"[28] It is, however, decisively to reject the idea that state sanctions are so widely and massively disproportionate as to make them coercive either systematically or in a significant number of cases.

---

[28] The U.S. Supreme Court's proportionality jurisprudence does not take us much farther, unfortunately. Compare *Solem v Helm*, 463 U.S. 277 (1983) (life imprisonment without possibility of parole imposed, under a recidivist statute, for passing a bad check, held "significantly disproportionate" and therefore "cruel and unusual" punishment) with *Hutto v Davis*, 454 U.S. 370 (1982) (forty years imprisonment for possessing eight ounces of marijuana not "cruel and unusual"). See also Joshua Dressler, *Understanding Criminal Law* 31–43 (New York: Matthew Bender, 1987).

A WRONGFUL MONOPOLY?

So far, the focus of the inquiry has been the relation between the state and the wrongdoer, and – for purposes of a moralized analysis of coercion – the question has been whether the state's relation is essentially one characterizable as prima facie wrongful. In the course of this investigation, we have noticed a discrepancy between what *other* individuals (or groups) are morally permitted to do to wrongdoers as a matter of moral self-help, and what the state may do. We have also noticed that the state often steps in to regulate and even to forbid moral self-help. These discrepancies between what the state presumes to do and what citizens otherwise might permissibly do suggests another powerful line of support for the view that law is coercive, and even that the state necessarily lacks moral legitimacy.

The argument is made by Charles Sayward,[29] and (as I will loosely paraphrase it) it goes like this:

Premise 1:   All victims of certain serious wrongdoings, and those acting on their behalf, have a right suitably to punish and exact compensation from their wrongdoers.

Premise 2:   An essential function of the state is to prohibit victims (and others) from suitably punishing wrongdoers.

Premise 3:   If it is an essential function of an institution to prohibit an action that one has a right to do, then that institution is illegitimate.

Conclusion: No state is morally legitimate.

The argument is logically valid while the conclusion is, in my view, plainly false, and so one of the premises must be false. Which one? Sayward thinks Premise 1 is "the least vulnerable," and so, for the apologist of the state, "the place to attack" is Premise 3. This premise looks vulnerable because sometimes it is legitimate to violate a right as, for example, where the fate of humankind hangs in the balance. This might also be the case if by failing to violate a certain right, "the total weighted amount of rights violations would be increased," and a defender of the state would argue that allowing untrammeled self-help would have just that effect. But the suggested line of attack, focusing on Premise 3, seems to concede that the state and its law is

---

[29]   Charles Sayward, "Anarchism and Rights Violations," *Critica* 105–16 (April 1982).

essentially coercive, because it is violative of rights – which is always prima facie wrongful – even though it is on balance justified in terms of the compensating reduction of the weighted net total of rights violations. In other words, even if the state is, on balance, legitimated by the strategy Sayward suggests, it remains convicted of coerciveness on a moralized analysis.

But is Premise 1 really so plausible? Here, we have to recall a distinction noticed earlier between two senses in which the term "right" may be understood. A person X has a right to ϕ in the sense of having a moral permission to ϕ just in case X violates no one's rights by ϕ-ing. This is what Hohfeld called a liberty, and what Gerald Postema calls an "unprotected liberty,"[30] to emphasize that others may permissibly interfere with X's ϕ-ing. X has a "protected liberty" (Postema) or "claim right" (Hohfeld) only if, in addition to the bare, unprotected liberty, others are forbidden to interfere with X's ϕ-ing. George Rainbolt gives a helpful example: If I give you a mere liberty to use my car on Saturday night, you have no right to complain if when you come to get it you find that I am using it already. If, in contrast, I give you a claim right to use my car, you do have a right to complain when you find that I am using it then, for I will have interfered with your exercising your liberty to use it, thereby violating your claim right. More to the point, if all that victims (or others) possess is a claim right to punish vis à vis the wrongdoer, *and a mere liberty vis à vis all others*, their rights are not violated if the state prohibits them from punishing (unless, of course, the state is the mere tool of the wrongdoer).

Sayward's argument assumes that Premise 1 states a general claim right, rather than a liberty, to punish. But, so stated, Premise 1 is false, as I will show in a moment. Premise 1 is true if it refers to a liberty unprotected against interference by any but the wrongdoer and his agents, but in that case the argument loses its validity. (If we were counting anarchical fallacies, this would be a fourth!) To see that Premise 1 is true only if understood in terms of a liberty to punish, consider what the world would be like if, in fact, a full claim right were involved. Robert Nozick puts it vividly, in considering how a regime of "open" punishment – that is, an equal claim right held by all – would work out in a generally well-behaved state of nature:

30 Gerald Postema, "Nozick on Liberty, Compensation, and the Individual's Right to Punish," 6 *Social Theory and Practice* 311 (1980); see also J. E. J Altham, "Reflections on the State of Nature," in Ross Harrison, ed., *Rational Action: Studies in Philosophy and Social Science* 133–45 (Cambridge: Cambridge University Press, 1979); David Schmidtz, *The Limits of Government* 33–53 (Boulder, Colo.: Westview, 1991).

Is it to be a system of the first actor's preempting the field? Will sadists compete to be the first to get their licks in? This would greatly magnify the problem of keeping the punishers from exceeding the bounds of deserved punishment and would be undesirable, the opportunities it offers for cheerful and unalienated labor notwithstanding. In a system of open punishment would anyone be in a position to decide upon mercy; and would another be permitted to negate this decision so long as the sum did not exceed the amount deserved? Could the offender have a confederate punish him only lightly? Would there be any likelihood that the victim would feel that justice had been done? And so on.[31]

As Nozick points out, these difficulties are additional to those that attend merely *compensatory* self-help, and they are not removed, but only compounded, by allotting some special status to the victim of the wrongdoing (who, of course, may be too intimidated to punish, or no longer around to do so). The conclusion Nozick is compelled to draw is that the right to punish is one held not individually but jointly in the state of nature, individuals (victims included) holding only "a right to a say in the ultimate determination of punishment." As Postema points out, Nozick's view of the individual's "natural" right to punish comes down to an unprotected liberty.

Those sympathetic to anarchism might suspect Nozick of treachery here or, at least, of a slackened diligence. John Simmons,[32] for one, defends "open" punishment as a natural right but concedes that it leaves no room for mercy, absent a universal dispensation, and, moreover, leaves those who withhold consent from government in possession of their natural right to preemptively deal with wrongdoers – of course on pain of being subject to punishment in turn should they punish mistakenly or excessively. (And so, too, the punishers' punishers – if the punishers were excessively or mistakenly punished for punishing – and so on.) "Pure" sadists are incapable of inflicting harm-*for*-wrongdoing, Simmons points out, which disqualifies them as punishers. But those sadists who possess *some* moral motivation would still be in business, presumably, gleefully meting out justice in full measure.

If Simmons is right about punishment, then Sayward's Premise 1

---

31 *Anarchy, State, and Utopia* at 138.
32 A. John Simmons, *The Lockean Theory of Rights* 121–66 (Princeton: Princeton University Press, 1992).

is a viable component in an argument capable of showing that law is essentially coercive. But do we really wish to commit ourselves to a view that entails, for example, that *if O.J. Simpson was really guilty of murder,* and if that were known to a person who had not surrendered his Lockean "natural executive right" to punish murder, then that person would have a protected liberty to deal with O.J. in whatever way natural law permits murderers to be dealt with, and to do so at anytime *before, during, or after* his trial? Few would chase even the loveliest theory so far.

SUMMARY

I conclude that the pre-reflective view, that law is coercive, cannot easily be sustained. And even if by some ingenious argument it were reaffirmed, that argument could not restore its former status as a social fact throwing, all by itself, a burden of justification onto the law and its functions. If law requires some special justification, that must be established by argument and no longer by utterance of the ritual shibboleth that the pre-reflective view has become.

This conclusion need not wait upon a resolution of the dispute between moralized and nonmoralized analyses of coercion. It seems that the purportedly nonmoralized analyses rely covertly on moral notions, but this reliance may be one of degree and the degrees may matter. In any case, the question (to paraphrase Jeremy Waldron's point about the concept of harm) is not which is the true conception of coercion, but "which conception answers more adequately to the purposes for which the concept is deployed."[33] To the extent that the concept of coercion has been deployed for the purposes of political theory, however, I think I have shown that neither the moralized nor the nonmoralized conceptions serve anywhere nearly as well as has long been assumed.

One disquieting corollary of any moralized account of coercion is that, to the extent a regime can truly be said to be promoting morality, the less coercive is the operation of its laws, other things being equal. This may mean that we will have to wait for agreement on moral truth before we can have any agreement about what and

---

[33] Jeremy Waldron, *Liberal Rights* 119–20 (Cambridge: Cambridge University Press, 1993). I owe this analogy to Alan Wertheimer.

where coercion is in the world. In that case, the concept of coercion may never be of much use to us again, except in tiny pockets of local agreement, such as those found within the law. This is no occasion for regret because, as I hope I have shown, the pre-reflective concept was never suited to bear the weight that political philosophy has asked it to bear.

Part Three

The Inner Sphere of Privacy Fallacy

"The inner circumference of the cell is formed . . . so . . . as not to screen any part . . . from the inspector's view."

Bentham, II Panopticon Letters

Chapter 7

The Private Sphere

The relation of law and morality is difficult to define, but it is of great importance. Discussing this relation raises troubling issues such as whether the law may ever require what is morally repugnant, or whether there is any moral requirement to obey the law simply because it is the law. These were the focus of earlier chapters but are separable from the issue I want to explore here, which is whether there may be valid moral requirements that may *not* validly be made requirements of law. The issue I want to examine is not so much one about what "law" and "morality" mean as it is about turf: Is there (can there be) any department of conduct that morality claims as exclusively its own, and which the law has no business penetrating? The view that there are some moral wrongs that the law may not properly right is tacitly and sometimes explicitly assumed by many participants in the unrelenting debate about the right of privacy.[1]

In what follows I will use the extremely barbarous term "strongly delegalized moral requirements" to refer to the putative class of moral requirements that are forbidden by morality itself to become legal requirements. In this discussion, I will mean by "law" the set of all legal requirements (existing at one place at a time) and by "morality" the set of all *valid* moral requirements (existing in that place at that time). Legal and moral requirements are distinguishable by the fact that there are state-maintained mechanisms for enforcing the former, but not necessarily the latter, type of requirement. (As the discussion to come will make evident, membership in the category of legal requirement is broader than what might at first appear.) The

---

[1] The landmarks of the constitutional progress of this debate are *Griswold v Connecticut*, 381 U.S. 479 (1965), *Eisenstadt v Baird*, 405 U.S. 438 (1972), *Roe v Wade*, 410 U.S. 113 (1973) and *Bowers v Hardwick*, 478 U.S. 186 (1986). For recent discussion of the underlying issues, see Symposium, "Law, Community, and Moral Reasoning," 77 *California Law Review* 475 (1989).

term "moral requirement" is meant roughly to invoke what Lon Fuller called "the morality of duty," as contrasted to "the morality of aspiration,"[2] but I mean the term "requirement" to extend to whatever morality requires, whether or not it would idiomatically be called a duty or an obligation, and to cover both prohibitions and positive injunctions, "shalt nots" as well as "shalts."

Some moral requirements are only "weakly" delegalized because the moral requirements that "delegalize" them do so only contingently. For example, utilitarian moral concerns might delegalize a certain moral requirement if the social costs of legal enforcement outweighed the benefits. In such a case, the requirements in question would be delegalized but only weakly so, because a shift in the balance of costs and benefits is always possible (however unlikely) and would remove the barrier of delegalization. Strongly delegalized moral requirements, on the other hand, are those whose delegalization is, in Ronald Dworkin's phraseology, a matter of principle, rather than of mere policy or expediency.[3]

Liberals and libertarians have a forensic if not a theoretical stake in defending the view that strongly delegalized moral requirements exist. Classical liberalism holds that individual liberty is a paramount value, and that legal curtailment of an individual's liberty to act is morally justified only if her conduct might cause harm to others or produce intolerable consequences of other kinds. A liberal need not claim that delegalized moral requirements exist, or are possible, for a liberal might hold that nothing can be a *moral* requirement unless harm to others, or some other consequentialist concern, so warrants. A liberal might, in other words, hold what Joel Feinberg calls a "perfect coincidence" view, according to which something like Mill's harm principle determines both what morality requires and what law may permissibly require. The perfect coincidence view entails that there are no strongly delegalized moral requirements.

Feinberg himself rejects the perfect coincidence view, but many liberals (including Mill himself, as I point out below) do not. For example, Ronald Dworkin apparently does not, and Anthony Woozley certainly does not. Other authors, including Ernest Nagel and Martin Golding, have expressed skepticism about the general project of

---

[2] Lon Fuller, *The Morality of Law*, rev. ed., 5–6 (New Haven: Yale University Press, 1969).

[3] For an elaboration of the distinction between "policy" and "principle," see Ronald Dworkin, *Taking Rights Seriously*, 22–8, 90–100 (Cambridge, Mass.: Harvard University Press, 1977) [hereafter, *Taking Rights Seriously*].

dividing morality into a part that may permissibly be legally enforced and a part that may not.[4] A point made by both Dworkin and Woozley is that counting something as a genuine moral requirement presupposes the existence of supporting reasons and that these reasons, in the absence of some bar, might legitimately be weighed by a legislature. This point is not decisive, however, for the existence of such a bar remains a possibility. My overall argument is designed to show that the existence of such a bar would be incompatible with the existence of the range of morally permissible forms of social enforcement that, I will claim, attach to any genuine moral requirement.

It is understandable why liberals would be tempted to follow Feinberg's lead and reject the perfect coincidence view. They are reluctant to claim that their principles circumscribe morality as well as law because to do so would embroil liberalism in controversies about the ultimate ground of value. Value is closely tied to religious belief, for many. Liberals are officially agnostic but sensitive to what Thomas Nagel calls "the politically suicidal aspect" of defending liberal doctrine by discrediting religion.[5]

Seeming to contradict or even to fail to reverence firmly entrenched conventional moral views can have the same suicidal aspect. To convince a popular audience, it is more effective to say, for example, that consensual sadomasochism is morally wrong *but* beyond the law's proper reach, than to say that it is morally permissible and *therefore* beyond the law's proper reach. And to confess that the law's reach is limited only because the net cost of extending it is simply too great – namely, that the moral requirement not to engage in sadomasochism is only *weakly* delegalized – will appear too calculating, too tentative, to appeal to an audience likely to suppose and encouraged to believe that a matter of principle is at stake.

Abortion is another example. According to a recent survey, one out of five American adults agreed *both* that "abortion is murder and

---

[4] Compare Joel Feinberg, *Harmless Wrongdoing*, vol. 4 of *The Moral Limits of the Criminal Law* at 124–5, 153–4 (New York: Oxford University Press, 1988), and Gerald G. Postema, "Public faces – private places: Liberalism and the Enforcement of Morality," in A. W. Musschenga, B. Voorzauger, and A. Soetman, eds., *Morality, Worldview, and Law* 153 (Maastricht, 1992) with *Taking Rights Seriously* at 253; Anthony Woozley, "Law and Legislation of Morality" in Arthur L. Caplan and Daniel Callahan, eds., *Ethics in Hard Times* (New York: Plenum, 1981); Ernest Nagel, "The Enforcement of Morals," *Humanist*, May/June 1968 at 18–27; and Martin Golding, *Philosophy of Law* 67 (Englewood Cliffs, N.J.: Prentice-Hall, 1975).

[5] Thomas Nagel, *Equality and Partiality* 157 (New York: Oxford University Press, 1991).

never the best course, even in a bad situation" *and* that preventing abortion is *"no business"* of the state.[6] It is unnecessary to attribute to these respondents the odd view that preventing murder is *generally* no business of the state; they can better be understood as implicitly relying on the existence of strongly delegalized moral requirements. One may, it would seem, consistently hold that abortion is a terrible wrong *and* that the state may not legitimately forbid it. Politically, it is more popular to deplore abortion while simultaneously defending abortion rights, than it is to take either the position that elective abortion is morally impeccable, or the position that it may be outlawed if the legislature so chooses.

Reformulating the abortion issue as one of "who decides?" rather than one of "who's right?" seems to open up a comfortable space in the middle. Michael Sandel has distinguished "naive" and "sophisticated" types of argument for, or against, morals legislation. According to Sandel, naive arguments hold "that the justice of laws depends on the moral worth of the conduct they prohibit or protect," while sophisticated arguments "bracket" substantive moral issues and invoke "a more general theory about the respective claims of majority rule and individual rights."[7] For sophisticated advocates of such legislation, bracketing means letting the majority decide; for sophisticated opponents, it means letting the individual decide. Each of these adversaries appeals to a "more general theory" to support its favored decision maker. The central point of this part of my essay, put in Sandel's terms, is that the "more general theory" that sophisticated liberals invoke involves an implicit or explicit denial of the perfect coincidence view and the coordinate assertion or assumption that strongly delegalized moral requirements exist, and further, that the "bracketing" of certain moral issues is what morality itself demands of politics.

---

[6] See *The N.Y. Times,* Aug. 3, 1989, at 10, col. 1 (emphasis added). To *The New York Times*/CBS News Poll, 68% of 978 adults polled responded that "even in cases where they might think abortion is wrong, the government has no business preventing a women from having abortion," and 35% of those who responded that "abortion is murder and never the best course, even in a bad situation" – 20% of all respondents – also responded that preventing abortion is "no business" of the state. See also *The N.Y. Times,* Jan. 16, 1998, at A16, col. 2: "Nearly 60 percent of those polled [say] that the Government should stay out of the decisions on whether abortion should be legal [sic]."

[7] See Michael J. Sandel, "Moral Argument and Liberal Toleration: Abortion and Homosexuality," 77 *California Law Review* 521 (1989).

An appealing picture is available to us if we deny the perfect coincidence view. We can picture the whole of morality to ourselves as consisting of a pair of nested, concentric spheres, surrounding our selves as their center. The space between the outer sphere and the inner is the space of political morality. Here, the state may add its sanctions to those of morality, or it may decline to do so, as a legitimately constituted legislature sees fit. But the inner sphere the state may not legitimately penetrate; this space is subject to morality's demands but is no business of the state. Resting at the center is the self – representable as a dimensionless point if morality is essentially social (of this, more later). To complete the picture, beyond the outer sphere lies a region in which the legislature may forbid or command what morality has not determined – the lawyer's mala prohibita – and I will remain officially agnostic on the question that occupied Chapter 1, whether the legislative fiat by itself imposes a moral requirement to obey.

This picture helps conceptualize two questions: (1) Is all morality *social?* and (2) is all morality *political?* As to the first question: By the slogan "all morality is social" I mean to express the position that a requirement of conduct is a moral requirement only if it is associated with a morally permissible social sanction. If all morality is social, in this sense, then it is fair to depict the self as a dimensionless point; if not, then it is misleading to do so. If some morality is not social, then a proper depiction would include a third, innermost sphere, which, though one of morality, is immune to social and of course legal sanctions.

The second question – "is all morality political?" – is distinct from the first. By the slogan "all morality is political" I mean to paraphrase the perfect coincidence view: Whatever morality requires the state *may* require. If all morality is political, then there is a perfect coincidence between the inner and outer spheres, and it is misleading to suggest that they are distinct. If it is false to say that all morality is political, then it is misleading – even dangerous – to confuse the inner and outer spheres. The view I defend here answers both questions in the affirmative: Yes, all morality is social, and Yes, all morality is political. All morality is political *because* it is all social. On this view, the proper picture consists not of two or three nested spheres but a single sphere – social, political morality – with a dot, the self – in the middle (or, like Wittgenstein's picture in the *Tractatus*, on the circumference of an egg-shaped world).

The super-simple picture I defend is not committed to any particular view of the reach, composition, or rigorousness of morality. Morality may be governed by one big principle or by a plurality of colliding principles, for all the picture shows. (I will consider later the suggestion that the fact of moral pluralism compels us to reject the perfect coincidence view.) The principle(s) of morality may have something to say about everything we do, in which case the moral sphere engulfs the world insofar as we act in it. Or, alternatively, there may be matters of moral indifference outside the sphere of morality. The shape of the sphere may be dented inward to exclude such things as "agent-centered prerogatives" – optimific acts that I am permitted to omit – and "agent-centered prohibitions" – optimific acts that I am prohibited to perform.[8] The picture I offer may oversimplify, but a defender of the more popular "nested spheres" picture is in no position to complain on this score. The question is: Which of the two possibly oversimple renderings is less misleading?

The perfect coincidence view and super-simple picture that goes with it of course do not entail any advocacy of state enforcement of the whole of morality. No sensible thinker has ever advocated that the state ought to enforce morality in every detail; and in fact some of the most monstrous follies of human history can be seen as attempts to fuse the moral and the political through and through. But one can consistently hold that morality in principle permits the law to add its sanction to each and every one that morality already carries, while denying that it would be wise, efficient, or desirable for there to be any more than a minimal, "night watchman" state, or while denying that any state is necessary or desirable at all. The issue is, as to each detail, what *is* wise, efficient, and desirable? These are political questions, to which some very bad political answers have been and no doubt will be given. It is tempting to forestall those bad answers by ruling out the questions, by denying the perfect coincidence view while appealing to the nested spheres picture. Tempting, I will argue, but untenable.

If there is a realm of morality that is not social, the question presents itself: What is it if it isn't social? I will argue that there is no sense to be made of the idea of a private moral *requirement*. In particular, I will argue that no one can convincingly maintain that some-

---

[8] See Shelly Kagan, *The Limits of Morality* (Oxford: Clarendon Press, 1989); Samuel Scheffler, *The Rejection of Consequentialism* (Oxford: Clarendon Press, 1982).

thing is a requirement of morality unless she is willing to recognize a range of morally permissible *social* measures designed to correct the individual's failure to observe that requirement. As Locke put it: "What duty is [i.e., moral duty], cannot be understood without a law; nor a law be known or supposed . . . without reward and punishment."[9] Having shown that morality is social, I will draw out some of the consequences of the claim that not all of it is permissibly political. To claim that perfect coincidence fails is to claim that the inner sphere is a region of *moral requirements* to which the state may not legitimately add its sanctions to those of morality. I will press the question: What account can be given of such requirements? One who believes that such strongly delegalized moral requirements are possible has to give an account of two things: (a) how such requirements arise and find rational support, and also (b) the range of morally permissible, *non*legal corrective measures that are associated with them. It is unclear how a liberal, for example, can give the first sort of account, because it will have to be congenial to the priority of liberty and the harm principle, and yet not so congenial that the requirement in question is legalizable. But even if such an account can be given, the liberal will find it difficult to give a plausible account of the contours of permissible, necessarily nonlegal, social correction.

Because Mill is such a central figure in the liberal tradition, it will be illuminating first to explore his view. In particular, I will show that, on Mill's account, for any morally permissible social enforcement measure, a less oppressive legal corrective is always conceivable, and that therefore the question whether such values as individual liberty and autonomy are better served by legal or by nonlegal correction of a moral transgression is always to be decided according to the nature of the case. I will then argue more generally that liberals (and everyone else) ought to accept the perfect coincidence view. But accepting this conclusion is not costless even in a generally just and well-governed polity; for, when specific issues of morals legislation arise, the perfect coincidence view requires those taking a liberal position to face the potentially awkward dilemma of having either to "bite the bullet" by explicitly contradicting popular moral notions, or to admit that their opposition to legal enforcement is based only on grounds of policy, not of moral principle.

---

[9] John Locke, *An Essay Concerning Human Understanding,* P. Nidditch, ed., Book 1, ch. 2, sec. 12 (Oxford: Oxford University Press, 1975).

MILL'S VIEW

The idea that there is an area of morality that is "not the law's business"[10] is usually traced to Mill. Mill does, in the introduction to *On Liberty*, speak of "rules of conduct . . . imposed . . . by opinion . . . which are not fit subjects for the operation of law," and of "a legitimate sphere of legal control" and to "what things are fit to be done by a government." And, in the fourth chapter, Mill distinguishes a category of conduct which, though "hurtful to others or wanting in due consideration for their welfare" does not violate "any of their constituted rights," in which case "the offender may then be justly punished by opinion, though not by law." These passages suggest that Mill's view was that delegalized – and perhaps strongly delegalized – moral requirements indeed exist. But Mill generally argues that the "harm" principle defines not only a limit beyond which law may not pass, but also a limit to morality, so the issue requires investigating.[11]

Mill divides personal faults into two categories. Members of the first concern the actor's "own good" but do not affect the interests of others, and therefore never merit social punishment although they may occasion the "disagreeable consequence" that others in their liberty may shun the actor's company, hold him in disesteem, and pass him over in the distribution of "optional good offices" not tending to his self-improvement. Into this category Mill places folly, "lowness or depravation of taste," rashness, obstinacy, immoderation, self-indulgence, and cupidity. Mill adds that these "are not properly immoralities and, to whatever pitch they may be carried, do not constitute wickedness." (Although Mill believes most strenuously in the virtue of self-improvement, he seems uncomfortable with the terms "duties to ourselves" and "duty to oneself.") To fit Mill's claim into the terminology I am using, doing what is for one's own good is never per se a moral requirement. And, although we may think ill of those who exhibit the vices of this first category, it is not proper to subject such persons to moral reproof.[12]

---

[10] This indelible phrase appears in paragraph 257 of the *Report of the Committee on Homosexual Offenses and Prostitution* (CMD 247) (1957), commonly known as the *Wolfenden Report*.

[11] John Stuart Mill, *On Liberty* at 8, 12, 91–2, Currin V. Shields, ed. (New York: The Liberal Arts Press, 1956) [hereafter, *On Liberty*]

[12] *On Liberty* at 94, 96.

Faults of the second category affect others and are "fit objects of moral reprobation and, in grave cases, of moral retribution and punishment." To this category belong rights violations, unjustified injury, and "unfair or ungenerous use of advantages over [others]; even selfish abstinence from defending them from injury." Dispositions to such conduct – such as cruelty, malice, envy, insincerity, irascibility, greed, and self-conceit – are also "properly immoral and fit subjects of disapprobation which may rise to abhorrence." But nothing is "socially obligatory unless circumstances render [it] at the same time [a] dut[y] to others." In other words, "moral disapprobation in the proper sense of the term" is appropriate only where conduct "violate[s] a distinct and assignable obligation to any other person" – although the existence of "a distinct and assignable obligation" to another is not, for Mill, a necessary feature of the duties of morality in general, as distinct from the duties of justice. Mill's puzzling summary is this: "Whenever, in short, there is a definite damage, or a definite risk of damage, either to an individual or to the public, the case is taken out of the province of liberty and placed in that of morality or law."[13]

The disjunction, "morality *or* law," suggests that Mill felt these provinces to be distinct, but he gives no indication that different principles should operate in the two provinces, and every indication that in each province the decision, whether to sanction conduct and to what degree, is governed by the answer to the general question "whether the general welfare will or will not be promoted by interfering with it." Mill makes it nearly certain that his view does not recognize strongly delegalized moral requirements, when, in the concluding chapter of *On Liberty*, he states the maxim: "For such actions as are prejudicial to the interests of others, the individual is accountable and may be subject either to social or to legal punishment *if society is of the opinion that the one or the other is requisite for its protection.*"[14]

In Mill's view the choice of remedies requires a calculation and comparison of the expected utilities of the available means and agencies. Once the harm principle justifies a sanction, Mill gives no hint that any principle dictates an a priori preference for private, that is, *merely* social, as against *state*, enforcement. Once the harm principle

[13] Ibid. at 95, 96, 99, 100. John Stuart Mill, *Utilitarianism*, Oskar Piest, ed., 60–2 (Indianapolis: Bobbs-Merrill, 1957) [hereafter, *Utilitarianism*].
[14] *On Liberty* at 92, 114 (emphasis added).

has been satisfied, the question of sanction is to be settled solely on grounds of utility, "the ultimate appeal on all ethical questions." As Mill put it in the introduction:

> If anyone does an act hurtful to others, there is a *prima facie* case for punishing him by law or, *where legal penalties are not safely applicable,* by general disapproval. . . . In all things which regard the external relations of the individual, he is *de jure* amenable to those whose interests are concerned, and, if need be, to society as their protector. There are often good reasons for not holding him to the responsibility; but these reasons must arise from the special expediencies of the case: either because it is a kind of case in which he is on the whole likely to act better when left to his own discretion than when controlled by any way in which society have it in their power to control him; or because the attempt to exercise control would produce other evils, greater than those which it would prevent.[15]

What, in Mill's view, distinguishes legal and merely social means of enforcing rules of conduct? He wrote:

> Society can and does execute its own mandates [as opposed to those issued "by the hands of its political functionaries"]; and if it issues wrong mandates instead of right, or any mandates at all in things with which it ought not to meddle, it practices a social tyranny more formidable than many kinds of political oppression, since, *though not usually upheld by such extreme penalties, it leaves fewer means of escape, penetrating much more deeply into the details of life, and enslaving the soul itself.*

The contrast Mill draws is multidimensional but, nonetheless, one of degree. "Civil penalties" are usually (but not always) more extreme than those of "prevailing opinion and feeling," but the latter are much harder to elude, much more minutely pervasive, and much more corrosive of individual personality. No wonder that Mill repeatedly announces that he intends his "one very simple principle" to set a limit to both legal and social control of the individual.[16]

Strongly delegalized moral requirements seem possible because the characteristics of being a legal requirement and of being a merely moral requirement differ.[17] Legal requirements are ultimately, if indi-

---

[15] Ibid. at 14, 15 (emphasis added); cf. *Utilitarianism* at 59–60.

[16] *On Liberty* at 7 (emphasis added), 13. Compare Sally Engle Merry, "Rethinking Gossip and Scandal," in Donald Black, ed. vol. 1, *Toward a General Theory of Social Control* 271 (New York: Academic Press, 1984).

[17] According to Louis Schwartz, co-author, with Herbert Wechsler, of the *Model Penal Code of the American Law Institute,* "Moral demands on human behavior can be higher than those of the criminal law precisely because violations of those higher

Table 2. *Means and Agents of Moral Enforcement*

		AGENTS	
		Private	State
MEANS	Suasive		
	Compulsory		Regulatory
			Criminal

rectly, compellable by some state-regulated mechanism; merely moral requirements are not necessarily compellable, although some certainly are. Any requirement of conduct may permissibly be enforced either through solely suasive means, or through means such as physical compulsion and threats thereof. This is a distinction between permissible *means* of enforcement, and it corresponds roughly to what Mill had in mind when he distinguished civil penalties and punishment "by opinion." Further, any requirement of conduct may be enforced privately (i.e., socially) only, or it may be enforced by the state. This is a distinction between permissible *agents* of enforcement, and it is one to which Mill gave less attention, for he felt that society had come in either case to be the ultimate agent of enforcement.

The two distinctions cut across each other and, for any requirement of conduct, create four possibilities: A requirement may be privately suasively enforceable, suasively enforceable by the state, privately compellable, or compellable by the state. A further division within the category of the state's compulsory means must be noted, namely, between regulatory and criminal sanctions. A map of the resulting territory is shown in Table 2.

In what follows, I will argue that nothing can be a moral requirement unless it carries a permissible sanction that can be located somewhere in this matrix. I will then try to show that it is implausible that the state should be barred by moral principle from employing the means of enforcement available to private actors. This is, I think, readily shown where compulsory means are privately available. Where the only privately available means of enforcement are

standards do not carry the grave consequences of penal offenses." Louis Schwartz, "Morals Offenses and the Model Penal Code," 63 *Columbia Law Review* 669, 685 (1963).

suasive, however, complications arise. These have to do with the fact that the state often cannot occupy the special roles whose occupants are in many instances the only morally allowable voices of suasion and censure, and have also to do with the fact that in any event the state seldom confines itself to purely suasive means. Therefore, I will have to show that from a Millian standpoint the moral grounds that justify private suasive enforcement also justify some form of state regulatory enforcement. Finally, I will argue that regulatory and criminal enforcement cannot be distinguished in any way that would enable one to hold that there are moral requirements that the state may enforce by regulation but by no form of criminal sanction.

Chapter 8

The Moral and the Social

Are unenforceable moral requirements possible? It is normally true of moral requirements that transgressions will create in some other person a grievance. If, without excuse or justification, I break your nose, steal your bicycle, falsely slander your name, or fail to repay your loan to me, you have, at the least, a right to complain, a claim to some sort of correction, and perhaps a right to prevent further transgressions. These rights are personal to you; they may not be asserted by just anyone. But, as has long been known, some moral requirements do not entail correlative individual rights of rectification. Mill, for example, noted the currency of the terms "perfect" and "imperfect" to distinguish between duties that do and duties that do not entail a correlative individual right to compel performance.[1] More recently, Derek Parfit has given a vivid example of a wrong giving rise to no grievance. A couple know that if they have a child now there is a risk that it will have a defect, but that the risk will pass if they wait. The couple decide to have a child now rather than wait, or are careless and then decide not to induce an abortion. The child is born with a handicap that a later-born child would not have had; but of course the child that is born would not exist at all had its parents followed advice and waited. So long as the child's life is at least barely worth living, the child has no grievance against its parents for their conduct, nor has anyone else. Even so, the parents have acted not merely badly, but wrongly.[2]

Parfit's example shows that there are moral transgressions that do not involve an individual grievance, understood to be, at a minimum, a right to complain that one has been done a personal wrong.

---

[1] John Stuart Mill, *Utilitarianism,* Oskar Piest, ed., 61–2 (Indianapolis: Bobbs-Merrill, 1957) [hereafter, *Utilitarianism*].

[2] Derek Parfit, *Reasons and Persons* 357–61 (Oxford: Clarendon Press, 1984).

Invariably, however, a moral requirement incumbent on a given person carries with it a moral permission of some sort, on someone else's part, to persuade that person to comply; it also carries with it a moral permission on someone's part to remonstrate if the requirement is not observed. If some such morally permissible persuasion and chastisement were not carried along, it would be false, I claim, to suppose that the relevant moral requirement existed.

True, the "disagreeable consequences" of being discreetly disesteemed, unrecommended, shunned, and passed over might conceivably be *all* that morality permits to be visited upon those who violate certain moral requirements – leaving reproach, censure, and ridicule entirely to the actor's conscience. Mill seems to have thought that where morally permissible correction is so limited, what is at issue is not "social obligation," and that the correction itself does not express "moral disapprobation in the proper sense of the term."[3] But Mill's (like Bentham's) is "a distinctively *legalistic* view of the nature of morality," as Gerald Postema has put it.[4] Therefore, Mill can't be appealed to, without begging important questions, to settle the issues I have raised. Let me now put Mill's views aside and proceed to clarify and defend what I mean when I say that morality is social.

THE MORAL, THE SOCIAL, AND THE PERSONAL

The roles of moral education and social sanctions must have a large part in any account of morality. What David Falk called the "social ought" often tends to eclipse the "personal ought" in discussions of

---

[3] A baffling passage in Mill makes one wonder whether this fully states his view; in *Utilitarianism*, he wrote: "The idea of a penal sanction, which is the essence of law, enters not only into the conception of injustice, but into that of any kind of wrong. We do not call anything wrong, unless we mean to imply that a person ought to be punished in some way or other for doing it, if not by law, by the opinion of his fellow creatures; *if not by opinion, by the reproaches of his own conscience*" (*Id.* at 60 [emphasis added]). The concluding clause involves "a step of some magnitude," as H. L. A. Hart has noted (H. L. A. Hart, "Legal and Moral Obligation," in A. I. Melden, ed., *Essays in Moral Philosophy* 106–7 [Seattle: University of Washington Press, 1958]). Here, Mill may simply be adverting to linguistic evidence rather than to his own view. Mill elsewhere opines that the "internal sanction" of conscience is "not innate, but acquired," which suggests that he would have agreed that punishment by conscience is parasitic upon punishment by opinion. Mill may in fact have regarded the view I state here as too weak; for he seems to have believed that the performance of any genuine moral duty is compellable or, at least, that a person under a moral duty has no right to complain if she is compelled. See *Utilitarianism* at 60–1.

[4] In correspondence (emphasis his).

the nature of moral requirements, that is, the "moral ought." The moral ought has seemed to be more stringent than any merely personal ought because its grounds are typically social and its force sufficient to override merely personal interests or commitments. The personal ought, unlike the moral and the social, seems renounceable merely by renouncing the personally chosen aim to which it attaches. The moral ought, in contrast, is an ought "twice over," for it dictates ends categorically as it does means hypothetically. Moreover, the social ought alone seems to carry the doubly binding force of reason and sanction.[5]

Falk gave the social ought, as pretender to be the exclusive moral ought, its due by calling it the "primary concept of the moral bond" – but primary only in the genetic sense and not in the logical. Although social norms and sanctions – "smiles or frowns, approval or disapproval, the promise of bestowing or the threat of withdrawing love" – are indispensable introductions to morality, they are merely preparatory to "mature moral thinking," which he characterized as "conscientious ought-abidance" governed by the totality of reasons whether socially grounded or not. He wrote, "It is inconsistent with the concepts of mature moral thinking to keep looking for the differentia of the authority of the moral commitments in one's social answerability for observing them." In other words, only a morally immature person or culture would confound the authority of morality with the existence *vel non* of social sanctions. But mature moral reflection, though not a matter of submission to society's will, is attentive to its needs and "favorable to its purposes." This double aspect is responsible for disguising the fact that "there really is a level on which public demands and the apprehension of incurring social guilt are irrelevant to the authority of a commitment considered as 'moral' "[6]

Falk's insights are compatible with maintaining that moral requirements entail permissible social sanctions and that, in this sense, the moral – even the "maturely" so – is indeed essentially social. For it is one thing to point out, as Falk does, that the authority of moral requirements "owes nothing" to the social pressures that may (or may not) happen to back them; it is quite another to say that a moral requirement may be incumbent on one while all other moral

---

[5] David Falk, "Morality, Self, and Others," in H.-N. Castañeda and G. Nakhnikian, eds., *Morality and the Language of Conduct* 40–7 (Detroit: Wayne State University Press, 1965) [hereinafter, Falk].

[6] Falk at 56, 60, 61, 62.

agents are forbidden to counsel its observance and chastise its transgression. Admittedly, to try to discern what morality requires by discerning what society (or some part of it) might permissibly chastise would seem to put the cart before the horse. But, although the view I am defending is not generally committed to such a procedure, it would be rash to reject it as a useful heuristic. Sometimes we don't know how seriously we take our own approval of or aversion to various types of conduct until we address the issue of sanctions. Thought experiments like Joel Feinberg's notorious "bus" examples[7] force us to confront a dissonance in our thinking between, on the one hand, the belief that merely offensive conduct is not wrongful and, on the other, the belief that it is permissible to compel others not to perform intimate hygienic chores in the immediate presence of unwilling others. If we judge that it is permissible for others to compel one not to ϕ on the bus then we have evidence that it is wrongful for one to ϕ on the bus.

UNDETECTED, UNDETECTABLE, ISOLATED, AND INCORRIGIBLE WRONGDOERS

The present question is: How could there be a moral requirement whose omission did not expose the actor to permissible moral reproach? I claim that no moral requirement can exist outside a space of social enforcement. But wrongdoers sometimes manage to evade detection, and it is possible to imagine a wrongdoer able to evade all detection (think of the ring of Gyges in the *Republic*). Does my thesis lead to the absurd conclusion that the undetected or the undetectable wrong is no wrong at all? No, but I do have to state my view more carefully: The undetected and undetectable wrongdoers violate a moral requirement only if their conduct is of a type that is permissibly subject to social correction when detected. To reiterate, social corrigibility is not the *ground* of a moral requirement, but it is its necessary concomitant.

My thesis, that morality is social, does not entail that, for example, Robinson Crusoe on his desert isle is subject to no moral requirements. Crusoe may, in fact, have duties to the island, its wildlife, its natural formations, and to the ecosphere, consistently with the thesis I am defending. What is ruled out is the possibility that Crusoe is

---

[7]   Joel Feinberg, *Offense to Others*, vol. 2 of *The Moral Limits of the Criminal Law* 10–13 (New York: Oxford University Press, 1985).

subject to moral requirements that no one might permissibly censure, reprove, or ridicule him for violating. If it is, indeed, as Mary Midgley has written, "the business of each not to forget his transitory and dependent position, the rich gifts which he has received, and the tiny part he plays in a vast, irreplaceable and fragile whole," how can it not be the business of all, when necessary, to remind him?[8]

The claim that someone must have a moral permission to censure the transgression of a genuine moral requirement does not entail that there must exist a moral permission to do whatever may be necessary to monitor and detect transgressions. The moral limits to permissible inquiry are typically narrower than those to permissible response, and few things could be more repugnant than the idea of an unconsented moral permission to do whatever is necessary to learn the moral truth about another person. Consider the case of adultery. Because marital fidelity is a moral requirement, it follows, on the view I am defending, that someone other than the actor has a moral right to censure violations (subject to "standing" and proportionality norms I will describe in a moment). This does not entail that anyone – even the aggrieved spouse – is permitted to extract the actor's confession under torture, open his mail, monitor his telephone conversations, place him under surveillance, or interrogate his associates to *discover* a transgression or verify a suspected one.

Conceivably, there are moral requirements that no one, other than the actor, has a moral right to know he has violated. It is not implausible to think that there is a moral requirement that we not indulge in erotic fantasies about the torture of children. Even so, if there is any moral right to ascertain whether another's fantasies are of this nature, it is surely a very circumscribed one. But if the requirement not to fantasize in certain ways is in fact moral, then in my view it must follow that the actor's legitimately detected transgressions subject him to permissible censure, remonstrance, and ridicule from *some* quarter other than the inner voice of conscience.

Here is a possible counterexample: Suppose a (visible) gunman is holding a number of innocent people hostage. Past experience tells us that any effort to persuade him to release his captives will cause him to kill them all instantly. Here, it seems true both that (a) the gunman is morally required to release the hostages, and (b) it would be morally impermissible for anyone to attempt to persuade the gun-

---

[8] Mary Midgley, "The Vulnerable World and Its Claims on Us," 39 *The Georgia Review* 739, 752–3 (1985).

man to do so.[9] How, then, can I maintain that a moral requirement always entails a permission to persuade the actor to comply?

Should I say, instead, that a genuine moral requirement entails *at least* a permission to persuade? In this case, more forceful affirmative measures to assure the safety of the hostages would surely be permissible even though, due to the touchy disposition of the wrongdoer, suasion and remonstrance would not. But the objector will avoid this reply by stipulating that the gunman will kill all the hostages instantly if anyone ever attempts anything – force, suasion, cajolery, *anything* – to cause him to comply with morality's requirement that he free the hostages. "Gee!" one now wants to say, "What kind of guy is this?!" The answer is that we are dealing with a *sociopath*, whom we ought not to regard as a moral agent in the full sense, and who is no more properly describable as being subject to moral requirements than a killer tornado would be. This knockdown counterexample fails.

Unfortunately, the thickets of moral catastrophe are not so readily avoidable, as the following variation shows. The sociopath is a Fagan who supervises the unwitting wrongdoing of a young Oliver, who does not know any better. Fagan credibly threatens to destroy humankind altogether if anyone so much as suggests to young Oliver that what he is doing is wrong. Here is a genuine case in which (a) Oliver is morally required to cease his wrongoing, and (b) it would be morally impermissible for anyone to attempt to persuade him to do so. Just as any proposed deontological constraint is subject to moral catastrophe counterexamples, so also is any deontological permission, including the one I am discussing. Adjusted accordingly, my claim is that any violation of a moral requirement entails a prima facie permission on someone's part to censure, remonstrate with, or ridicule the wrongdoer. But notice that only this rather outré example was capable of forcing a qualification. This, I think, exhibits, rather than undermines, the importance of the necessary permission I have identified.

There are limits to permissible private suasion and chastisement, of course, and these may be more stringent where it is less than obvious what morality requires or whether a moral requirement is at issue. As Falk put the point, "To say 'you ought to' to another is always a kind of interference; and the propriety of *saying so* (as dis-

---

[9] I owe this example to Steve Rieber. Julia Driver poses a similar case in her "The Suberogatory," 70 *Australasian Journal of Philosophy* 286, 291 (1992).

tinct from having a judgement about it) varies with the case."[10] For example, even those who think it obvious that a pregnant woman is morally required to take care to avoid doing harm to her unborn child would admit that they are constrained from offering unsolicited advice to her about her smoking or drinking.[11] In a case like this, comment may properly come only from those who are specially related to her – parent, sibling, child, doctor, spouse, lover, or a close-enough friend. (Sometimes legitimate detectors of a transgression are not permissible remonstrators – hence gossip and scandal to close the circuit.) In the event that it is evident no such person exists, or that such persons are unwilling to give counsel, then it must be morally permissible, and only seemingly presumptuous, for a stranger to comment.

Any decent moral regime will mandate moral limits to social pressure, as Ferdie Schoeman stressed. Given the mutual vulnerability between actors that morality essentially entails, unless such limits exist, the individual personality would be inappropriately at the mercy of social pressures. It is clear that where a violation of another's *rights* is concerned, social pressure and even compulsion are allowable, subject to norms of standing and proportionality. "Standing" norms limit and order the range of those who may appropriately complain – if I forget to return a borrowed item, the lender may complain but a stranger to the transaction may not. The lender may scold me or, if necessary, file suit, but she may not cane me for this transgression because proportionality norms limit what may be done to enforce this moral requirement.

My claim is that a moral requirement of a given actor presupposes the existence of some other or others that at least potentially have a sufficient interest in what she does to have a right to tell her what they think. The moral standing and proportionality norms that apply in given circumstances and in various types of case can be expected to vary in stringency, but they may never leave an omission immune from reproof. Moreover, the necessarily permissible suasion and remonstrance must be of a recognizably moral strain – they must be consistent with the assumption that they are licensed by the fact that a moral requirement of the actor is at issue. Therefore, the "sufficient interest" on another's part has to be understood as restricted to a

---

[10]   Falk at 56 (emphasis in original).
[11]   I owe this example to the late Ferdie Schoeman; see, generally, Ferdinand David Schoeman, *Privacy and Social Freedom* (Cambridge: Cambridge University Press, 1992).

subset of that other's legitimate interests, that is, to those interests that are implicated because the actor's performance of some moral *requirement* is at stake. "Sufficient interest" does not encompass the larger set of legitimate interests containing what would suit the other's preferences on some other ground, or what would comport with the other's notions of what would merely be ideal or *commendable*.

Consider this example: Suppose I am walking down the street and pass a blind man. He has dropped his cane and is groping for it. Although it would cost me nothing to help him, I step around him and over his cane and proceed on my way. I was observed at a distance by a person whom I now pass. If I was morally required to give assistance (as I think I obviously was) and the facts of the situation are evident to the onlooker, I think the onlooker is entitled to say something like this: "I saw what you did. It was rotten of you not to help. How would you like it if you were in his shoes?" (Or "What if everybody were as callous as you?") Even though there is a presumptive moral standing requirement not to offer unwelcome comment to strangers on the street, the onlooker acts properly if, but only if, the interest he takes is in my inexcusable omission of a moral requirement. He would, on the other hand, be a merely officious intermeddler if he were to say, "I saw what you did and I just didn't like it. It didn't please me at all," or "Excuse me, but what you just did was hardly commendable. I don't mean that sarcastically, because I don't think you were morally required to do otherwise. You were, in fact, morally free to do what you did – but I don't commend you for it."

One might say, "What's *wrong* with officiously intermeddling if the onlooker has a *right* to free speech?" In other words, it might seem that because the onlooker may not be *compelled* to be quiet, there is nothing wrong with his speaking his mind *whether or not* what he is commenting on is my failure to meet a moral requirement. But this is an error. This description of the case depends upon the false assumption that what the onlooker does is wrong only if his silence is compellable. Moral standing requirements, which are in their turn subject to proportionality requirements, are not normally permissible to enforce by compulsion. But they are enforceable by censure and remonstrance – sternly so in a proper case.

This is, of course, not to deny that in many cases strangers do no wrong by offering unwelcome comment on an actor's performance – but I doubt that this is such a case. Why? Because the closer we come to being understood as making a moral point, the stronger the moral stricture against offering merely casual comment becomes. The stranger's gratuitous opinion as to whether or not a pop fly went foul is tolerable even if careless; but if he wants to opine as to which of two strangers was next in line at the grocery checkout, he'd better be sure of his ground. This is because there is an issue of fault in the air. My not having helped the blind man is neither a small matter *nor* is it none of the stranger's business – it is a moral matter. Even so, we need not say that the blind man has a *right* to my assistance. If I have a right to do the wrong I have done here, the blind man cannot complain that I have violated a right of his; but it is nonetheless a *wrong* that I have done.[12] If it is not wrongful then – *judge* me as you will – it is no one's business to *censure* me.

THE "SUBEROGATORY"

The blind man example is worth looking at as a potential member of the category of the "suberogatory" that Julia Driver has described.[13] The suberogatory is the realm of the bad, but not wrong; of nice things that it would be praiseworthy to do (or omit) but not necessarily blamable to omit (or do). Declining to return a favor on a certain occasion may be merely bad; so also refusing to donate a kidney to a twin, who otherwise will die; so also, perhaps, having a frivolous abortion or destroying a piano for amusement. These are cases in which failing to do good is not morally forbidden, analogously to the more discussed case of the *super*erogatory, where doing good is not morally required. The wrongful is what opens the actor to permissible censure, while the merely bad only opens the actor to being thought ill of and, of course, to the "reproaches" of conscience, such as they may be.

We can now distinguish four categories of conduct: the unjust, which is grievance-creating; the wrongful, which though not necessarily grievance-creating does expose the actor to permissible reproach, censure, and ridicule; the merely bad, which does not necessarily open the actor to any more than self-reproach and the discreet ill-judgment of others; and the innocent. The line between the wrongful and the merely bad may seem evanescent, but it explains some moral phenomena that are not otherwise easy to account for. In

[12] See Jeremy Waldron, "A Right To Do Wrong," 92 *Ethics* 21–39 (1981).
[13] Julia Driver, "The Suberogatory," 70 *Australasian Journal of Philosophy* 286 (1992).

particular, it explains why the onlooker may censure my failing to help the blind man, but he may not censure my failure to give a nearby beggar twenty dollars; and in neither case may the blind man and the beggar justly complain that *I* have violated their rights (although the beggar's condition, if destitute, may very well represent a rights violation of another sort).[14] My failing to help the beggar is, if anything, merely bad. The duty of beneficence does not require me to help everyone I can on every occasion. It is praiseworthy if I do so on this occasion, but not wrongful if I don't. It is either innocent (because I have discharged the duty in other ways) or merely bad (because I haven't and perhaps won't).

This division is somewhat overlapping, and pigeonholing particular act-types is subject to a degree of cultural variation. What may seem wrongful to the man or woman on the street in Seattle or Berlin may be merely bad in Berkeley and perhaps innocent in New York. To harken back to an earlier example, Mr. Robinson from Chapter 1 violates a standing norm if my crossing the street against the light is innocent or merely bad; he does not if it is wrongful or unjust. The point to be taken here is that our standing norms reflect the fact that conduct that is wrongful, that is, contrary to a moral requirement, opens us to moral censure in a way that merely bad conduct does not.

SELF-CONCERNING DUTIES

There seems to be a category of moral requirements – call them *self-concerning duties* – that by their very nature legitimately concern the actor only. I use the term "self-concerning duty" rather than the more familiar term, "self-*regarding* duty" because the latter tends to confuse matters. Clarity is served by replacing the latter with a trio of terms: a "self-concerning" duty is one whose omission legitimately concerns no one other than the actor who is bound; a "self-*directed*" duty is one having as its aim the improvement of the actor or her lot; a "self-*grounded*" duty is one whose basis lies in the nature of the actor herself. None of these three types is necessarily correlated with a right to complain, or *grievance*, on another's part if they are omit-

---

[14] Joel Feinberg speaks of such claims as stating rights only in a "manifesto sense." Joel Feinberg, "The Nature and Value of Rights," 4 *The Journal of Value Inquiry* 243, 254–5 (1970).

ted. In this respect they are alike. The terminology offered here makes it possible to pose the question whether self-directed or self-grounded duties may be self-concerning.

Many would claim that there is a moral duty to respect oneself. Thomas Hill has argued that certain servile personalities – which he calls the Uncle Tom, the Self-Deprecator, and the Deferential Wife – violate this duty.[15] Persons who without good reason denigrate their own moral status transgress a requirement of morality. This duty of self-respect does not share all of the logical features that other types of duty have. Unlike transgressions of the duty to respect others, transgressions of the duty to respect oneself do not necessarily entail another's right to demand that one respect oneself (although they might if the actor's servility sufficiently diminished the respect accorded, say, her child or parent). The person who violates her duty of self-respect cannot idiomatically be said to violate her correlative right to insist that she respect herself. But these disanalogies do not refute the position that the duty of self-respect is a genuine moral duty and figures prominently in a category of duties to oneself that can be coherently defined.

The duty of self-respect is one that can be classified as both self-directed and self-grounded. The actor owes the duty *to* herself in the sense that she especially stands to gain if the duty is met. She owes it to herself also in the sense that *her* personhood is the source of the duty. But is this a self-*concerning* duty in the sense I have isolated? Is it, in other words, a duty whose omission at least sometimes legitimately concerns no one other than the actor herself? Hill does not address our question, but does make this suggestive observation:

> To say that the duty to avoid servility is a duty to oneself would indicate that, though sometimes a person may justifiably reproach himself for being servile, others are not *generally* in the appropriate position to complain. Outside encouragement is *sometimes* necessary, but, if any blame is called for, it is *primarily* self-recrimination and not the censure of others. (My italics.)[16]

If the duty of self-respect is a moral requirement whose omission *ever* concerns the actor alone, then it stands as disproof of my thesis

---

15 Thomas E. Hill, Jr., "Servility and Self-Respect," 57 *Monist* 87 (1973), reprinted in his *Autonomy and Self-Respect* (Cambridge: Cambridge University Press, 1991) [hereinafter, Hill].

16 Ibid. at 102.

that there are no self-concerning duties. But is this what it is? Resolving this issue is complicated by the fact that a breach of the duty of self-respect normally involves a pattern of conduct, rather than a one-off instance. Some duties are breachable straight away – my single failure to return a borrowed item is a breach of duty to do so – but others aren't. My occasional (posttenure) bowing and scraping before a despised senior colleague may or may not violate my duty of nonservility. Surely, another who upbraids me for my servility must have a pattern, rather than a single instance, in view. Let us suppose that this is what is present. Should we say that servility is wrongful or that it is merely bad? In other words, is the servile person one who is entitled to be left alone to reproach himself, suffering only the discreetly unspoken adverse judgment of those who perceive his vice? Or does he open himself to permissible censure and reproof at the hands of some suitably positioned other?

I think it would trivialize the duty of self-respect to classify its breach as an instance of the suberogatory, or what I have been calling the merely bad. Notice that the servile person, as Hill imagines her, may be perfectly happy in the subjective sense of the word – contented, cheerful, even in command of an impressive rationale purporting to justify her subordinate station in the scheme of things. If there is a permission to point out her moral flaw it can't be explained by an overriding duty to help relieve suffering. Her suffering may, in fact, only begin with the forced realization of her vice. Suppose that, despite the encouragement of others, the Deferential Wife insists on adopting her husband's views and tastes in all things, or the Uncle Tom persists in counting himself a grateful member of an inferior race, and that neither is disposed to self-recrimination on this score. It would seem to me that either their conduct is censurable by others or it is not contrary to a moral requirement.

A PRIVATE MORALITY IMAGINED

It is difficult to understand how morality can both impose a genuine requirement of conduct and insulate the actor from the only independent means of knowing that and how her conduct varies from what is required. This would be less mysterious if morality or some part of it were not imposed on us at all, but chosen. Certainly the duty of self-respect is not a chosen duty – those who reject it in favor of, say, a duty of self-abasement are not thereby freed of it. But duties are quite commonly the product of choices. I may have a duty to pay you five dollars because I have chosen to buy your Mel Tormé recording and there is a general (unchosen) duty to perform contractual promises, for instance. Of course, this chosen duty is not a self-concerning one; I owe *you* the five dollars. But why could there not be a chosen duty that was self-concerning? Why could I not tailor the duty so that I was answerable for violating it only to what Holmes (misleadingly) called "the vaguer sanctions" of my own conscience?

The difficulty with the idea of a wholly self-concerning moral requirement is not vagueness – for it needn't be any vaguer than the most precise requirement of social morality. The problem is epistemic, and what vagueness there may be aggravates this. The epistemic problem is that if social enforcement is impermissible then there is to that extent no way for the actor to know whether she is doing what is required or merely thinking she is. Working out the hypothesis that there is a self-concerning moral requirement that such-and-such is not so very different from trying to imagine the world-view of a tribe, one of whose tabus is *"Never* correct what anyone says." Unless such a tribe were fantastically lucky, its worldview would be hopelessly indeterminate even to itself. The problem is thus not merely epistemic – it has ontological import, for what we can't imagine coming to *know* is *pro tanto* what we can't meaningfully assert to *be*. A "private language" of morals is as incoherent as one of sensations, or interior beetles-in-boxes. "It makes no more sense to suppose we invent the moral law for ourselves," as Gerald Dworkin has put it, "than to suppose that we invent the language we speak for ourselves."[17]

Suppose I commit myself to pursue some high aspiration that is, from the standpoint of social morality, entirely supererogatory. Although I fulfill whatever duties of beneficence social morality imposes, I resolve to do more. Let me make the aspiration as concrete as possible: I resolve to spend one morning each week working in a homeless shelter. Assume that I am able to do this in a way that creates no legitimate expectation that I will continue in it – the requirement is entirely self-concerning. One morning I oversleep and real-

---

[17] Gerald Dworkin, *The Theory and Practice of Autonomy* 36 (Cambridge: Cambridge University Press, 1988). Compare also Ludwig Wittgenstein, *Philosophical Investigations*, G. E. M. Anscombe, trans. 3d ed., ¶¶ 94e–100e (New York: Macmillan, 1958), and G. W. F. Hegel, *Phenomenology of Mind*, J. B. Baillie, trans., rev. ed., 149–60 (New York: Harper, 1967).

ize that seven mornings have elapsed since my last appearance at the shelter. Have I violated my requirement? If so, will my working two mornings during the coming week fulfill the commitment or will it merely correct a failure? If the former, may I, without violating my commitment, wait until the end of the month and do three mornings work over a long holiday? If that is permissible, may I liquidate my commitment by writing a check at the end of the year to the shelter, to enable it to hire someone to do what I would have done as a volunteer worker?

I think it is obvious that, if the matter concerns me and me only, I am not only free to reinterpret my self-imposed requirement to suit my present pleasure, I am condemned to do so because I am in no position to know whether I have done what I was required to do or simply replaced the requirement with another. (For that matter, *did* I commit myself, or did I merely propose to investigate what it might be like to labor under such a commitment?) The drift needn't be in the direction of laxity. I might make the discovery that much of a morning's work at the shelter consists of socializing, and I might begin to wonder whether I am required to stay longer to make sure I am doing a full morning's-worth of work. In doubt, I resolve to stay longer. But is this now personally supererogatory with respect to my already socially supererogatory undertaking? Unless the requirement is opened to another's view I have no way of knowing whether I am keeping faith or merely thinking I am.

Surely, one wants to say, I can discuss this with someone without thereby violating the hypothesized self-concerning nature of the moral requirement. But it won't do to say that a wholly self-concerning moral transgression might be corrected by another *on the actor's request only.* This would leave it wholly up to me whether the present occasion was one as to which a detached opinion was necessary, and, again, its being needed would collapse into my thinking it so. Therefore, to enlist another to serve effectively as a check, I must open myself to comment, criticism, and censure from another on terms beyond my control. But now, notice, we are already close to giving up on the idea of a wholly self-concerning moral requirement. Even though the supposed requirement flows solely from *my* commitment to *my* ideal – and is thus entirely self-directed and self-grounded as I have defined these terms – it cannot be wholly self-*concerning* without threatening to lose all shape.

But, assuming that the need to surrender control is granted, does this show that my éminence grise has an *interest* in my observing my ideal? It does not. But, because it does not, I am worse off both motivationally and epistemically than I would be if another *did* have an interest in my commitment to an ideal. Think of quitting smoking. Our neo-Puritanism is not so ascendant, yet, that anyone could claim that not smoking, *tout court,* is morally required. Those with close associates and dependents may be morally required to limit their smoking or quit because of other, more general moral principles. But suppose I owe it to no one else to quit. Whatever interests there are – my own and others' – are not sufficient, let's suppose, to impose upon me a moral requirement that I stop smoking. Nonetheless, upon mature reflection I resolve to pursue an ideal of good health and, thereby, impose upon myself a moral requirement to quit or cut down. Here, my ideal seems clear enough to free me from the need for social reinforcement. But what does pursuit of good health *require,* once I have made it my socially supererogatory ideal? Does it require cold-turkey absolute abstinence, or that and more? Or is what I've required of myself simply the quitting, which must be absolute, and is neither in need of supplementation by other health measures (exercise, diet, medical checkups) nor compensable by any?

If my ideal of health requires simply and only what I from time to time think it requires, it seems to trivialize the moral to insist that what is involved here is a moral requirement. But if I were to endow another with an interest – say, I promise my spouse or a colleague that I will quit – that makes the door to the moral swing open in a way that even a litany of the solemnest private vows cannot. The other of course needn't be said to have a *claim* in order to have an interest in what I do that brings it into public light sufficiently to give it a shape that would otherwise remain hopelessly inchoate. Kant, the most determined champion of duties to oneself, saw that they "consist . . . in guarding, each in our own person, the dignity of mankind. A man will only reproach himself if he has the idea of mankind before his eyes. In this idea he finds an original, with which he compares himself." To suggest that that ideal of mankind might be maintained in isolation from the possible reproaches of others ignores Kant's admonition that "while we should make ourselves a fixed center of our principles, we should regard the circle thus drawn around us as one that also forms the all-inclusive circle of those who, in their attitude, are citizens of the world." Whether we begin with an idea of morality as originating in social convention, or as originating in a "self-regarding" duty to perfect one's own soul, we cannot in the end surrender or deny its essentially social dimension.[18]

Morality, I have argued, is social in the sense that by transgressing its requirements we render ourselves censurable, even fit for ridicule by others. Nietzsche – no friend, as Brian Leiter puts it, of morality "in the pejorative sense" – in fact complained of "the moral judgment" that it is the "chief means" by which the "weak and mediocre . . . weaken and pull down the stronger."[19] But, as Annette Baier has said, "*No* version of morality will work unless we keep ourselves more or less equally vulnerable to the same sorts of wounds."[20] Morality itself imposes limits, as we have noticed, to the permissible means of social enforcement, and this raises the question whether, within those limits, there is an additional moral limit that debars the state from employing the very same means available to some private person. This question is the subject of the following chapter.

---

[18] Immanuel Kant, *The Doctrine of Virtue* VI 473/145 and *Education* IX 489/103. These quotations are taken from Robert B. Louden, *Morality and Moral Theory* 18 (New York: Oxford University Press, 1992). Citations are to the German Akademic edition.

[19] Friedrich Nietzsche, *The Will to Power* ¶ 345, Walter Kaufmann and R. J. Hollingdale, trans. (New York: Vintage, 1968); and see, generally, Brian Leiter, "Nietzsche and the Morality Critics," 107 *Ethics* 250–85 (1997).

[20] Annette C. Baier, "Moralism and Cruelty: Reflections on Hume and Kant," 103 *Ethics* 436, 453 (1993) (emphasis added). See also P. M. S. Hacker, "Sanction Theories of Duty," in A. W. B. Simpson, ed., *Oxford Essays in Jurisprudence (Second Series)* 131–70 (Oxford: Clarendon Press, 1973).

Chapter 9

The Social and the Political

Are there moral requirements whose permissible means of enforcement are not available to the state? Some things that are morally required of an actor are such that it is morally permissible for properly situated others to *compel* her compliance. The law is shaped by a recognition that in some instances what would otherwise be a battery, or worse, is justifiable by the fact that the would-be defendant acted to enforce a moral requirement, for example, the moral requirement that the would-be complainant refrain from violating the defendant's moral right to bodily integrity or property. This is sometimes explained by reference to what would be permissible in a state of nature. However we regard the matter, there are, as far as I can see, no instances of privately compellable moral requirements that are not permissibly legally enforceable. Here is a possible example: Suppose that all children are morally required to obey their parents' reasonable bedtime rules, and suppose that the parents may physically compel the child's compliance. It could be argued that this requirement is strongly delegalized because legal intervention would violate moral principles that protect the integrity of the family.

This example would be worrisome if it presented a genuine example of a moral *requirement,* but I don't think it does. Children are relatively deficient in knowledge and judgment. This is why their parents are entitled to make special rules for them until they are of "suitable age and discretion." But this very same immaturity makes it odd to say that children are morally required to follow these rules; a child does not breach a duty or ignore a moral obligation when it ignores them. Not everything that is permissibly compellable is a *moral* requirement incumbent upon the person who may permissibly be compelled.

Another example: A distraught mother begins to spank a young child. Assume that corporal punishment in this context is morally wrong but does not threaten physical or serious emotional harm to the child. The father points out the impropriety but the mother persists. The father, aware that the mother's severity is the product of other concerns by which she has been overwhelmed, gently restrains the mother and separates her from the child long enough to calm her. Here, the father has physically compelled the mother to comply with the relevant moral requirement, but principles of family integrity seem to exclude any state agent's taking similar steps.[1]

This example, I think, trades on several ambiguities. We have to imagine that the harm the mother is doing is sufficient to render what she does wrongful, yet not wrong enough to constitute serious abuse. It is true that in many cases of this sort we feel that strangers to the situation cannot be sufficiently attuned to its nuances to be able to distinguish ragged-appearing discipline from abuse. But it is also true that an overwrought parent may not be the best judge on certain occasions! The composed father seems ideally suited to know whether the child is being wronged and whether intervention with gentle force is necessary. But if the father is absent or indifferent, I cannot agree that a more distant relative, a family friend, and a state-employed social worker – assuming each to be legitimately present in the home – would be morally foreclosed from using the same measured degree of gentle force.

Remember that what we have assumed is that the mother's use of force against the child is *wrongful*. Making this assumption without vividly painting its grounds leaves us with two sorts of doubts that occlude our judgment. The first has to do with the wrongness of the mother's conduct: Does it flow from an assumed categorical moral truth that corporal punishment is always wrongful, or from other facts and principles? Note also that abuse (like servility) is as much a matter of patterns as of one-off occurrences: Is this spanking wrongful because part of a pattern or wrongful in itself? The second doubt has to do with the presumably vast difference between the mother's knowledge of the child, its susceptibilities, dispositions, and so forth, and anyone else's. Both mother and father, we tend to assume, are vastly superior interpreters of their child's and each other's needs

---

[1] I owe this example to George Rainbolt. Compare D. Olds, J. Eckenrode, C. Henderson, et al., "Long-Term Effects of Home Visitation on Maternal Life Course and Child Abuse and Neglect," 278 *Journal of the American Medical Association* 637–43 (1997), reporting that nurse home-visit programs bring about significantly lower rates of child abuse in disadvantaged homes and improve a range of other outcomes as well.

and tolerances. This, I think, is what inclines us to believe that the father can detect a wrong to the child in the situation better than anyone else, and that he also can tailor the use of force upon the mother to keep it within bounds. It is one thing to say that it is best that the father intervene, and quite another to say that only he may. The example trades on our predisposition to believe the former, but it cannot show the latter.

I can think of no significantly different examples, and so I conclude that any moral requirement that is enforceable by private compulsion is permissibly enforceable by some legal compulsory means. The law exists, after all, to eliminate the hazards of a regime of private enforcement, and the law achieves this end by presuming largely to monopolize compulsory means, as Hobbes and Locke explain. There are in fact many moral requirements that the state and *only the state* may permissibly enforce by compulsion, for example, paying taxes, ceasing public nuisances. The argument that this monopoly is itself wrongful was examined and dismissed in Part Two.

There are, however, many moral requirements whose performance may not be compelled by any private person. The blind man example in Chapter 8 is a probable instance. The onlooker may permissibly chastise me, but he may not lay hands on me, drag me back, and force me to retrieve the blind man's cane. The question then becomes, are there suasive means of enforcement that the state may not permissibly pursue, even though some private person may? It seems to me that there are not, but the issue is obscured by the fact that the state rarely is in a position to offer personalized moral advice, and it seldom contents itself with doing so. Because the state cannot in principle occupy certain roles, such as spouse, parent, or friend, its morally permissible suasive efforts seem to be seriously curtailed. Therefore it will be necessary to explore the question: Are there moral requirements that, though subject to permissible private suasive enforcement, are not proper subjects of legal enforcement?

MANY GRADES OF LEGAL INVOLVEMENT

Law affects conduct in multifarious ways. Like it or not, "We live in and by the law," as Ronald Dworkin has reminded us,

> It makes us what we are: citizens and employees and doctors and spouses and people who own things . . . we insist on our wage, or refuse to pay our rent, or are forced to forfeit penalties, or are closed

up in jail, all in the name of what our abstract and ethereal sovereign, the law, has decreed.[2]

The paradigm instance of a legal requirement is a criminal statute that makes certain conduct punishable by imprisonment. But statutes impose fines as well as confinement, and taxes as well as fines. Paying these is a legal requirement. And the criminal law concerns not only what statutes prescribe, but also sentencing once a violation is proven. The defendant whose sentence may be enhanced for failure to show remorse after the fact is, in a perfectly natural sense, being legally required to show remorse.[3] And the criminal law is not the whole of the law. Civil courts order contracts to be performed, property to be handed over, money to be paid, and children to be given up by their parents. To the extent that helping out with the dishes and abstaining from profanity may properly affect the result in a child custody suit, there is an attenuated sense in which these things are legally required.

This messiness means that the *delegalization thesis*, that strongly delegalized moral requirements exist, can be held in various forms. A moderate form is the thesis that certain moral requirements may not permissibly be enforced by threats of imprisonment or of corporal or capital punishment. An extreme form is the thesis that certain moral requirements are strongly delegalized "all the way down"; that is, certain moral requirements have no business affecting any legal outcome insofar as conformity with that outcome is compellable. I will explore the extreme and moderate views in turn.

THE EXTREME DELEGALIZATION THESIS

The extreme form of the thesis is not very plausible. What facts about a moral requirement would show that its affecting any legal result would violate a moral principle, that is, some other moral requirement? Facts about individual autonomy and integrity come to mind. Consider the man who fails to help the blind man recover his cane. He acts selfishly and in a way that merits censure, one might argue, but visiting legal consequences would impermissibly impinge upon his autonomy. This answer is unsatisfactory because it appeals to the

---

[2] Ronald Dworkin, *Law's Empire* vii (Cambridge, Mass.: Harvard University Press, 1986).

[3] See my "Liberalism, Legal Decision Making, and Morality 'As Such,'" 10 *Oxford Journal of Legal Studies* 505 (1990).

very boundary that is at issue. Surely the man's conduct would be proper to consider in some legal contexts such as a child custody proceeding or a parole hearing – and, if considered, it might very well determine the outcome.

Another example: the expectant mother who smokes and drinks despite the risk to her unborn child. A defender of the extreme view could argue that just as a stranger could not properly comment on her conduct, the state may not attach consequences to it. This position appeals to an analogy between the state and the officious intermeddler, while implicitly rejecting analogies between the state and those in special roles, such as the physician. Unless this selective use of analogy can be supported, it is question begging. Such support seems unlikely, and in any case it is implausible to suggest that the woman's conduct could not permissibly be taken into account in deciding, for example, her fitness to be a custodial parent or her entitlement to recover damages against a tobacco company or distiller for injuries to her own health. Of course the weight such facts should be given in isolation may be slight, but it is hard to imagine a moral barrier to their being weighed at all that is not also a barrier to thinking them contrary to a moral requirement.

Here is another possible example. I am morally required to show my wife that I love her. (The love I have for her is itself not morally required for the reason that it is not within my power to love and not love.) It may at first seem a bit much to suggest that the state might permissibly require me to show the love I feel. But until recently "mental cruelty" was (and in some jurisdictions still is) grounds for divorce, and judges in family courts today routinely adopt and modify custody decrees with a view toward encouraging estranged parents to cultivate and express what warm feelings for each other that remain, if only for their children's sakes.[4]

The extreme position is defensible only if at least one of the following two propositions is true: (a) legal correction is per se oppressive of liberty or autonomy in a way that private correction is not, or (b) legal correction, though not different in kind from private correction, is in fact always more oppressive. But neither is true. Legal correction can be very mild. The "lingering death" imposed for various

---

[4]   See, e.g., *Linda R. v Richard E.*, 561 N.Y.S.2d 29 (App. Div. 1990), where Dad's inability to acknowledge Mom's contribution to Kids' upbringing cost him custody, and cf. *Quiner v Quiner*, 59 Cal. Rptr. 503 (Ct. Apps. 1967), where the court ordered Mom, as a condition of having custody of Kid, not to say bad things about Dad. George Rainbolt forced me to deal with this example.

offenses in imperial China stands at the opposite extreme from, for example, the five-dollar parking ticket or the five mil sales tax. But each is an example of an exaction imposed by a legal system, a legal requirement. Moral suasion and remonstrance, on the other hand, can be very hard. The sermon on hell in *A Portrait of the Artist As a Young Man* is a good example of the extremes to which moral suasion can be carried, and *The Scarlet Letter* of the extreme possibilities of remonstrance.[5] I find it difficult to believe that imposing a fine of five dollars for each failure to render aid to the blind man in circumstances like those described is *inherently* more offensive to one's liberty, autonomy, or privacy than the suasion and remonstrance that is licensed in virtue of the fact that one has acted contrary to a moral requirement. A violator might well prefer to pay the five dollars and be spared the "moral reprobation . . . retribution and punishment" of which Mill spoke.[6]

It could be argued that legal correction fails to respect the agent as an autonomous being, unlike private suasive correction, which essentially constitutes an appeal to the agent in her capacity as rational chooser. This argument proves too much if it means that the threat of legal correction precludes free choice. Anyone who has ever driven on a highway knows this to be false. Moreover, it is unclear why a criminal statute cannot be understood to be both an appeal to the citizen's moral sense and a threat. As Mill points out, moral suasion may involve "moral reprobation . . . retribution and punishment," without ceasing to be an appeal to us in our capacity as rational actors.

Perhaps it could be argued that although the fine may not be so oppressive as to preclude free choice, it is inherently more objectionable than suasion because the actor cannot exercise virtue – or act morally in a Kantian sense – by complying with the threat the fine represents. Insofar as this objection involves an appeal to the authority of Kant, Barbara Herman has shown that it is far from clear that Kant's view rules out any moral worth of the ordinary run of actions

---

[5] Hester Prynne was of course *legally* required to wear the scarlet letter but, in itself, the letter was only marginally more burdensome than the garment to which it was sewn. The efficacy of legal punishment depended on its stimulating private means of enforcement that would in perhaps lesser degree have been used anyway. There are indications in the text that the legal punishment forestalled even more drastic private measures.

[6] If the addition of the fine and moral reproof were to exceed a due proportion between crime and punishment, then a downward adjustment would, of course, be in order – but this nicety does not deflect the point made in the text.

performed with mixed motives of duty and inclination, much less need it disparage the moral virtue of those acting on such motives.[7] In any case, the appeal to autonomy misfires as an objection to the view I am defending; for if an actor's conduct is morally worthy only to the extent that her choice is unaffected (consciously or otherwise) by its consequences for her, why should it matter whether the constraining consequences are legal or merely social in nature?

AN APPEAL TO NEUTRALITY

Another response here is an appeal to the *neutrality thesis*, namely, the thesis that the state acts illegitimately if it seeks to impose a particular conception of the good upon those who might reasonably disagree. The idea is that the inner sphere of morality is governed by controversial conceptions of the good, while the outer sphere is governed by public values no reasonable person could reject. The neutrality thesis has been advocated in one form or another by a number of contemporary political philosophers, John Rawls most notably.

Drawing upon the idea that there is a diversity of goods that persons in the free exercise of their moral powers might reasonably choose to pursue ("the fact of reasonable pluralism"), the fact that moral judgment is ineluctably hindered when our limited intelligences confront the complexity of human affairs ("the burdens of judgment"), and the presumed coercive nature of the state,[8] Rawls derives both the "Liberal Principle of Legitimacy" – constraining the exercise of political power (and examined in Part Two) – and also a "duty of civility":

> Since the exercise of political power itself must be legitimate, the ideal of citizenship imposes a moral, not a legal, duty – the duty of civility – to be able to explain to one another on . . . fundamental questions how the principles and policies they advocate and vote for can be supported by the political values of public reason.[9]

Rawls's neutrality idea thus comprises two components: a moral

---

[7]   Barbara Herman, "On the Value of Acting from the Motive of Duty," 90 *Philosophical Review* 359–82 (1981).

[8]   Rawls also invokes what he calls the "fact of oppression," namely, the fact that no comprehensive doctrine could possibly attain universal assent without the application of coercive state power. John Rawls, *Political Liberalism* 37 (New York: Columbia University Press, 1993) [hereafter, *Political Liberalism*].

[9]   *Political Liberalism* at 137, 216–17.

principle circumscribing the legitimate exercise of state power, and a separate principle defining a moral duty incumbent upon all citizens of the just (or nearly just) state. The Liberal Principle of Legitimacy defines what the state may properly do; the duty of civility delimits what citizens may properly ask the state to do.

The key notion is that of the "political values of public reason." It is contrasted to what Rawls terms "comprehensive philosophical doctrines." His view is that in a liberal society there will always be an ineliminable (and ever proliferating) plurality of conflicting comprehensive religious, moral, and philosophical doctrines that citizens will naturally be tempted to try to impose upon one another (directly or indirectly) through the political process. Although no such doctrine can count as "reasonable" if it rejects the idea of democracy, all relevant comprehensive doctrines will encompass tenets that, though reasonable for adherents to hold, nonadherents might reasonably reject. Therefore, the dynamics of political life would be unstable, and the liberal state would tend to delegitimate itself, unless political discourse were confined to positions that can be defended with reference to a core of ideas that Rawls calls "the political values of public reason." As long as these values enjoy an "overlapping consensus" of support from the diverse, competing, comprehensive (and reasonable) doctrines represented in society, the problem of stability is manageable.[10]

What are these "political values of public reason"? Whereas nonpublic reason may make an appeal to what is "right and true" without limitation, the content of public reason is a set of substantive principles of justice and "guidelines of inquiry" compatible with each citizen's status as "free and equal" and that, as far as possible, "rest on plain truths now widely accepted, or available, to citizens generally," or, in other words, "presently accepted general beliefs and forms of reasoning found in common sense, and the methods and conclusions of science when these are not controversial." The doctrines that survive this screening will necessarily be liberal but will not be identical in their principles, much less in their details. An orderly political contest over time is to decide which among them "if any, is most reasonable." The duty of civility requires, however, that citizens not vote in any way that they would not be permitted publicly to advocate. Although discussion and decision making within "background culture" associations such as churches and labor unions need only be

---

[10]   Ibid. at 131–58.

guided by the "social reason" appropriate severally to them, and within families by "domestic reason," in the political arena and wherever the application of political power is at issue, each individual's participation both in discussion and (by voting) in decision making must be circumscribed by the values of public reason.[11]

Rawls rejects the suggestion that this conception of neutrality entails moral skepticism or antirealism, and he disavows his own earlier intimations that morality as a whole might be reconstructed on the foundations of the theory of justice. The duty of civility, then, is not intended to govern the social enforcement of morality generally – even though "the fact of reasonable pluralism" and the "burdens of judgment" would seem to be as telling in the sphere of social enforcement as they are in the sphere of the political.

Why the discontinuity between Rawls's basic project and Mill's? That is, why does Rawls propose to delimit the political only, while Mill embraces as his necessary task that of circumscribing the social as well as the political? I think the difference might be accounted for simply by the fact that Rawls conceives the state as peculiarly coercive, while Mill saw state and society both as equally prone to oppress the individual. This tendency to concentrate on the state and other large organized mechanisms as a "basic structure" separable from the moral situation of individuals characterizes Rawls's approach to distributive justice as well, as G. A. Cohen has pointed out.[12] It would also account for Rawls's reluctance to pursue his early classification of the *family* as part of the "basic structure," as Susan Okin and others have noted.[13] If the duty of civility were applicable to individuals on all moral questions, *whether or not posed in the context of political action*, its scope will of course have been dramatically enlarged.

Thus enlarged, the duty of civility would pull us toward the perfect coincidence view. The duty of civility, so viewed, would function in much the same way as the standing and proportionality norms that govern the social enforcement of morality. Much as standing norms limit and set priorities as to who may complain, comment, or censure,

---

[11] Ibid. at 216–27.
[12] G. A. Cohen, "Where the Action Is: On the Site of Distributive Justice," 26 *Philosophy & Public Affairs* 3–30 (1997).
[13] Susan Muller Okin, *Justice, Gender, and the Family* 22, 96–7, 108 (New York: Basic, 1989). Rawls reaffirms that the family is "part of the basic structure" but, again, appears to deny that principles of justice apply to families, directly anyway, in "The Idea of Public Reason Revisited,"64 *The University of Chicago Law Review* 765, 787–91 (1997).

and just as proportionality norms limit the degree and form of social pressure brought to bear, the duty of civility, so conceived, would take special account of relevant features of the subject matter of enforcement. Suppose, for example, that reasonable people may disagree as to whether spanking a child is wrong, but that there is no room for reasonable disagreement as to whether chaining a child to the furnace in the basement overnight is wrong. The duty of civility would allow both legal and social sanctions against the parent who chains the child in the basement; but it would forbid advocating or voting for a legal ban on spanking, and would also – if expanded to encompass the social – forbid the use of social pressure. One proviso: Rawls allows that within associations, such as churches, and within families, social pressure might be appropriate in this case even if justified solely by an appeal to "the whole truth" about the proper discipline of children.[14]

On this interpretation, Rawls seems to leave some room for social morality. "Social reason," as he conceives it, is tied to associations such as churches, labor unions, and faculties, his stock examples. "Domestic reason" – distinguished, without explanation, from social reason – is tied to the family. The rest is governed by "public reason." The sanctions of "social reason" as Rawls conceives it are avoidable by resigning membership in the relevant association: Change churches, drop out of the union. Because the sanctions such associations bring to bear are not political, that is, not essentially coercive, they need not be subject to the discipline of public reason.

If Rawls is right, there is no social morality apart from the focus of some intermediate association. When we apply social sanctions we must be "coming from" somewhere, that is, invoking the norms supported by some group or another – although there are "personal values," in Rawls view, "there is no such thing as a private reason." Outside such groups there lies only the state, the "social union of social unions." Social sanctions are nothing much to worry about, perhaps, because they either (a) emanate from a social union that the aggrieved individual may either take or leave, or (b) emanate from the state and are therefore subject to the rigor of public reason. Either

---

[14] Another caveat Rawls has in reserve has to do with whether the legally permissible forms of family discipline are a "constitutional fundamental." Rawls gives no clue as to whether it is, and he is noncommittal as to whether the strictures of public reason apply only to constitutional fundamentals or "all the way down" to reach such matters as tax policy, regulation, and subsidies. See *Political Liberalism* at 214 & n.3.

way, no point of origination remains for social pressures motivated by reasons that one may reasonably reject. Political pressures are governed by public reason; social reasons emanate from groups that one may avoid; and domestic reasons can be escaped by moving away from home or reaching the age of majority.

Looked at another way, though, Rawls's neutrality appears less favorable, even inimical, to the perfect coincidence view. It looks inimical because it partitions moral requirements into two classes: those that are consistent with public reason, and those that are grounded only in some comprehensive doctrine (even liberalism, as a comprehensive doctrine, is excluded from public reason, according to Rawls). The inner sphere of morality could be defined as that determined by the true comprehensive philosophical doctrine, whatever that is, if it is. The inner sphere is strongly delegalized because to advocate or advance its legal enforcement would be to violate the duty of civility. The outer sphere, on the other hand, is occupied by the product of the political values of public reason, determined by the overlapping consensus of reasonable comprehensive doctrines. It is a politically enforceable morality consistent with, or at least not too seriously at odds with, each of the reasonable comprehensive doctrines represented in society.

But does Rawls, in fact, allow for an inner sphere? If not, his is a perfect coincidence view. The inner sphere, recall, is a sphere of genuine moral requirements. Although Rawls is avowedly agnostic on the question whether there are, in fact, any such things, he does make clear that the demands of competing comprehensive views are ones that it would be reasonable to reject. If the inner sphere is composed entirely of moral demands that it would be reasonable to reject, it is difficult to see how they could be permissible to enforce even by merely social measures. Rawls's suggestion is that these requirements are permissible to enforce because, and insofar as, they are ones that we affirm by subjecting ourselves to those very pressures. They are self-imposed, "freely accepted, politically speaking," even if not in any other sense. Thus, if one's Mormonism exposes one to social pressure to cease one's adultery, the permissibility of the social pressure rests in one's acceptance of Mormonism, not in the wrongness of adultery. But if this is the correct reading of Rawls, the inner sphere collapses to the dimensionless point of personal acceptance, which I may avoid simply by switching doctrines. On inspection, Rawls's may turn out to be a perfect coincidence view *malgré lui*.

Whether or not Rawls's is a perfect coincidence view, there are several general points to be made. The first is the unlikelihood that there is, in fact, a duty of civility as Rawls and others have defined it. Kent Greenawalt and Michael Perry have pressed the point that it demeans religious believers to suggest that, in voting or discussing public issues, their comprehensive views are ones that they may consult only to the extent that they overlap with the views of nonbelievers.[15] It would be unreasonably onerous as well, in its imposing a strenuous motivational hygiene on everyone holding (as all are assumed to hold) a comprehensive view, for all as citizens would be duty bound to take care that their grasp of "the whole truth" not contaminate the permissible "public" set of reasons that alone may properly motivate political discourse and conduct. Michael Moore has argued that if in fact an actor has both reasons r and q to ϕ, and does ϕ, she cannot be said to have chosen to ϕ for reason r rather than reason q.[16] Whether Moore is correct about this or not, it is no doubt difficult to *know* that one has ϕ-ed for reason r rather than reason q. If, for example, I know I am biased against Ivy League graduates but also have independent doubts about a particular job candidate, I may never know whether my vote against him was tainted by bias.

The duty of civility is satisfied, apparently, as long as the actor's act is at least a partial product of a public reason. Normally, though, where we judge that an action produced by a mixture of proper and improper motives is sustainable, we would hold that the best course is for the actor to try to extirpate the improper motive altogether from his psychology. As to the nonpublic reasons furnished by comprehensive doctrines, Rawls would reject such an approach. Would he then say that it is permissible for an actor to allow nonpublic reasons to influence her advocacy and voting on public matters *so long as they do not causally predominate* in determining her action? This would license sailing very close to the wind. But the only alternative would be to require the actor wholly to disable her nonpublic reasons in matters having a political bearing. This, as Perry and Greenawalt observe, is a stricture as hard to accept as it would be to implement.

It might be argued that implementation of the duty of civility

---

15   Kent Greenawalt, *Religious Convictions and Political Choice* (New York: Oxford University Press, 1988); Michael Perry, *Love and Power* (New York: Oxford University Press, 1991); George Sher, *Beyond Neutrality: Perfectionism and Politics* (Cambridge: Cambridge University Press, 1997).
16   Michael Moore, "Authority, Law, and Razian Reasons," 62 *Southern California Law Review* 827, 878–83 (1989).

should not trouble us too much, because a supreme judiciary, as exemplar of public reason, can tidy things up – as in fact the Liberal Principle of Legitimacy seems to require. At least as to matters of "constitutional fundamentals," an expert judiciary, Rawls proposes, shall "appeal . . . to a political conception of justice [namely, public reason] to distinguish those questions that can reasonably be removed from the political agenda ["once and for all"] and those that cannot."[17] Judges, if not citizens, can be counted upon to sort out the ideas implicit in the political – as opposed to the social – background culture and separate them from what are merely projections of their own or some other, perhaps even dominant, comprehensive view. But this simply transfers the difficulty from the citizen's shoulders to the judge's. No one, not even the fairest, the most dispassionate, can – like a mirror held to a mirror – reflect nothing but what is reflected in an "overlapping consensus" of viewpoints that she judges to be reasonable ones to reflect.[18]

A METRIC OF SOCIAL PRESSURE?

Although I think there is much to these points, I would like to stress another, namely, that society does not so neatly decompose into an overlapping montage of voluntary "social unions" in the way Rawls indicates. Each of us is constantly subject to nonlegal social pressures that do not emanate from co-members of any identifiable voluntary association. I ignore here the adventitious groupings – the Hoosiers and other "granfaloons" that Kurt Vonnegut has brilliantly mocked – that lack the regularity and cohesiveness necessary to support an identifiable set of conduct requirements. Whether we bowl alone or in leagues, most of the people we urbanites encounter are strangers. Even so, there are norms of common decency that we share (most of us) if we share little else. Many of these norms are moral requirements, and many of them are enforceable by quite seri-

---

[17] *Political Liberalism* at 151.
[18] Rawls's assurance, *Political Liberalism* at 236 n.23, that his view of adjudication does not differ "in substance" from Ronald Dworkin's, rests on an understanding of how "fit" with the body of legal precedent operates as a curb on a Dworkinian judge's reference to political moral *truth*. Ken Kress has shown that Dworkin's position is unstable, and tends inexorably to favor moral truth over fit. See Ken Kress, "Precedent, Coherence, and Moral 'Mathematics' in Adjudication," unpublished MS; see also Larry Alexander and Ken Kress, "Against Legal Principles," in Andrei Marmor, ed., *Law and Interpretation: Essays in Legal Philosophy* (Oxford: Clarendon Press, 1995).

ous, if rarely compulsory, means. Moreover, many of our more intimate relationships have no explicit ground rules. "Friendship" and
"Romance" are not clubs with bylaws that we may consult before
joining up. Yet here, too, the way we conduct ourselves opens us to
manifold pressures that we can hardly be said to have been free, at
the threshold, to take or leave, much less to pick and choose among.
To classify such norms as parts of "the social, not the political . . .
'background culture,'"[19] as Rawls does, is to evade rather than to
address the issues raised by the fact of the social enforcement of
morality.

Mill's observation about social enforcement bears repeating here:
Although merely moral requirements are "not usually upheld by
such extreme penalties" as legal requirements are, private suasive
enforcement "leaves fewer means of escape, penetrat[es] much more
deeply into the details of life, and enslav[es] the soul itself." These differences can be explained. If we consider the perceived extremity of a
sanction to be equal to its actual extremity discounted by the probability the actor assigns to its occurrence, any given degree of perceived extremity can be attained either by combining a low probability of "conviction" with an extreme penalty, or by combining a higher
probability of conviction with a lesser penalty. Social rather than legal
enforcement may be attractive because it combines relatively low
administrative costs (police, courts, etc.) with a relatively high probability of conviction. Thus, social enforcement may not only deliver a
given level of perceived extremity of sanction at a lower administrative cost, it may do so by employing less extreme penalties.[20]

Legal sanctions typically increase in abrupt fashion as the actor
passes from a permitted to a forbidden level of activity, whereas

---

[19] *Political Liberalism* at 14.
[20] For a discussion of the dynamics of the choice between public and private enforcement through the legal system, and of the factors that govern the choice between
different combinations of severity and probability to achieve a given expected
cost to the criminal, see Richard Posner, *Economic Analysis of Law*, chs. 7, 22, 3d ed.,
(Boston: Little, Brown & Co., 1986). Posner argues that the problem of the insol-
vent defendant largely accounts for the great degree to which criminal law relies
on nonpecuniary penal sanctions rather than tort remedies to achieve its ends, but
this misses the deeper problems that Jules Coleman has identified. See Jules L.
Coleman, *Markets, Morals, and the Law* 153–65 (New York: Cambridge University
Press, 1988). For an historical account of a regime combining extreme penalties
and private prosecution, see Douglas Hay, Peter Linebaugh, John G. Rule, E. P.
Thompson, and Cal Winslow, *Albion's Fatal Tree: Crime and Society in Eighteenth-
Century England* (New York: Pantheon, 1975).

social sanctions do not. Mill's observation that legal requirements are typically upheld by "more extreme penalties" can be understood as referring not only to the relative severity of legal enforcement, but also to the fact that the *abruptness* with which the law responds to incremental increases in activity level stands in contrast to the more continuous nature of social enforcement. We are capable of expressing social disapprobation in nearly continuous fashion – think of the gradually raised eyebrow – whereas legal sanctions tend to jump at one in a more extreme-seeming (because abrupt) way.[21]

Mill also stresses that private suasive correction is not only intrusive, it can erode the spontaneity of individual choice more surely and more extensively than any concern on the agent's part to avoid mild or remote legal consequences. There are, as we have seen, moral and even legal limits to the extent and nature of suasive correction. Officious intermeddling is sometimes morally impermissible, and suasion or remonstrance that lapses into harangue or harassment is also impermissible. But these limits are diffuse and wide. No matter how much we may relish abstract discussion, only the sturdiest and most self-certain of us are likely to remain unmoved and unbothered by the more strenuous forms of permissible suasion and censure where our actual, impending or completed practical decisions are at issue. It is curious that Mill disparaged as mere "notions of politeness" the standing requirements that limit our exposure to officious commentary on our faults, those "merely bad" traits that Mill would not confuse with wrongs and thought not proper objects of censure.[22]

Mill held that private suasive correction, unlike legal repression, can "enslav[e] the soul itself." We can understand this as a reminder that the boundary between self and state is much harder to confound than the boundary between soul and soulmates. Heretics, for example, so typically form subcultures in which heresy is orthodoxy that it is reasonable to view such associations as practically necessary to the very maintenance of heresy. Moreover, it is hard to imagine how an individual could, without lapsing into pathology, persevere in any course of conduct that was universally thought wicked, whether or not it was illegal. We are not noumenal egos; we know ourselves through our associations and our understandings of how we are as

21 See Robert Cooter, "Prices and Sanctions," 84 *Columbia Law Review* 1523 (1984).
22 John Stuart Mill, *On Liberty*, Currin V. Shields, ed., 94 (New York: Liberal Arts Press, 1956) [hereafter, *On Liberty*]. See also Ferdinand David Schoeman, *Privacy and Social Freedom* 24–36 (Cambridge: Cambridge University Press, 1992).

others know us.[23] A barrier to legal correction alone would leave the individual's identity, as well as her liberty, exposed to potentially devastating social assaults.

Following Mill, we can conceptualize every instance of social control as an ordered quadruple whose values are a severity measure, an avoidability measure, a pervasiveness measure, and a measure of the effect upon individuality. These measures are comparable and additive (let's pretend) and yield a measure of the total burden upon liberty of any given means of social control. Typically, civil penalties exceed private suasive methods in the severity measure, but not in the others. On Mill's view, then, for any given private suasive means of enforcement there exists a conceivable, less burdensome state-imposed, ultimately compulsory means. Therefore, if Mill is generally correct, and these additional assumptions are not too fanciful, there will always be a possible, state-imposed means of enforcement that is less oppressive, on balance, than the most burdensome, though permissible, private, suasive means.

One may, of course, object by saying that this ignores the fact that private and legal forms of correction differ in that the latter are state-imposed and backed by the awesome machinery of the state, and they therefore differ *intrinsically*. But what is the moral significance of this point? I suspect that it isn't simply question-begging, but only because I sense here an implicit appeal to the pre-reflective view that *law is essentially coercive*. That would be an intrinsic difference that would morally count but, as argued in Part Two, the pre-reflective view – as dear as it is to modern political theorists – cannot be maintained.

On another tack, one might object that my point can be shrugged off because it depends upon assumptions of comparability and additivity that are – I confess it – at best fanciful, at worst nonsensical. In answer, I would point out two things. The first is that if legal and social forms of correction are incomparable, this fact is as much an embarrassment for one who attacks the perfect coincidence view as it is for me, its defender. To the extent that my picture is simpler, and adopting it does not necessarily license any consequence that can be characterized as "worse" than its more complicated alternatives, I'd say the simpler picture wins. Secondly, whether or not the measures I have invoked can be domesticated to the satisfaction of an econo-

---

23   On this subject, see, generally, Michael Sandel, *Liberalism and the Limits of Justice* (Cambridge: Cambridge University Press, 1982).

metrician is really beside the point. The fact is that, in most every case that is likely to come up, we are able to agree approximately as to what would be more and what would be less oppressive in pairwise comparisons.

Legal correction is often less intrusive than the *least intrusive* morally permissible, available form of private suasive correction. Suppose I am driving on a public highway with my young children. I am driving carelessly but cause no actual harm, and suppose my driving this way violates a moral requirement. Suppose that another private person observes my driving and perceives that it is creating a sufficiently great risk of harm to myself and the children to give him a moral permission to censure me for it. In these circumstances the least intrusive suasive correction available to him might be something like following me, catching up with me, waving me over, and complaining – politely – about my driving; in others words, doing what the nicest police officer would do in the circumstances. My suspicion is that most of us would find this considerably more galling than being cautioned or even ticketed by the police. And more than galling – humiliating, infuriating, baffling, and discombobulating. In a word – intrusive. One now fairly commonplace automobile bumper sticker reads: "Don't like my driving? Dial 1-800-EAT-SHIT." The idea behind this (if there is one) might be unpacked this way: "If my driving isn't bad enough to call forth legal correction, then *no one* has a right to censure it."[24]

Any genuine moral requirement entails the existence of some permissible social means of enforcement. This is the vulnerability that is inseparable from the nature of our moral being – being laid open to possible reproof, censure, and ridicule *over and above* others' mere harboring of adverse judgments. And, as Jeremy Waldron has put it "the line at which mere prescription and admonition stop and coercion begins is a fine one. Even the mere expression of disapproval – the raised eyebrow or the icy stare – may be felt as a positive show of force."[25] Law's expressions of disapproval, too, may be harsh and direct, or they may be slight and remote. The extreme position, that some moral requirements cannot legitimately affect any compellable legal outcome, rests on the assumption that legal correction is either

---

[24] Cf. Aristotle, *Nicomachean Ethics* 1180^a 22–24, W. D. Ross, trans. (Oxford: Oxford University Press, 1966) [hereafter, *Nicomachean Ethics*]: "And while people hate *men* who oppose their impulses, even if they oppose them rightly, the law in its ordaining of what is good is not burdensome" (emphasis in original).

[25] Jeremy Waldron, "A Right To Do Wrong," 92 *Ethics* 21, 30 (1981).

per se or in fact more oppressive than any of the associated social enforcement measures that might be taken. These assumptions cannot be sustained, as I have shown, and the extreme view must therefore be abandoned.

IS CRIMINAL PUNISHMENT DIFFERENT?

The extreme view has proven to be untenable, but the moderate view may not be. The extreme view is vulnerable because it forbids any legal consequence to attach to certain moral transgressions. The moderate view does not forbid all legal consequences to attach, but only those of a certain type, that is, imprisonment or corporal or capital punishment. The moderate view thus seems more reasonable; after all, imprisonment seems importantly different from other burdens that the state may impose on us. But, looking behind this appearance, what separates regulation from punishment? Unless some principled distinction between regulation and criminalization can be drawn, every example of permissible regulatory enforcement of a moral requirement is a problem for the moderate version of the delegalization thesis.

Joel Feinberg offers a principled basis for such a distinction in his essay "The Expressive Function of Punishment."[26] According to Feinberg, punishment needs to be understood as distinct from mere penalty. Penalties include such things as "parking tickets, offside penalties, sackings, flunkings and disqualifications" while "imprisonment at hard labor for committing a felony" is an example of a punishment. Feinberg rejects the idea that the distinction can rest on severity alone, even though penalties typically are the less severe; and he rejects the idea that penalties can be characterized as "retroactive licensing fees" in contrast to punishments, which are not. Rather, Feinberg differentiates the genus of "authoritative deprivations for failures" – to which both punishments and penalties belong – according to an "important additional characteristic" common and peculiar to punishments. This characteristic is what Feinberg calls "a certain expressive function." Punishment, he argues, "is a conventional device for the expression of attitudes of resentment and indignation, and of judgements of disapproval and reprobation, on the part either of the punishing authority himself [sic] or of those 'in whose name' the punishment is

---

[26] Collected in Joel Feinberg, *Doing and Deserving* 95–118 (Princeton: Princeton University Press, 1970).

172

inflicted." Feinberg's point is very much in keeping with the spirit of Mill, who had written that "the chief mischief of the legal penalties [imposed on unpopular belief] is that they strengthen the social stigma . . . which is [what is] really effective."[27]

If Feinberg can establish that a criminal legal requirement is backed by a threat (*viz.*, of punishment, rather than mere penalty) that is different in kind from what backs a merely regulatory legal requirement, then there is a way to maintain the moderate version of the delegalization thesis. The advocate of the moderate view will admit that moral requirements may permissibly become regulatory legal requirements, but she will deny that all moral requirements may permissibly become criminal legal requirements. She will be able to do this by exploiting the discontinuity between penalties and punishments. She will admit that for each private suasive enforcement measure there exists a possible, less oppressive regulatory legal enforcement measure; but she will deny that there always exists a possible, less oppressive criminal legal enforcement measure. She can do this because every criminal legal enforcement measure will carry a special characteristic not shared by its otherwise equally severe regulatory counterparts – namely, the symbolic stigma.

Can this work? It is true that regulatory legal requirements do not generally *independently* constitute moral requirements, and it is true that to add a "symbolic stigma" to what would otherwise be a mere regulatory offense (a mere malum prohibitum) is to attach a consequence different in kind from mere penalty. But the delegalization thesis concerns types of conduct that are supposed already to be morally required, and whose omission is therefore already necessarily stigmatized. And so what criminalizing the omission of a moral requirement adds is not indignation or a judgment that a type of conduct is morally wrong, for those must already have existed.

Criminalizing the omission of a moral requirement changes two things. It creates an ultimately compulsory remedy where, possibly, no morally permissible private compulsory remedy had existed. And it expresses the state's remonstrance in addition to the necessarily permissible private remonstrance that otherwise exists. The first change is not necessarily different from the change that would be brought about by regulating the omission, and there is reason to doubt that any moral requirement can be morally immune from regulatory enforcement. The second change adds to – but does not orig-

---

[27] *On Liberty* at 39.

inate – the category of those who may permissibly remonstrate with the offender for his omission. Therefore the necessary minimum net difference between regulating and criminalizing is the addition of the state to the category of those who may permissibly remonstrate. The moderate version of the delegalization thesis is tenable only if it is plausible to hold that there is a moral principle that makes it impermissible for the state to remonstrate about the omission of some moral requirement.

The inquiry has now come full circle. Earlier I suggested that because particularized state suasive enforcement is often unavailable, it would be necessary to examine whether the state could permissibly enforce, by its typically compulsory mechanisms, moral requirements that no private person was free to compel. I then gave an affirmative answer to this question with respect to regulatory measures, leaving only the question whether there are principled grounds to believe that criminal punishment may not be employed to enforce at least some moral requirements. Now, it appears that the search for an answer to *this* question returns us to the earlier one: Is it ever morally improper for the state suasively to enforce a moral requirement?

Above I noted that the class of those who may permissibly remonstrate with a person about her omission of a moral requirement is sometimes limited. I also suggested, though, that circumstances may operate to open this class; for example, when no one occupies the roles that ordinarily carry such a permission. Like it or not, we see that the state is often the only dependable inheritor of these roles when – as increasingly happens – they fall vacant. Their having responsible tenants is at best a contingent matter, and the circumstance that they often do have responsible tenants cannot be a basis for strongly delegalizing any moral requirement.[28]

There is no denying that criminal punishments are typically more severe than regulatory penalties and typically more burdensome upon liberty than private suasive enforcement measures. But it is likewise true that private compulsion is more severe than suasion. A nebulous idea of proportionality governs both legal and private enforcement. The moderate version of the delegalization thesis is interesting only if it holds that some moral requirement enforceable by private means of overall burdensomeness b is not enforceable by

---

[28] Aristotle seems to regard the state as the primary custodian of moral education, a role devolving to parents only when the state is in default. See *Nicomachean Ethics* at 1180^a 29–32.

criminal legal means having an overall burdensomeness of b or less; but holding this seems unreasonable. The moderate version cannot be defended by appealing to the fact that we would object to the state's locking up the petty malefactor and throwing away the key; we would likewise object to any private person's doing this. What counts is what others do to the individual and, as Mill saw, whether what is done is done privately or by law makes no fundamental difference.

But Mill did not tell the whole story; and in a way it remains untidy. There is a gap between there being a necessary permission on someone's part to chastise wrongdoers and there being a claim right on the state's part to punish wrongdoing. Although social pressure can be oppressive, punishment *stigmatizes* – that is, it expresses a corporate adverse judgment of the wrongdoer and facilitates the adverse judgments of citizens generally. A permission to do something does not convey any protection against interference – but a claim right does. So punitive measures by the state normally differ from other social enforcement in two ways: (1) They claim to affix an "official" stigma expressing the disapproval of society as a corpus, and (2) they are applied with a claim right not to be preempted, hindered, or duplicated by any person or group acting on its own.

Two points should be made about this gap. The first is that even if the *idea* of private or "open" punishment is not incoherent, a *regime* of private punishment cannot be coherently imagined. This is what led Nozick to the reluctant conclusion that there is one right – the right to punish – that is irreducibly social. This very incoherence compels the further conclusion that what the state, as society's agent, exercises is not merely a permission but a claim right, that is, a permission to punish that is exclusive and protected against interference. The second point is that this ineliminably social nature of punishment does not subjugate the individual to *any further degree than morality itself already claims to do*. As argued above, however light the social burden on wrongdoing may be, the state's may be set lower, and it also will typically carry compensating procedural benefits.

SUMMARY

In the pluralistic, complicated, and increasingly fragmented world we inhabit, there are good reasons to refer to the state a greater-than-traditional share of the task of moral correction. For one thing, private correction is less reliable than it may have been when ties of family, religion, and community were stronger. For another, private correction can be irregular, unfair, scary, risky, and invasive. State responsibility for moral oversight may on balance be to the benefit of those overseen; whether it is or is not cannot be settled a priori.

Mill's fears of social tyranny have not yet, in the postindustrial West at least, been realized – "Mill had scarcely any prophetic gift," as Sir Isaiah Berlin tersely put it.[29] What Mill did not and perhaps could not foresee was the degree to which mobility and urbanization have eroded the bases both of the social enforcement that moral requirements entail and of the reflective consensus that, some would argue, moral requirements presuppose. To the extent that social tyranny appears less of a threat than Mill envisaged, legal tyranny appears more of one. This fact has made it tempting to recast Mill's doctrine as one defining the limits of law alone, or of criminal law alone, rather than a limit to social control generally. I have tried to show that this is a mistake.

To grant that something is a moral requirement is to authorize some means of social enforcement. To those of us who find popular notions of morality too narrow, it may be tempting to ignore the "moral" point in order to concentrate our forces at the perimeter of the law. This gambit leaves the legitimacy of social enforcement unchallenged; but the thought may be that this can be readily evaded and that the cost of contesting the moral territory is too high. However sound this might seem as forensic strategy, I think I have shown that it is philosophically untenable.

It is easy to picture morality divided into an outer sphere and an inner sphere. Morality is not offended if the state helps police the outer sphere, but the inner sphere is another matter. The law may not enter here; morality itself forbids it, and forbids it absolutely, not as a mere matter of policy. This is a powerful, though inaccurate, picture. Because of its power, it is hard to resist using this image when the legislature threatens to penalize what is morally innocent. Appealing to this picture may help block bad legislation while finessing the politically very bloody debate about what is and is not morally wrong. The perfect coincidence view rejects this seductive and expedient picture. Some will say that the perfect coincidence view (true or not) should remain an esoteric doctrine – as Sidgwick thought utilitarianism should be – until the passions the privacy

---

[29]   Isaiah Berlin, *Four Essays on Liberty* 183 (New York: Oxford University Press, 1970).

debate has stirred recede. But the reasons to resort to such an expedient can only be ones founded in despair of moral reasoning or of democratic politics, or of both.

Morality, we may discover, is strenuously demanding, much more so than we generally now believe. If that turns out to be so, the view I am defending would seem to have the disquieting corollary that the state may be strenuously demanding too. If the moral life includes a duty of beneficence requiring deep sacrifices at the expense of the good life then, my view must hold, the political life may require them as well. This is a real concern but, so put, it overlooks the ways in which political institutions may introduce "a normative division of labor into human life,"[30] in Thomas Nagel's phrase, reconciling the moral and the personal as, otherwise, might require a choice between heroic self-transformation and piggish indifference. Whether our political institutions will undertake and achieve such a division will depend, in part, on the perceived legitimacy of their doing so.

[30]   Thomas Nagel, *The View from Nowhere* 207 (New York: Oxford University Press, 1986).

Conclusion: The State for What?

"The two parties which divide the state [are those] of Memory and [of] Hope."

Emerson, "The Conservative"

My argument against the three fallacies is now done. In some ways, I hope, the later parts have reinforced those they follow. The conclusion of Part One was that legitimacy entails a prima facie duty not to interfere with the state's administrative prerogatives. The possibility that such a duty in fact exists, and that there are in fact legitimate states, should be reinforced by the conclusion of Part Two, that law is not essentially coercive. If law were essentially coercive it would be that much harder to believe there is a prima facie duty not to resist it. Similarly, if Part Three was successful, it showed that the state may enforce whatever morality may; and this conclusion should make the conclusion of Part Two more credible – that law is least coercive where its requirements track those of morality.

Once the three fallacies I set out to expose are out of the way, what then? Exposing the first fallacy tells us only that a legitimate state is one whose administrative prerogatives impose on us a prima facie duty of noninterference. I have given some reasons to think that there is such a duty, but to prove that there is would require further moral argument. Exposing the second fallacy tells us only that some moral argument has to be made in order to show that state action bears a special burden of justification, or that state action bears an inherent moral stigma. It also tells us that such an argument cannot be founded on the premise that law is coercive; but it does not foreclose the possibility of a different argument on different premises. Exposing the third fallacy tells us only that the law may legitimately reach wherever morality reaches, but it does not even begin to tell us where that is. Again, further moral argument is needed to know that.

179

My general aim has been to establish that a legitimate state is possible, but, to establish a conclusion, it is never enough to expose the fallacious arguments for its denial. Even so, I hope I have at least exposed some areas where moral argument is possible and necessary, where formerly it had been thought irrelevant or unnecessary.

The account I have given accords legitimacy only to those states that at least approximate an ideal of justice about which I have said next to nothing. Although justice is indeed to be the "first virtue" of the state, what that virtue entails – and whether there are others – is a subject far larger than what I can address here. I hope it will suffice to point out that justice and legitimacy, though related, are not coextensive. A just state may be illegitimate and a legitimate state unjust. How can this happen? A legitimate state may be unjust because in certain circumstances the only practical alternatives are far worse, or even less just, or both. Classical Athenian democracy was unjust (think of slavery and its treatment of women) but legitimate; any unjust but consented-to regime has a claim to legitimacy that we may deny but cannot ignore. By the same token, a just state may be illegitimate, for example, if it is so unpopular that it would be better, all things considered, if a little justice were sacrificed to gain the allegiance of a contrary populace.

Both of these last examples show that the idea that consent is essential to legitimacy has deep roots. We explored some of the ramifications of this idea in Part One, where we considered the question what was the most suitable criterion of state legitimacy. There we rejected the Strong Legitimacy Thesis, which would deem legitimate only those states as to whose laws their subjects had a general duty to obey. One of the shorings that we considered for the duty to obey the law was consent – express, implied, or hypothetical. We acquiesced in the conclusion that a general duty to obey the law cannot be founded on the idea of consent, for the reasons we considered there.

But many have thought that political legitimacy is nonetheless tied to consent – if not via the intermediate idea of political obligation, then more directly. In other words, as Jeremy Waldron has argued, consent might stand as the criterion of legitimacy even though it may not adequately ground political obligation. Waldron points out that consent theories of legitimacy are of two contrasting types: one voluntaristic, emphasizing the individual's willing assent, and the other rationalistic, pursuing the hypothetical consent idea. The two are irreconcilable in the sense that "if emphasis is placed on the role of will in the individual choice of government," as the voluntaristic conception does, "then hypothetical consent will not be viewed as an adequate substitute for the actual consent of the citizen."[1] Since, as we have seen, actual consent can at best only support a transient, relativized, and enfeebled legitimacy in modern circumstances, the hypothetical consent route is the only one capable of reinforcing the common intuition that just or nearly just states are not hopelessly incapable of legitimacy.

Pursuing the criterion of hypothetical consent has led many – John Rawls most prominently – to the position that any legitimate modern state must be *neutral* with regard to a wide range of different, equally reasonable visions of the good life.[2] This follows because if the state's legitimacy depends on its being able in ideal circumstances to secure the assent of all reasonable persons, the state cannot simply take sides in fundamental controversies. The state has a responsibility to ensure that each of its decisions can be justified to each one of its reasonable citizens, and justified in terms that each can freely accept. On this view, a legitimate modern state is one that confines itself to enabling its citizens to choose among and pursue any of an almost limitless variety of possible lifestyles and carefully avoids expressing any preference within that range. This the state will do by implementing procedures to ensure that opinions which are either unreasonable or nonneutral do not influence its decisions.

Working out this idea depends on maintaining the distinction between outcomes and what Rawls calls "constitutional essentials."[3] Reasonable dissensus about outcomes should not foreclose the state's legitimately taking a side; otherwise, the state would be paralyzed. What matters is that the process by which state decisions are made is one to which assent cannot reasonably be withheld. But process here cannot be merely formal – what legitimacy demands is that public discussion be governed by the duty of civility, which means that a legitimate state is one in which political discussion, debate, and voting itself are sufficiently widely conducted within the bounds of a "public reason" confined to premises and rules of inference that make no crucial appeal to moral truth or to any compre-

---

[1] Jeremy Waldron, "Theoretical Foundations of Liberalism," 37 *Philosophical Quarterly* 127, 140 (1987).

[2] See John Rawls, *Political Liberalism* (New York: Columbia University Press, 1993) [hereafter, *Political Liberalism*]; see also Bruce A. Ackerman, *Social Justice in the Liberal State* (New Haven: Yale University Press, 1980); Thomas Nagel, *Equality and Partiality* (New York: Oxford University Press, 1991).

[3] *Political Liberalism* at 137, 216–17.

hensive view of the good for humanity. The hypothetical "would consent" is supported by insisting on limiting the options under discussion to ones to which all *could* consent without indoctrination or duress. The duty of civility must in turn be made concrete by "guidelines of inquiry" that, like courtroom rules of evidence, specify when "the trial would be better without the evidence," that is, without appeals to controversial truths.

Rawls and others advance what could be termed "ideal moderator" theories. This kind of theory tries to minimize substantive constraints on state legitimacy in favor of what it conceives as procedural ones: A legitimate state is one that can be conceived as an ongoing conversation that observes certain rules of discourse that disallow appeals to premises that reasonable participants may not share.

The perennial objection to ideal moderator theories is that the constraints they place on the range of permissible options and viewpoints are not rooted in reason or "reasonableness" alone, and that they are not merely procedural – they are themselves controversial, nonneutral, substantive moral views that many people cannot submit to or accept without doing violence to their convictions. The progression – from consent, to hypothetical consent, to hypothetical consent as to "constitutional essentials," to an ideal discussion limited to a short list of favored alternatives to be evaluated by abstract but tendentious criteria of rationality – has seemed to many to make manifest the unworkability of consent as the criterion of political legitimacy.[4]

Joseph Raz also approaches the issue of legitimacy rationalistically, but in a quite different way. According to Raz

> The normal way to establish that a person has [legitimate] authority over another person involves showing that the alleged subject is likely better to comply with reasons which apply to him (other than the alleged authoritative directives) if he accepts the directives of the alleged authority as authoritatively binding and tries to follow them, rather than by trying to follow the reasons that apply to him directly.

---

[4] See Michael J. Sandel, *Liberalism and the Limits of Justice* (Cambridge: Cambridge University Press, 1982); William Galston, *Liberal Purposes* (Cambridge: Cambridge University Press, 1991); Michael J. Perry, *Love and Power* (New York: Oxford University Press, 1991); George Sher, *Beyond Neutrality: Perfectionism and Politics* (Cambridge: Cambridge University Press, 1997); Stephen Gardbaum, "Why the Liberal State Can Promote Ideals after All," 104 *Harvard Law Review* 1350 (1991).

There may be other ways of justifying an exercise of authority, but this Normal Justification Thesis captures the "normal way" and is an expression of a *service conception* of authority, namely, that its "role and primary normal function is to serve the governed," not by imposing "completely independent duties on people" – which authority has no right to do – but by helping them fulfill duties based "on reasons which already independently apply." Authority makes a difference because it preempts the citizen's directly acting on those independent reasons: "The fact that a [legitimate] authority requires performance of an action is a reason for its performance which is not to be added to all other relevant reasons when assessing what to do, but should exclude and take the place of some of them."

Raz's conception of legitimacy does not involve any strict "screening" of independent reasons: If reason r in fact applies to person X, giving rise to a duty to ϕ, and X would be likelier to comply with r by submitting to a legal duty to ϕ than by acting on r herself, then a political authority may legitimately impose on X a duty to ϕ, even though X might reasonably reject both r and the duty to ϕ. Normally, reasons r will apply to X in virtue of goals X has adopted, but they may not, for example, if they relate to X's goals but X doesn't appreciate the fact, or if they are biologically based, or, more typically, if reason r is implicated in a social coordination problem.[5]

Raz's account of legitimacy is shaped by its inclusion in a wider moral view that is avowedly perfectionistic: There is a best sort of life; it is a life of autonomy; the state may and must promote this life; it may do so by limiting choice in order to enhance autonomy in the wider sense. So long as the state acts within the general bounds of this role it acts legitimately.

It is better to avoid exaggeration when stating the contrast between the "service conception" and the "ideal moderator" approaches to legitimacy. In the broadest, most impressionistic form, it is the difference between being helpful and being civil. Often it is possible to be both, of course, but being helpful is a "success" concept, while being civil is not. I wasn't helpful if I sent you down the wrong path, no matter how sincerely I thought it was the right one. But I was civil to you if I sincerely tried to be, even if I said the wrong thing. Contrariwise, I may have been helpful even though I didn't particularly care to be; but I can't have been civil in contradicting

---

[5]   Joseph Raz, *The Morality of Freedom* 53, 56, 59, 47, 46, 290–2 (Oxford: Clarendon Press, 1986).

everything you said, even though I was right. Being helpful means doing what is good for us, even if we never appreciate it. Being civil means taking our feelings into account even if they are wrong-headed.

Roughly speaking, a service conception of legitimacy makes better sense if we suppose that there is a good to be served, even if that good is closely tied to what the individual chooses as her own goals. An ideal moderator conception of legitimacy, on the other hand, makes better sense if we suppose that there is no such good apart from the way it is regarded. A good valve job on my car may seem lousy to me, yet be good. But a good conversation involving me has got to include my viewpoint as an aspect of its assessment – it wasn't a good conversation if it left me feeling bored or (more to the point) belittled.

The service conception and the ideal moderator conception have affinities that soften the contrast between them. The ideal moderator is there (so to speak) to help us decide what we, together, want to do about the problems of living together. This quest for an agreement about fair terms of cooperation (or, at least, coexistence) presumes that that is how we are best to be served. The service conception proceeds from the assumption that what is of service to us is in large measure what helps us achieve our often conflicting individual goals. A big part of this will involve registering and paying heed to what those goals are. But this basic difference remains: Autonomy is an input for the ideal moderator, while for the service conception autonomy figures more importantly as output. Consent is the benchmark of legitimacy for the ideal moderator, but consent has a secondary and even supernumerary role for the service conception. Legitimacy, on the service conception, depends on what moral reasons there are and how they are best complied with, whereas the ideal moderator view avoids and even excludes such questions if their answers are not within the "overlapping consensus" of reasonable opinion.

In my view, the service conception is the better one because it alone has a horizon that takes meaningful account of the human future. Of course, on either view, the living must speak and decide for those to come. But the ideal moderator takes our ends as given and (subject to a certain amount of tidying up) equally worthy. It includes the voices of those yet to be born by appointing the living as their proxies. This slights the fact that the needs, values, and interests – even the identities – of those to come are a function of the choices the living now make. The service conception, on the other hand, sees human ends as a function of circumstance and cultivation, and as possibly not of equal worth. It is capable of envisaging different human futures as objects of present policies that reflect our best, present thinking about what would be the better ways to continue our collective story. Ideals are a personal matter, as seen from the perspective of the ideal moderator, who is "ideal" only in the sense of, ideally, having no ideals.

Idealism run amok has done so much more visible injury than civility has that it might seem silly to suggest that the scope for ideals in politics ought to be enlarged. But this is the common tendency of the arguments I have been advancing. A greater and acknowledged scope for moral argument in politics is nothing other than a greater and acknowledged scope for ideals. Mistakes and excesses are bound to occur, but if we cannot trust ourselves to discuss and collectively pursue any controversial ideal then we are indeed an unfortunate and transient race.

Index

Index

Index

Marxists, Marxism, 3, 73, 84–5, 102
Midgley, Mary, 143
Mill, John Stuart, 97, 128, 133–7, 160,
    167–70, 173, 176
monopoly, 55, 89, 120–3, 157
Moore, G. E., 93
Moore, Michael, 166
morality
    of aspiration, 128
    of duty, 128
    inner sphere of, 3, 131–2, 161, 165–7
    nested-spheres picture, 3, 132, 176
    outer sphere of, 131–2, 161, 165
    in pejorative sense, 154
    super-simple picture, 132
morals legislation, 32–3, 130, 133, 176–7
More of *Austin v Loral* case (Case 4),
    75–6, 101
murder, 13, 21, 52–3, 123, 129–30

Nagel, Ernest, 128
Nagel, Thomas, 90, 129, 177
natural executive right, 123
natural law, 9
Nazi Germany, 9–11, 22, 55–6, 96, 111
necessity, as ground of duty, 28, 52
neutrality thesis, 161–7, 181
Nietzsche, Friedrich, 154
98–Pound Weakling case (Case 11), 82–3,
    96, 101
"No Difference" Thesis, 41
Normal Justification Thesis, 182–3
Nozick, Robert, 81, 89, 100, 101, 107–8,
    122, 175
Nozick's Drug Dealer case (Case 13),
    100
Nozick's Slave case (Case 12), 99–102

Oberdiek, Hans, 77
original sin, 88

Parfit, Derek, 83, 139
participation, 19
perfect coincidence view, 128, 131–3,
    163, 165, 170, 176
Perry, Michael, 166
Plea Bargain case (Case 7), 79–80, 97,
    101, 102, 115
pluralism, 132, 161–3

Portrait of the Artist As a Young Man, A,
    160
Postema, Gerald, 121, 122, 140
presumption
    of illegitimacy, 88–91
    of liberty, 28, 91–3
    of moral rectitude, 33
    of security, 93
prima facie
    duty, 10–12, 14
    illegitimacy, 73
    wrong, 95, 109, 120–1
privacy
    inner sphere of, *see* morality, inner
        sphere of
    right of, 127–30
private language, 151
private morality, 132
promises, 15–16, 59
proportionality
    and disproportionality cases, 117–
        19
    norms, 143, 145–6, 163–4, 174–5
Proximity Thesis, 47, 48, 68, 70
public goods, 20, 21
Publicity Principle, 68
punishment, 121–3, 172–5 (*see also*
        enforcement, sanctions)
    capital, 59–60, 80, 97, 158
    corporal, 155–7, 164
    expressive function of, 172–3
    moral, 135
    open, 121–2, 175
    and regulation contrasted, 172
    social, 134

Rainbolt, George, 61–2, 121
Rationality, Principle of, 88
Rawls, John, 30, 57, 89–90, 92, 111, 116,
    161–7, 181–2
Raz, Joseph, 10, 14, 37–8, 39, 41, 44,
    182–3
reason, reasons
    content-independent, 12–13, 50, 52–3
    double counting of, 13–14
    moral, 10–11, 27, 48
    and prima facie duty distinguished,
        12, 27
    public reason, 161–5

190

Index